Collins

Social Studies for Jamaica

GRADE 7

T0340523

Series Editor: **Farah Christian**

Collins

William Collins' dream of knowledge for all began with the publication of his first book in 1819. A self-educated mill worker, he not only enriched millions of lives, but also founded a flourishing publishing house. Today, staying true to this spirit, Collins books are packed with inspiration, innovation and practical expertise. They place you at the centre of a world of possibility and give you exactly what you need to explore it.

Collins. Freedom to teach.

Published by Collins
An imprint of HarperCollins*Publishers*
The News Building
1 London Bridge Street
London
SE1 9GF
UK

HarperCollins*Publishers*
Macken House,
39/40 Mayor Street Upper,
Dublin 1,
D01 C9W8,
Ireland

Browse the complete Collins Caribbean catalogue at
collins.co.uk/caribbeanschools

© HarperCollins*Publishers* Limited 2024

10 9 8 7 6 5 4 3

ISBN 978-0-00-841396-5

MIX
Paper | Supporting responsible forestry
FSC
www.fsc.org
FSC™ C007454

This book contains FSC™ certified paper and other controlled sources to ensure responsible forest management.

For more information visit: www.harpercollins.co.uk/green

British Library Cataloguing in Publication Data
A catalogue record for this publication is available from the British Library.

The publishers gratefully acknowledge the permission granted to reproduce the copyright material in this book. Every effort has been made to trace copyright holders and to obtain their permission for the use of copyright material. The publishers will gladly receive any information enabling them to rectify any error or omission at the first opportunity. See page 300 for acknowledgements.

Series editor: Farah Christian
Author: Laura Pountney
Reviewer: Kayon Williams
Editorial consultancy: Oriel Square Limited
Publisher: Dr Elaine Higgleton
Product developer: Saaleh Patel
Development editors: Megan La Barre, Bruce Nicholson and Helen Cunningham
Copy editor: Lucy Hyde
Typesetters: Siliconchips Services Ltd UK and Jouve India Pvt Ltd.
Mapping: Gordon MacGilp
Cover design: Kevin Robbins and Gordon MacGilp
Cover photo: Kwanza Henderson/SS
Production controller: Lyndsey Rogers
Printed and bound by Ashford Colour Press Ltd

Contents

How to use this book

This page gives a summary of the exciting new ideas you will be learning about in the unit.

This is the topic covered in the unit, which links to the syllabus.

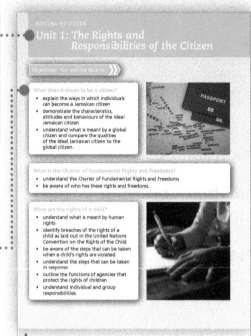

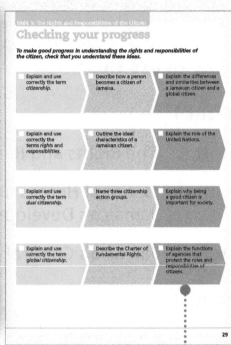

These lists at the end of a unit act as a checklist of the key ideas of the unit.

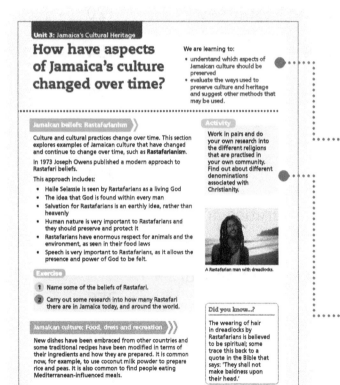

Learning objectives tell you what you will be learning about in the lesson.

Activity features allow you to do practical activities related to the topic.

Project and Research features allow you to work on your own or in groups to explore the topic further and present your findings to your class or your teacher. Along with the Activity features, and higher order thinking questions, the Project and Research features reflect the STEM/STEAM principles embedded within the curriculum.

Try these questions to check your understanding of each topic. Green questions test recall; yellow questions require critical thinking and application of facts; and orange questions require higher order thinking, analysis and/or extended learning activities.

These are the most important new social studies words in the topic. Check their meanings in the Glossary at the end of the book.

Discussion features allow you to work in pairs, in a group or as a class to explore the topic further.

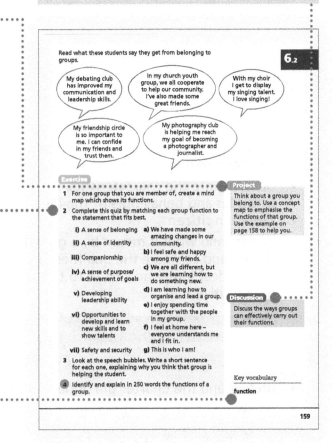

These end-of-unit questions allow you and your teacher to check that you have understood the ideas in the unit by applying the skills and knowledge you have gained.

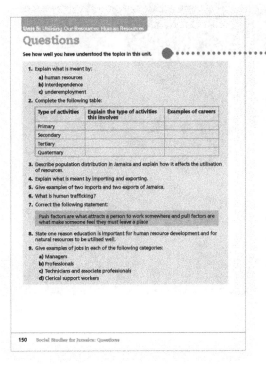

Unit 1: The Rights and Responsibilities of the Citizen

Objectives: You will be able to: ⟩⟩

What does it mean to be a citizen?

- explain the ways in which individuals can become a Jamaican citizen
- demonstrate the characteristics, attitudes and behaviours of the ideal Jamaican citizen
- understand what is meant by a global citizen and compare the qualities of the ideal Jamaican citizen to the global citizen.

What is the Charter of Fundamental Rights and Freedoms?

- understand the Charter of Fundamental Rights and Freedoms
- be aware of who has these rights and freedoms.

What are the rights of a child?

- understand what is meant by human rights
- identify breaches of the rights of a child as laid out in the United Nations Convention on the Rights of the Child
- be aware of the steps that can be taken when a child's rights are violated
- understand the steps that can be taken in response
- outline the functions of agencies that protect the rights of children
- understand individual and group responsibilities.

Individual and group civic responsibilities

- assess issues involving the rights, roles and responsibilities of citizens in relation to the general welfare of society.

How to take action

- participate in citizen action
- explore examples of citizen action in Jamaica.

What does it mean to be a Jamaican citizen?

We are learning to:

- explain the ways in which an individual can become a Jamaican citizen
- demonstrate the attitudes and behaviours of the ideal Jamaican citizen.

What does citizenship mean?

A **citizen** is someone who belongs to a nation, or country. If you are a citizen of a country, you will have particular rights, freedoms and responsibilities.

A citizen of a country is usually someone who was born there, but there are other ways in which one may become a citizen. Did you know it is possible to be a citizen of two countries? This is called dual citizenship.

However, not everyone living in a country is a citizen of that country. Many people move to other countries to work and study. They may live there permanently but this does not make them a citizen of that country. The legal word for someone who is not a citizen in a country in which he or she is living is an **alien**.

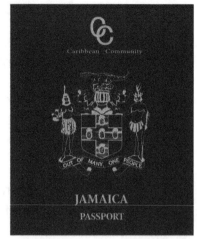

Being a citizen of Jamaica means you can apply for a Jamaican passport.

Who can be a citizen of Jamaica?

The following people can become citizens of Jamaica:

- people born in Jamaica
- people born outside Jamaica who have Jamaican parents or grandparents. This is called citizenship by **descent**
- people who have married a Jamaican citizen
- people who have lived in Jamaica for more than five years

Naturalisation is a process where a foreign person becomes accepted as a citizen of another country. In Jamaica, a person may become naturalised after living in the country for five years.

The government of Jamaica may have someone who is a foreign national deported to his or her own country. **Deportation** is where someone who is not a citizen is forced to leave a country. This usually happens if that person breaks an immigration law.

> **Did you know...?**
>
> Parliament has the power to grant, deny or remove (denaturalise) the citizenship of anyone who has applied, depending on the circumstances. Also, a person may voluntarily give up their citizenship. This is called a renunciation.

> **Did you know...?**
>
> Citizenship can also be applied to the use of technology. A **digital citizen** is a person who is using technology to be a good citizen.

Key vocabulary

citizen

alien

descent

naturalisation

deportation

digital citizen

oath ceremony

When a person applies for naturalisation, which means to become a Jamaican citizen, they must attend an **oath ceremony**. This is a special event for 'new Jamaicans' as they are formally welcomed. They are given a welcome package which includes:

- information to read about the history, culture, customs and traditions of Jamaica
- a Jamaican flag
- an application form to apply for a Jamaican passport.

During the ceremony, new citizens must read out the oath of allegiance:

'I (insert name) do swear that I will be faithful and bear true allegiance to Her Majesty Queen Elizabeth the Second, Her Heirs and Successors according to the Laws of Jamaica and that I will faithfully observe the laws of Jamaica and fulfil my duties as a citizen of Jamaica. So help me God'.

Case study

When someone is born, their birth is registered with the relevant authorities and a birth certificate is issued. In Jamaica, the Registrar General's Department oversees registration of births. If a child is born in a hospital, the child is registered by the hospital's Registration Officer. If a child is born outside a hospital, it is the parent's duty to register the child. It is law in Jamaica that a child must be registered within six weeks of its birth.

All individuals and businesses in Jamaica must have a Taxpayer Registration Number (TRN). This is so that they can be employed, or employ people, and pay taxes to the government. When applying for a TRN, a driver's licence or a passport, National Identification card or birth certificate have to be provided.

What documents should a Jamaican citizen have?

In order to be a Jamaican citizen, you need to have one or all of the following documents:

- birth certificate
- National Insurance Scheme (NIS) number
- Taxpayer Registration Number (TRN)
- voters identification card
- passport.

Exercise

1 What is an 'oath ceremony'? Why is it important?

2 Write definitions for these terms in your own words:

   a) right   **b)** freedom   **c)** citizen.

3 Explain why each of these documents are important.

4 Read the case study. Find out the process involved in applying for a birth certificate and TRN.

Activity

Create a citizenship portfolio. Collect and organise pictures and copies of the documents each person should have as a citizen and make a portfolio of these. See if you can find older versions of citizenship documents and see how they are different to the current ones.

What is the ideal Jamaican citizen?

We are learning to:

- understand the characteristics of the ideal Jamaican citizen
- understand why each characteristic is important.

There are a number of characteristics which make a person a good citizen.

I love my country. I understand the history of Jamaica.

I know the national anthem. I stand when it is playing.

I obey the law.

I vote in elections.

I pick up litter.

I know my rights and responsibilities.

I respect the rights and freedoms of others.

Activity

In small groups, role play examples of good and bad citizenship. Perform your role play to the rest of the class.

Exercise

Look at the diagram above.

1 Who do you know who is an 'ideal Jamaican' citizen?

2 Name two important events in the history of Jamaica.

3 Can you think of two things that you do that are not in the diagram above, which show you are a good citizen?

The image above shows that a Jamaican citizen should have ideal characteristics. Some of these include:

- being **law abiding**, which means you accept and abide by the laws and rules of the country

Project

Using pictures from magazines or the internet, make a poster collage to show examples of good citizenship.

Key vocabulary

law abiding

patriotic

civic activities

- being **patriotic**. A patriotic person is one who has a strong sense of love, support and dedication towards his or her country
- participating in **civic activities**, for example: voting, volunteering, being part of group activities, such as community Labour Day activities and International Coastal Clean-up day.

Activity

Look at the mural in the photograph. In pairs, work together to identify what characteristics of the ideal Jamaica citizen the mural shows. Write a paragraph for each characteristic identified.

Then, working together, create your own mural showing the characteristics of the ideal Jamaica citizen. Write text to explain your reasons for the mural.

Looking after your environment is part of being a good citizen.

Children's mural in a bus stop, Port Antonio, Jamaica.

Exercise

Read the information above.

4 List three characteristics of an ideal Jamaican citizen.

5 Describe and draw a national symbol of Jamaica.

6 Give two examples of ways you can 'respect the environment'.

Global citizen

We are learning to:

- understand what is meant by a global citizen
- compare the qualities of the ideal Jamaican citizen and the global citizen.

You have explored what it means to be a Jamaican citizen. As well as being a Jamaican citizen you are also a **global citizen**, which means you are a member of the world community. As a global citizen it means you are:

- aware that you are a part of a country and the wider world
- willing to take an active role in your community as well as the wider Caribbean or at an international level
- willing to work with other people to make our planet more equal, fair and more sustainable
- willing to develop the skills to be able to make a difference locally and globally and believe you can make a difference.

Global citizens are aware that they are part of the wider world.

Exercise

Read the information above and answer the following questions:

1 Explain what a 'global citizen' is.

2 State two characteristics of the global citizen.

3 What does it mean to make the world 'more sustainable'?

How is being a Jamaican citizen similar and different to being a global citizen?

Jamaican citizen	Global citizen
Follow the laws of the country	Respect the laws of your country and other countries
Be proud of your country	Respect other people's culture
Be active in looking after your environment	Be active in looking after your environment
Learn the history, customs, and traditions of your country	Find ways to make the world more equal and fairer to everyone
Respect the rights and freedoms of others	Learn the skills to be able to work with people all over the word
Volunteer and participate in community activities	Believe you can make a difference to the world through your actions

Who is an Economic Citizen? ❯❯

An **economic citizen** is someone who becomes a citizen of a country because they have invested money into that country in some way. This route to citizenship is sometimes pursued by persons who live in countries that are politically unstable and is also used as a way of securing citizenship in another country.

Case study

A wealthy businesswoman, Sarah wants to live in Jamaica and become a citizen. She can do this by investing money in businesses and properties in Jamaica. So, Sarah is expected to invest around US $500 000 for a period of around 10 years. The Jamaican government can use some of this money financing new projects in the country, to help develop its economy.

Discussion

What are the benefits of introducing economic citizenship in Jamaica? Some people suggest that people being able to 'buy citizenship' is a problem. What do you think?

Activity

1. Plan a day of action for your class, or even your school.

2. In small groups pick an issue that affects Jamaica and create an information leaflet and a poster about what action can be taken to address the issue.

   Some of these issues might include:

   • environmental issues such as endangered animals or plants

   • global warming

   • reducing waste

   • raising awareness of global problems such as poverty

   • creating better awareness of world events.

3. Organise a series of activities that can be done in the community or school to address any one of the issues.

Exercise

4 Make a list of similarities between Jamaican citizenship and global citizenship.

5 How different is a citizen of Jamaica from a global citizen?

6 Write a paragraph explaining how you play the role of being a citizen in Jamaica.

Key vocabulary

global citizen

economic citizen

What is the Charter of Fundamental Rights and Freedoms?

We are learning to:

- understand the Charter of Fundamental Rights and Freedoms
- be aware of who has these rights and freedoms.

In Jamaica, the constitution was written in 1962. A **constitution** is an important set of laws which outlines how the government will be set up as well as setting out the powers and rights of the individual. Here is an extract:

Chapter 3 of the Jamaican Constitution was amended in 2011 to include the Charter of Fundamental Rights and Freedoms Act. This charter says that it *"provides that every person, regardless of race, place of origin, political opinions, colour, creed or sex, is entitled to certain fundamental rights and freedoms"*.

There are many fundamental rights and freedoms included in the charter. These include:

- The right to life
- The right to personal liberty
- Freedom of movement
- Freedom from inhuman treatment
- Enjoyment of property
- Freedom of conscience
- Freedom of association
- Respect for private and family life
- Freedom from discrimination.

The Charter also declares that "all persons are under a responsibility to respect and uphold the rights of others".

Discussion

Discuss situations where freedoms and rights as set out by the Charter can be breached or violated. How might the government respond to this?

What is meant by rights, freedoms and responsibilities

You will recall that a citizen has particular rights, freedoms and responsibilities. A **right** is something to which you are entitled. For example, you have the right to an education. A **freedom** is having the power to do something, for example you have the freedom to practise a religion.

A **responsibility** means the things you need to do as a citizen of your country. For example, in Jamaica one responsibility you have is to obey the law.

The rights, freedoms and responsibilities of all Jamaicans are outlined in what is known as the **Charter of Fundamental Rights and Freedoms**.

You have the freedom to practise a religion.

Who has fundamental rights and freedoms? ▶▶▶

Fundamental rights and freedoms are given to most citizens of Jamaica. Full rights and responsibilities may not be given to some individuals.

For example, the following individuals are not allowed to vote in elections:

- people in prison
- people who have severe mental health issues
- children: you cannot vote until you are 18 years old.

How are the rights of citizens protected? ▶▶▶

Individuals can make reports to the authorities about situations in which their human rights are not fully observed or recognised. Individuals and groups may also turn to organisations that are set up to help support people who have experienced violation of their human rights.

What organisations are involved with protecting the rights of citizens? ▶▶

If citizens' rights are violated in some way, there are a number of organisations that you can go to to get help in Jamaica and beyond.

The Citizens Advice Bureau Jamaica (CAB) ▶▶▶

The CAB is an organisation which helps people with legal advice, preparing documents for citizenship, and advising people on how to get a job. You can make an appointment to go and see them, visit their social media pages or call them on the phone for help.

Jamaicans for Justice (JFJ) ▶▶▶

JFJ is an organisation that helps hundreds of Jamaicans each year by providing legal services in response to human rights violations, and campaigns for social justice causes. They work with the community to help support groups that need assistance and educate people about the importance of human rights.

These organisations may also help to lobby the government. A **lobby group** is a group of people who seek to influence the government make changes to or act on a particular issue.

Lobby groups work by writing to the editors of newspapers, setting up their own social media sites and writing blogs, producing videos about the issue, and attending meetings to share their desired forms of change.

Exercise

1. Why is it good that children themselves can report human rights violations?

2. What other rights are prisoners unable to have?

3. Why are prisoners unable to have these rights?

4. Think of two reasons for and against lowering the voting age to 16.

Key vocabulary

constitution

right

freedom

responsibility

Charter of Fundamental Rights and Freedoms

lobby group

What are the rights of a child?

We are learning to:

- understand what is meant by human rights
- identify breaches of the rights of a child as laid out in the United Nations Convention on the Rights of a child.

Human Rights ⟩⟩

The **United Nations** is an organisation made up of 193 countries, which was established in 1945 after World War II to protect peace and security. The United Nations introduced the idea that all individuals should be entitled to human rights. **Human rights** are fundamental or important rights that every person is entitled to have.

The Universal Declaration of Human Rights (UDHR) was adopted by the United Nations in 1948 after the suffering experienced during the World Wars in the first half of the 20th century. It was the first international statement about human rights and its main aim is to promote basic rights and freedoms for all people.

All countries that are members of the United Nations signed the declaration, and in doing so they agreed to promote respect for human rights. It has since been built into the constitutions and laws of most countries around the world.

There are 30 articles in the declaration. Read the first five articles below and then answer the questions in the exercise.

Article 1: When children are born, they are free and should be treated in the same way. They have reason and conscience and should act towards one another in a friendly manner.

Article 2: Everyone can claim the following rights, despite:

- being a different sex
- having different skin colour
- speaking in a different language
- thinking different things
- believing in different religions
- owning more or less
- being born in another social group
- coming from another country.

It also makes no difference whether the country you live in is independent or not.

Article 3: You have the right to live, and to live in freedom and safety.

Article 4: Nobody has the right to treat you as his or her slave and you should not make anyone your slave.

Article 5: Nobody has the right to torture you.

In 1990 The United Nations wrote what is called the 'Convention on The Rights of the Child'. These are human rights that are particularly written for children. By 2019, 181 countries agreed to abide by these rights. In total there are 54 parts or articles in the convention. All of these rights are connected to each other and all are seen as equally important. This set of rights places a duty on governments in the following areas of children's lives:

- The right to life
- The right to their own name and identity
- The right to be protected from abuse or exploitation
- The right to an education
- The right to have their privacy protected
- The right to be raised by, or have a relationship with, their parents
- The right to express their opinions and have these listened to, and where appropriate, acted upon
- The right to play and enjoy culture and art in safety.

The United Nations flag.

Discussion

Working in groups, discuss factors that affect child rights. Why are the rights of some children violated? What action should be taken by the government when children's rights are not respected?

Exercise

1 What does it mean by saying 'this set of rights places a duty on governments'?

2 Visit the United Nations website (search for 'What is the UN convention?') and find five more child rights to add to the list.

3 Working in pairs, find out about parts of the world where children's rights are not respected. Suggest two examples where rights have been denied to these children.

Key vocabulary
....
United Nations

human rights

What happens when the rights of a child are not upheld?

We are learning to:

- be aware of the steps that can be taken when a child's rights are violated
- understand the steps that can be taken in response.

When a child's human rights are not met, it is said that their rights are being violated.

In this section, we explore what happens when children's rights are violated, and what can be done to address the situation. Here are some examples of situations in which children's rights have been violated.

Case study 1

Rohingya children deprived of education

Due to conflict, many families in Myanmar were forced to flee the country. Many families ended up moving to Bangladesh, where they have been unable to access education.

Rohingya child refugees from Myanmar, in Kutupalong refugee camp near Cox's Bazar, Bangladesh.

Case study 2

Torture of boys in Egyptian prisons

Children as young as 12 have been tortured in Egypt's prisons. Hundreds of children have been detained by Egypt's security forces since the military took power in 2013. They are often arrested without being given a reason, or because they were simply taking part in public protests.

Case study 3

Lack of access to education for children with disabilities in Iran

For most children with disabilities in Iran, going to school is impossible. For the few who are able to attend, the experience is often difficult. There are many reasons for this, including the fact that children with disabilities have to have a medical assessment, they cannot gain access to the school building, and they may face discrimination in school.

Exercise

1 Which child rights are being violated in each of these three case studies?

2 What could the government do to improve the situation in each case?

3 Why do you think it might be harder for children to report human rights violations than adults?

Case study

UNICEF, the United Nations International Children's Emergency Fund, was established in 1946 to help deal with the needs of children in post-war China and Europe. By 1950, UNICEF had expanded to help and support children and women in countries all over the world. In 1953, it changed its name to the United Nations Children's Fund (still UNICEF), when it became a permanent part of the United Nations.

Today, UNICEF works in over 190 countries to help save children's lives, to defend their rights, and to help them fulfil their potential.

The aims of UNICEF are that:

- every child has the right to grow up in a safe and inclusive environment
- every child has the right to survive and thrive
- every child has the right to learn
- every child has the right to an equitable chance in life
- every child can be reached in emergencies
- every girl has the right to fulfil her potential
- innovation should drive results for every child
- solutions should be delivered to reach every child at risk
- date should be used to drive results.

UNICEF works in some of the world's most difficult, dangerous and toughest places, and helps to save children's lives with vaccines, clean water and food. Children often suffer the most during and after armed conflicts. Organisations such as UNICEF help to support children who have lost their homes or family during conflicts. Other organisations like the Red Cross and Save the Children are also involved in this type of help.

Source: UNICEF website.

Exercise

4 What is the role of UNICEF?

5 In groups, discuss the reasons why children may not report human rights violations.

Activity

Carry out research into two other organisations who help children around the world. Find one example for each organisation of who they have helped in recent years.

Activity

In small groups discuss the functions of citizens' rights organisations. Then carry out research into a current campaign by the Jamaicans for Justice. Write a report describing the campaign and how it helps promote citizens' rights. You may present your report through an oral presentation, a blog entry online, a video recording or a display for others to view.

Rohingya children in Bangladesh have been supported by UNICEF.

Key vocabulary

UNICEF

Which parts of the government are responsible for children's rights?

We are learning to:

- outline the functions of agencies that protect the rights of children
- understand individual and group responsibilities.

The Jamaican government also have a role to play in protecting children's rights. There are several agencies of the government that focus on this area. They work hard to make sure that children are protected and their rights are respected and upheld. Here we explore two of these agencies.

Case study 1

Child Protection and Family Services Agency (formerly Child Development Agency (CDA))

- This agency's mission is to protect children, empower families and secure the future for children.
- Their role is to promote child-friendly policies and develop programmes which strengthen families. These include fostering and adoption programmes as well as counselling services.
- The agency is made up of social workers and other child protection specialists.

Case study 2

Office of the Children's Registry

- The main role of the Children's Registry is to receive reports of children who have been, are being or are likely to be abandoned, neglected, physically or sexually ill-treated, or are otherwise in need of care and protection.
- The Children's Registry also manages a national alert and response system for the safe return of missing children in the shortest possible time.
- They place great emphasis on the development of ways to prevent and reduce child abuse and to locate missing children.

Exercise

1 How do both of these agencies protect the rights of children?

2 How is the alert system helpful in protecting children?

3 What else do you think the government might do to help protect children, for example, what might they learn about in school?

Did you know...?

In 2017, 4 365 children were in need of care and protection in Jamaica.

Children can now report violations of their rights (Geneva 2014)

United Nations child rights experts have introduced a new rule that allows children to complain directly to the United Nations Committee on the Rights of the Child about alleged violations of their rights. "Today marks the beginning of a new era for children's rights. Children are now further empowered as this new rule recognises their ability to exercise and claim their own rights," four United Nations child rights experts said.

"We hope that this new treaty will give voice to children's concerns and allow their problems to be resolved."

Teenagers have rights too!

Teen journalists who are members of the Jamaica Youth Advocacy Network have been calling for attention to be paid to the rights of teenagers as well as children.

Two decades ago (1989), world leaders made an historic agreement through the Convention of the Rights of the Child (CRC), which acknowledges that governments, caregivers and stakeholders must respect, promote and fulfil the rights of all children within the society.

Internationally, this was the first instrument to incorporate civil, cultural, economic, political and social human rights. The convention outlined the rights of each and every child to survival; to develop to the fullest; to protection from harmful influences, abuse and exploitation; and to participate fully in family, cultural and social life. Here they report on child rights in Jamaica.

Jamaica has made significant strides in recognising children's rights by ratifying the CRC in 1991 and passing the Child Care and Protection Act of 2004. While this is significant, more efforts and work must be done to ensure laws, policies and programmes show serious efforts to build a protective and enabling environment for the development of all our children.

Spokespersons for the Youth Advocacy Network call for better standards in children's services, detention centres and ask that all teenagers are provided with opportunities to learn. They state that:

'as young people, we must recognise the important role we play in good governance. We must encourage and make public officials accountable to children and youth, thereby ensuring that our rights are protected and advanced. We must make all Jamaicans aware about the importance of children's rights. We must raise awareness that children's rights are human rights. As UNICEF emphasises, "children's rights are not special rights, but rather the fundamental rights inherent to the human dignity of all people"'.

Activity

Carry out research into the Jamaica Youth Advocacy Network and Jamaica's Office of the Children's Advocate. Write a paragraph about the work they each do and their role in protecting children's rights.

Children's rights are human rights.

Individual and group civic responsibilities

We are learning to:

- assess issues involving the rights, roles and responsibilities of citizens in relation to the general welfare of society.

What are the civic responsibilities of citizens? Why are these important?

Part of being a good citizen is being informed about how you can help to make society work well.

Civic responsibility

Your **civic responsibility** is the obligation you have as a citizen of your country. You have the right and freedom to do certain things in your country, but responsibilities go with these rights. Some of these responsibilities are individual and some happen in groups. Examples include:

- paying taxes when they become due
- working with others of different cultural backgrounds, religions or ethnicity
- respecting the freedom and rights of others
- getting involved with what happens in your country, including voting and commenting on laws and bills
- helping wherever you can to make your country a better place to live, such as keeping your country clean and helping other people when they need help.

One civic responsibility is to vote in elections.

Discussion

Working in groups, discuss what you think are your most important civic responsibilities. Share your ideas with other groups.

Individual and group civic responsibilities

Individual	Group
Being keen to learn	Helping people around you who need it
Voting	Working with people from other backgrounds
Being well-rounded	Commenting on laws and bills that might affect you and other people
Being individually productive	Respecting the rights and freedoms of other people
Help nation building	Respecting the views of other people
Being proud to be Jamaican	Helping to educate other people to be a good citizen
Paying your taxes	Reporting rights violations where you see them
Picking up litter	Getting involved with community events

Activity

Look at the table on page 22. Which of these civic responsibilities are you already carrying out? What could you do more of?

Case study 1

John works in a hotel and in his spare time volunteers at a youth group. He attends community meetings and helps out at litter pick mornings. He makes sure that he pays his tax bills and enjoys being involved in community events and festivals. He has two children and believes that it is important that they see him volunteering and being involved in community life.

Case study 2

Nelly is unemployed and spends a lot of time on her own. She walks her dog and doesn't speak to many other people. She often watches TV or plays on her computer games. Nelly is aware that her neighbour is elderly and doesn't have many visitors.

It is everyone's responsibility to look after our environment.

Activity

Who is a better citizen, John or Nelly? Give reasons for your answers. What more could each do to improve their roles as active citizens?

Litter picking is a civic responsibility that everyone can get involved in.

Exercise

1 Make a list of all the ways that carrying out civic responsibilities adds to the general welfare of a society.

2 Discuss in groups what happens to society as a whole if people do not carry out their civic responsibilities.

3 Write an essay in which you explain four ways that you can show your civic responsibility. Your essay should have an introduction and a conclusion as well as four short paragraphs of content. The essay should be about 150 words.

Key vocabulary
....

civic responsibility

How to take action

We are learning to:

- participate in citizen action
- explore examples of citizen action in Jamaica.

So far you have learned about what it means to be a citizen, and how to be a good citizen. You may wish to become more involved in the issues that concern you, meaning that you become an active citizen. Your actions could be an attempt to make a difference at a local, national or global level. You can do this in a number of different ways.

- You can collect signatures for a petition you have written.
- You could contact the local media.
- You could take part in a protest.
- You could lobby on behalf of a group that is interested in resolving a problem.
- You could help raise funds to help a cause.
- You could volunteer in your community.

Discussion

In small groups discuss which issue you might want to take action on. Explain to the rest of your group why you feel strongly about this issue and then think of what you can do to become more active in helping this cause.

Different examples of citizen action

Here are some examples of **active citizenship** in Jamaica.

Case study 1

Respect Jamaica

Respect Jamaica is an anti-discrimination group, launched in 2014, aimed at promoting inclusion and equality for all Jamaicans, regardless of social identity and status. The programme aims to tackle stigma and discrimination by raising public awareness of how both affect individuals. They have organised and trained over 100 young people in social advocacy to improve public understanding of discrimination/human rights. Young people form an important part of their anti-discrimination activities across Jamaica.

Case study 2

Extinction Rebellion Jamaica

Extinction Rebellion (XR) believe that the climate crisis is becoming an emergency and that more has to be done to protect the planet from further destruction. The aim of XR is to create a fairer world and therefore one goal is to eliminate poverty. Very few people would argue that there is not a link between poverty and education; in Jamaica there are problems with poverty and it is increasing, but XR believe this could be improved by state investment in solar-powered schools and renewables.

XR argue that the effects of climate and ecological disruption that we are experiencing now are nothing compared to what could come. They argue that unless more is done by the government and individuals, we will see:

- biodiversity loss
- sea level rise
- desertification
- wildfires
- water shortage
- crop failure
- extreme weather.

Case study 3

The Jamaican Society for the Prevention of Cruelty to Animals (JSPCA)

The JSPCA has been working in Jamaica for more than one hundred years. Its main mission is to promote the compassionate treatment of animals through education, advocacy, veterinary care and the placing of unwanted animals in loving homes. They strive towards improvement of the conditions of animals in the pounds and abattoirs, as well as the racetrack and riding establishments in Jamaica.

One of their major goals is to amend the 1965 Cruelty to Animals Act and the Pound Laws, increasing the fines to levels that will constitute a real deterrent and give them more authority to take suitable action against those who inflict harm, pain or suffering on animals.

Exercise

1 In small groups, create a table that summarises each example of citizenship action.

2 Organise a day of action in your school to raise funds for a citizenship group of your choice, with information about what your group aim to do and why you think it is worthy of support.

3 Carry out research into one of the three case studies and in your group, write a presentation on the group, its aims, its successes and its current activities. Explain what you can do to get more involved.

Key vocabulary

active citizenship

25

Questions

See how well you have understood the topics in this unit.

1. A/An _____ is a person who belongs to a nation, or a country.

   a) individual
   b) citizen
   c) alien
   d) member of the public

2. _____ is where a foreign person becomes accepted as a citizen of another country.

   a) Naturalisation
   b) Immigration
   c) Citizenship
   d) Deportation

3. A _____ is something to which you are entitled.

   a) role
   b) responsibility
   c) right
   d) law

4. Jamaica's constitution was written in:

   a) 1768
   b) 1988
   c) 1962
   d) 1946.

5. True or False? There are no specific children's human rights.

6. Correct this statement: A global citizen is someone who understands the best way to be an ideal citizen in Jamaica only.

7. Outline three characteristics of an ideal Jamaican citizen.

8. Write a short definition of the following terms:

   Economic citizen
   Human rights
   Civic responsibilities

9. Make a list of the documents a Jamaican citizen should have.

10. Which two of these articles are part of the Rights of the Child?

   a) The freedom to break rules without punishment

   b) The right to life

   c) The right to choose an education

   d) The right to be raised, or have a relationship with, their parents

11. Give two examples of civic responsibilities.

12. Explain what the role of government agencies are in protecting children, give examples.

13. Give two examples of groups that carry out citizenship action in Jamaica.

14. Find a blog or newspaper article about a lobby group in Jamaica and the work it is doing. How successful has this group been? Why do you think it was successful or not?

15. Imagine that you work for a citizenship action group in Jamaica. Write an essay of about 200 words describing what your group is involved in and how your actions are helping individuals or groups.

Grade 7 Unit 1 Summary

Citizenship

In this chapter, you have learned about:

- What it means to be a citizen and to have citizenship
- Who can be a citizen of Jamaica and the documents a Jamaican citizen possesses
- The characteristics that make a good citizen and why they are important
- What is meant by the term 'global citizen'
- The qualities of the ideal Jamaican citizen and how these compare to the qualities of global citizen
- What it means to be an economic citizen
- What is meant by the terms: rights, freedoms and responsibilities.

The Charter of Fundamental Rights and Freedoms

In this chapter, you have learned about:

- Who has fundamental rights and freedoms
- What the Charter of Fundamental Rights and Freedoms is
- How the rights of citizens are protected
- Organisations involved in protecting the rights of citizens
- What the Citizens Advice Bureau is and the types of services it offers
- What the Jamaicans for Justice organisation is and the types of services it offers.

Human rights

In this chapter, you have learned about:

- What is meant by the term 'human rights'
- What is meant by the term 'Rights of the Child' and what these rights are
- What happens when the rights of a child are not upheld
- How the Jamaica government ensures that children's rights are protected.

Civic responsibilities

In this chapter, you have learned about:

- The rights, roles and responsibilities of citizens and how they relate to society
- The meaning of the term, 'civic responsibility' in terms of individuals and groups
- Different examples of how citizens can take action at local, national and global levels

Checking your progress

To make good progress in understanding the rights and responsibilities of the citizen, check that you understand these ideas.

- [ ] Explain and use correctly the term *citizenship*.

- [ ] Describe how a person becomes a citizen of Jamaica.

- [ ] Explain the differences and similarities between a Jamaican citizen and a global citizen.

- [ ] Explain and use correctly the terms *rights* and *responsibilities*.

- [ ] Outline the ideal characteristics of a Jamaican citizen.

- [ ] Explain the role of the United Nations.

- [ ] Explain and use correctly the term *dual citizenship*.

- [ ] Name three citizenship action groups.

- [ ] Explain why being a good citizen is important for society.

- [ ] Explain and use correctly the term *global citizenship*.

- [ ] Describe the Charter of Fundamental Rights.

- [ ] Explain the functions of agencies that protect the roles and responsibilities of citizens.

Unit 2: National Heroes and Their Contributions to Jamaica's Development

Objectives: You will be able to:

What does it mean to be a national hero?

- discuss the characteristics of a hero
- assess the extent to which national heroes fit these characteristics.

Who are Jamaica's national heroes and how did they contribute to Jamaica's development?

- gather information from multiple sources
- use selected details to compile a biography of Jamaica's national heroes.

What are the awards and honours conferred upon Jamaicans?

- understand the national awards and honours given to Jamaicans.

Who are some other outstanding Jamaicans?

- compare the descriptions of national heroes from different sources
- identify how each source treats the contributions to national development made by the national heroes.

How should we value the contribution made by these individuals?

- assess the way we value and remember Jamaican heroes
- suggest other ways that heroes may be honoured.

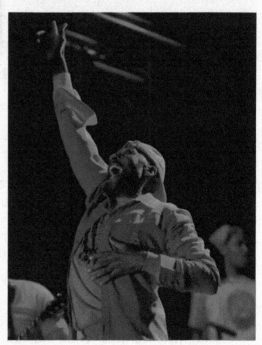

What does it mean to be a national hero?

We are learning to:

- discuss the characteristics of a hero
- assess the extent to which national heroes fit these characteristics.

Who is a hero?

In this section we explore Jamaica's national heroes. There is some debate about what is meant by a **hero**. Here are some different definitions of 'hero':

1. 'A person who is admired for their courage, outstanding achievements or noble qualities.'

2. 'A hero is someone who has done something brave, new, or good, and who is therefore greatly admired by a lot of people.'

3. 'Somebody who has good qualities.'

Exercise

Read the information above and answer the following questions.

1 Have a look at the different definitions above.

2 Which definition do you think is best and why?

3 In your view, does somebody have to be famous in order to be a hero?

4 Explain what is meant by 'noble'.

A hero, then, is a person who is admired for their courage, outstanding achievements or noble qualities. There are many outstanding individuals who have contributed to the development of Jamaica in a wide range of fields including politics, economics, the arts, sports and entertainment.

Heroism refers to acts that reflect brave or admirable qualities where:

- the actions are done in service of others who are in need, whether it is for an individual, a group, or a community
- the actions are performed voluntarily, without being asked

- the individual recognises the potential risk or sacrifice they are making by taking these actions
- the heroic individual willingly accepts the sacrifice they may be making.

Heroes carry out these actions without any expectation of reward or gaining anything.

Case study

Mary Seacole (born 1805 – died 14th May 1881)

Mary Seacole was an influential Jamaican nurse who put her own life in danger to treat wounded soldiers during the Crimean War. Seacole was determined to take care of her "sons", the British troops. After being turned away at least four times for being black, Seacole decided to set up her own British hotel in Turkey. There, Seacole worked day and night as a nurse and could even sometimes be seen on the battlefield tending to soldiers. Her bravery and selflessness make her a truly remarkable person and war hero.

Mary Seacole.

The term 'hero' can be used to talk about men or women, but the word '**heroine**' is often used for female heroes.

Sometimes a person acts in heroic ways, which are not recognised until much later, even after they have died. We call this kind of person an '**unsung hero**'.

Unsung heroes might be seen as even more brave and special because maybe they did not experience any form of recognition or praise during their lives.

When someone becomes a famous hero and acts in a way which is seen as particularly important by a country, they are sometimes called a '**national hero**'.

When a hero makes a particular contribution to a country, which means that the country moves forwards or progresses in some way, it is said that they contributed to the **development** of a country.

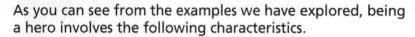

As you can see from the examples we have explored, being a hero involves the following characteristics.

Discussion

In small groups, make a list of all the qualities of a hero. Place them in order of importance, explaining why you have put them in that order.

1. **Bravery** – Heroes often put their lives, jobs and families at risk in the actions that they take.

2. **Moral integrity** – A hero will stick to what they personally believe in, their morals and values, regardless of what is happening around them.

3. **Conviction** – A hero will act in line with their convictions, a special set of beliefs that set out for them, what is right or wrong. The convictions a person has will shape the actions that you take. They shape how you react in different situations.

4. **Self-sacrifice** – Heroes are willing to give up their own needs and wishes in order to help others.

5. **Selflessness** – A hero is selfless, meaning that they are more concerned with the needs of others rather than their own needs.

6. **Determination** – A hero shows great determination, meaning that they do not give up reaching a goal, they can resolve problems and find solutions to obstacles that they experience.

7. **Inspirational** – A hero acts in ways which inspire other people to act the same way. They make people feel positive and hopeful, even in difficult times.

8. **Honesty** – A hero is truthful to themselves and others even if it costs them personally as a result.

9. **Helpful** – A hero is someone who thinks about how they can help other people, rather than always putting their own needs first.

10. **Protective** – A hero will think about shielding others from harm, not just themselves. 'Harm' might mean discrimination, physical or emotional harm.

11. **Courage** – A hero is brave even in very difficult circumstances.

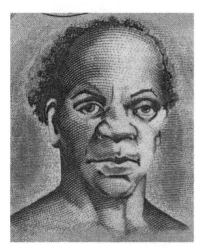

Samuel Sharpe had moral integrity, he fought to end enslavement.

Paul Bogle was selfless, he was hanged for fighting for his beliefs.

Mary Seacole showed great bravery in taking care of people even in dangerous battlefields.

Exercise

5   Make a table of the above characteristics and find an example of a Jamaican hero who exhibits this characteristic and why.

6   Which of the qualities above did Mary Seacole display through her actions?

7   Think of a person you know in your own life who exhibits some of the characteristics of a hero and write a short passage on why this is.

8   Research the history of Mary Seacole. How do you think she developed these characteristics?

Activity

Write a letter to the editor of your local newspaper, explaining why someone you know should be considered a hero.

Key vocabulary

hero

heroism

heroine

unsung hero

national hero

development

Who are Jamaica's national heroes and how did they contribute to Jamaica's development?

We are learning to:

- gather information from multiple sources
- use selected details to compile a biography of Jamaica's national heroes.

There are seven national heroes: six men and one woman. Each hero made significant contributions to Jamaica's social and political development by fighting for what they considered to be right. Some, such as Nanny of the Maroons and Sam Sharpe, fought against the system of **enslavement**, while Paul Bogle, George William Gordon and Marcus Garvey fought against the injustice and systems of inequality that people faced even after enslavement ended. This fight continued with Norman Manley and Sir Alexander Bustamante who both looked out for the poor working class and helped to secure Jamaica's independence from Britain.

Nanny of the Maroons.

Profile

Nanny of the Maroons (born around 1686 – died around 1740s)

Nanny was a leader of the Maroons at the beginning of the 18th century. She was known by both the Maroons and the British settlers as an outstanding military leader. She was a symbol of unity and strength for her people during times of crisis.

Profile

Samuel Sharpe (born 1801 – died 23rd May 1832)

Samuel Sharpe was the main person whose actions led to the 1831 Slave Rebellion, which began on the Kensington Estate in St James, Jamaica, and which was largely instrumental in bringing about the **abolition** (ending) of enslavement.

You can find more information on Nanny of the Maroons, Samuel Sharpe and Jamaica's other national heroes at the Jamaica Information Service web site. Go to 'Information', then 'National Heroes'.

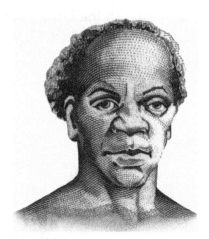

Samuel Sharpe.

Profile

Paul Bogle (born 1822 – died 24th October 1865)

Problems in Jamaica with poverty and injustice led Bogle to lead a protest march to the Morant Bay courthouse on 11th October 1865. The government tried to stop the protest, killing seven men. The protesters set fire to the Court House and other buildings nearby. Several officials were killed too.

- Peasants rose up and took control of the parish for two days. The Governor responded by ordering troops to capture the peasants and stop the rebellion. Nearly 400 people died and 300 were arrested. Even more people were flogged and punished before order was restored.
- Bogle was hanged on 24th October 1865.
- By the end of 1865 a Royal Commission was sent to investigate the events. The Governor was suspended and recalled to England, eventually dismissed.

Bogle's demonstration led to important changes in the way that the government worked and also led to a shift in attitudes. His actions showed how strongly people felt about being treated fairly. It led to fairer courts and it brought about a change in official attitudes, which made social and economic development more possible.

Paul Bogle.

Profile

George William Gordon (born 1820s – died 23rd October 1865)

- Born to an enslaved mother and a planter father who was a lawyer (or attorney) to several sugar estates in Jamaica, George William Gordon had educated himself and became a landowner in the parish of St Thomas.
- Gordon began life as a politician. This was not easy as the people he wanted to help could not vote and had very little power.
- He divided his own land into smaller sections and sold off these sections to people as cheaply as possible, then he organised a market system, so that people could sell their produce at fair prices.
- Gordon urged the people to protest against and resist the oppressive and unjust conditions under which they were forced to live. Gordon was arrested and charged for being involved in the Morant Bay Rebellion in 1865.
- He was illegally taken to court and, even though there was a lack of evidence, Gordon was convicted and sentenced to death. He was executed on 23rd October 1865.

George William Gordon.

Discussion

What important changes did Gordon make that have shaped Jamaica today? Draw a poster which summarises the life story of Gordon with the key events in his life.

Norman Washington Manley (born 4th July 1893 – died 2nd September 1969)

- Manley was a brilliant student, soldier and athlete.
- After serving in the First World War, Manley returned to Jamaica as a barrister.
- During the Great Depression, where there were high rates of unemployment, he began to see how difficult life was for the workers. He began to give his time and legal skills to help them.
- In order to improve conditions for the workers in 1938, Manley helped to set up the People's National Party.
- At the same time, Manley fought hard to make sure that all adults were able to vote. He was successful in 1944, when the **universal suffrage** (meaning all adults could vote) was approved.
- He served as the colony's chief minister from 1955 to 1959, and as the premier from 1959 to 1962.
- He helped to improve agricultural production and put more land to use in the 1950s.
- In 1958, he helped to introduce measures to give more children access to secondary school education.
- In 1960, he helped to introduce a pension scheme for sugar workers.
- Manley was a strong believer in **democracy**: a society which gives everyone a say in how Jamaica should be governed.

Norman Washington Manley (right).

Profile

Marcus Garvey (born 17th August 1887 – died 10th June 1940)

Marcus Garvey was an inspirational figure for civil rights.

In Jamaica he founded the Universal Negro Improvement Association (UNIA) in 1914.

He organised the first important American Black nationalist movement (in New York) which existed 1919–1926. It is thought that he had up to two million supporters by 1919. He urged African-Americans to be proud of their race and return to Africa, their ancestral homeland. He taught that people should be proud of their African culture and of Jamaica he said, "A people without a knowledge of their past history, origin and culture is like a tree without roots."

In Jamaica, he formed the People's Political Party in 1929 and although he was unsuccessful in national elections, he won a seat on the Kingston and St Andrew Corporation (KSAC).

Marcus Garvey died in 1940, but in 1964, his body was returned to Jamaica, where he was born, and he was declared the country's first national hero in 1969.

Marcus Garvey.

Exercise

1 What contribution did Norman Manley make to Jamaica?

2 Why do you think Norman Manley is a national hero of Jamaica?

3 Research Mr Manley's achievements then create a timeline summarising these.

4 Why do you think Marcus Garvey is such an inspiration to Jamaicans?

Case study

Sir Alex Bustamante (born 24th February 1884 – died 6th August 1977)

- When Sir Alexander Bustamante began to act politically the country was still a **Crown colony**.
- Bustamante realised it was important for the poor and the working class to be given more say in how Jamaica was run.
- Pay and working conditions were poor in the 1920s and 1930s. Unemployment was high.
- Bustamante wrote letters in newspapers calling for the problems of the poor and working class of Jamaica to be recognised.
- Bustamante became the champion of the working class.
- On 8th September 1940, Bustamante was detained at Up Park Camp, for seventeen months.
- In 1943 he founded the Jamaica Labour Party (JLP), with himself as head. The first general election under Universal Adult Suffrage came in 1944 and the JLP won 22 of the 32 seats.
- Sir Alexander became the first Prime Minister of Independent Jamaica in 1962.

Sir Alexander Bustamente.

Project

In groups you will research two of the national heroes in Jamaica. Use a range of sources to explore the biographies of each, with images and a timeline. When you have gathered all the information together design a PowerPoint with any photos and drawings that you have found. Then present your project to the class.

Activity

1. Do you believe the actions of the national heroes were justified? Explain your answer.

2. Explain what contributions were made by any of the national heroes to Jamaica's development.

3. Explain how the actions of the national heroes affect your life today.

Key vocabulary

enslavement

abolition

universal suffrage

democracy

Crown colony

What are the awards and honours conferred upon Jamaicans?

We are learning to:

- understand the national awards and honours given to Jamaicans.

Different types of awards ⟩⟩

The award system in Jamaica was established through an Act of Parliament, called *The National Honours and Awards Act* in 1968. The way this works is that the Governor-General is the Chancellor of each type of award and the Prime Minister of Jamaica advises the Governor of who he thinks could get an award. There are six types of awards or '**orders of awards**.'

Heroes Day ⟩⟩⟩

Heroes Day in Jamaica is usually in October. It is a public holiday, dedicated to the memory of seven official national Heroes. On National Heroes Day, six heroes and one heroine are remembered for their heroic acts that led to greater freedom and a fairer, better country.

Apart from remembering these past heroes, modern day heroes are also recognised and given awards on National Heroes Day. This is called Jamaica's government-run '**honours system**' that is meant to encourage all noble, heroic acts.

Did you know...?

There are also many special, festive events on National Heroes Day, including musical performances, dancing, cricket and soccer matches, art and craft exhibits, agricultural shows, and more.

Discussion

How do you celebrate Heroes Day? Discuss in small groups, as well as thinking about why Heroes Day is an important day for Jamaica.

Description and criteria for each order

The Order of the National Hero is conferred upon any citizen of Jamaica who has given the most highly regarded form of service to the country; it is highest honour given to any citizen of Jamaica Anyone receiving this award can use 'The Right Excellent' before their name and can also be known by the title of 'National Hero of Jamaica'.

Examples:

- Paul Bogle
- Sir Alexander Bustamante
- Marcus Garvey
- George William Gordon
- Norman Manley
- Nanny of the Maroons
- Samuel Sharpe.

Marcus Garvey, was awarded the Order of the National Hero in 1969 posthumously.

Description and criteria for each order	
The Order of the Nation is the second-highest Jamaican order introduced in 1973. This is often awarded to Governor Generals and to those people who have held the office of Prime Minister. People who receive this award are given the title 'The Most Honourable' or they can use 'Order of the Nation' after their names. Their husbands and wives can also use these titles.	 Patrick Allen (Governor General).

Examples:

- Patrick Allen (Governor General)
- Florizel Glasspole
- Edward Seaga
- Kenneth O.Hall.

The Order of Excellence, introduced in 2003, is the newest addition to the Jamaican honours system. It is given to foreign heads of state or government.

Thabo Mbeki (South Africa).

Examples:

- Thabo Mbeki (South Africa)
- King Juan Carlos I of Spain
- Jakaya Kikwete (Tanzania).

The Order of Merit is the fourth-highest Jamaican order as of 2003, and it is meant for any citizen of Jamaica who has achieved an important international distinction in science, the arts, literature or any other area. It can be given to members of other countries. People who receive this award can be called 'The Honourable' or 'Order of Merit' or 'OM'.

Bunny Wailer.

Examples:

- Jimmy Cliff
- Professor Manley Elisha West
- Bunny Wailer.

The Order of Jamaica is the fifth most important award in Jamaica. It is awarded to any Jamaican citizen of outstanding distinction. Like the Order of Merit, this can be given to foreign individuals too. Members of this order are entitled to the title 'The Honourable' or 'Order of Jamaica' or 'OJ'.

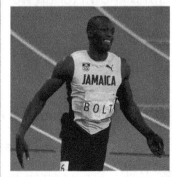
Usain Bolt.

Examples:

- Howard Aris
- Usain Bolt
- Sue M.Cobb
- Amy Bailey.

Description and criteria for each order

The Order of Distinction is the sixth most important award in Jamaica. It has two levels or ranks, Commander and Officer. In this order, as well, honorary memberships may be given to foreign nationals at the rank of Commander or Officer.

Examples:

- Carl Abrahams
- Patrick Brown
- Lloyd Brevett
- Heather Little-White.

Lloyd Brevett.

Case study

Jimmy Cliff (who was originally named James Chambers) was awarded the Order of Merit, the highest honour that is granted by the Jamaican government for achievements in the arts and sciences. Born in 1948, Jimmy Cliff is a ska and Reggae musician, who plays many different instruments, sings and acts. He had his first hit, 'Hurricane Hattie' aged just 14. He is known for his hugely popular songs such as 'Many Rivers To Cross' and 'You Can Get It If You Really Want'. Cliff played an important role in helping to make Reggae popular around the world and he was one of five performers who entered into the Rock and Roll Hall of Fame in 2010.

Jimmy Cliff's music has appeared in major films such as:

- Cocktail – which featured his single 'Shelter Of Your Love' (1988)
- Cool Runnings – which featured his cover of Johnny Nash's 'I Can See Clearly Now' (1993)
- Lion King – where he collaborated with another musician on 'Hakuna Matata' (1995)
- Something's Gotta Give – which featured 'You Can Get It If You Really Want' (2003).

Cliff is known for his work helping raise the profile of refugees around the world. He is still working today on various musical projects.

Jimmy Cliff performing in Portugal, 2008.

Exercise

1 Carry out research on one person from each order.

2 Explain why each person got their award, writing a brief biography of their lives.

3 Write a short essay, no more than 150 words on why it is important to have awards in society.

What are the criteria that are used for different awards?

Each award is given for different reasons or criteria. Using the information in the table (below) explain what characteristics are necessary for each type of award.

The table below should help:

The Order of the National Hero	1. Bravery 2. Moral Integrity
The Order of the Nation	3. Conviction 4. Self-sacrifice
The Order of Excellence	5. Selflessness 6. Determination
The Order of Merit	7. Inspirational 8. Honesty
The Order of Jamaica	9. Helpful 10. Protective
The Order of Distinction	11. Courage

Exercise

4　What does the word 'criteria' mean?

5　Using the examples used in this unit or your own examples, describe the characteristics each person that received an award displayed.

6　Do you think that there are any other criteria that might be useful to determine if someone should be given an award?

Project

Awards aren't just for famous people. As a class, you are going to come up with some awards for students and teachers at your school. Here are the steps you should follow:

1. Plan the awards you would like to create. What will the awards be for? For example, you might have an award for good leadership or sportsmanship.

2. Once you have agreed, your teacher will put you in groups and ask you to create them. Think about how you want them to look and then use paper or card to make them. You can draw or use pictures from magazines or the internet.

3. Have a class vote to decide who should get each award.

4. Plan and conduct an awards ceremony.

Key vocabulary

orders of awards

Heroes Day

honours system

Who are some other outstanding Jamaicans?

We are learning to:

- compare the descriptions of national heroes from different sources
- identify how each source treats the contributions to national development made by the national heroes.

This section looks at the work of other individuals in various fields and their contribution to Jamaica's cultural, social and economic development.

Science ❯❯

People who work in science and technology can make enormous changes to human lives. Scientists and researchers are always making new discoveries that can help to treat diseases and save lives.

Profile

Dr Thomas Lecky (1904 – 1994 Jamaica, pioneering cattle breeder)

- He noticed that cattle in Jamaica were not suited to the environment, so he spent many years breeding cattle to make them more suitable for the local farmers.
- In 1951, he made his first breakthrough with the Jamaica Hope cattle – a specially bred milk-producing cow. The new breed revolutionised how dairy farming was done in Jamaica and scientists from all over the world went to Jamaica to see how this was done.
- He later developed the Jamaica Red for better beef and the Jamaica Black which was more suited for cooler parts of the island. His work inspired animal breeders to follow in his footsteps, but more importantly improved the lives of the cattle farmers in Jamaica.

The Jamaica Red Cow was developed by Dr Thomas Lecky.

Research

Research the life of a Jamaican scientist. Write a brief report, including some biographical detail and their main achievements. Create a three minute PowerPoint presentation on your research to the class.

It isn't just politicians and scientists who play an important role in Jamaican life. Artists, including musicians, can also be hugely significant.

Profile

Robert Nesta Marley (born 6ᵗʰ February 1945 – died 11ᵗʰ May 1981)

- Bob Marley was a Jamaican singer, songwriter and musician.
- He was not the first person to sing Reggae, but his work brought Reggae together with other music types and made Reggae more visible all over the world.
- He became known as a Rastafari icon and was one of the best-selling music artists in the world.
- He died in 1981 and was given a special state burial in Jamaica.

Bob Marley statue outside the National Stadium, Kingston.

Exercise

1 Why are developments in medicine and science so important?

2 Why do you think it is important to share such expertise?

3 How did Dr Thomas Lecky improve the lives of farmers in Jamaica?

4 Write a letter to someone of your choice to thank them for their contribution to the development of Jamaica. Outline in your letter how you feel about being from Jamaica and how you would like to contribute to its development.

5 Do some research on the roots of Reggae music. Where did it come from and why is it so important to the culture of Jamaica?

6 Explore other Reggae musicians and explore what made them popular.

7 Why is it important for heroes of the arts world to be recognised?

Research

Conduct surveys with your friends and family to find out who they think are outstanding Jamaicans. Share your findings with the class.

Key vocabulary

cultural

social

Cricketers and athletes head up the lists of famous Jamaicans who have made significant contributions, not only to their sports but also to the **cultural**, **social** and economic developments of Jamaica.

Profile

Shelley-Ann Fraser Pryce (born 27th December 1986)

- She was the first Jamaican woman to win 100m gold at the 2008 Olympic Games.
- She was the first woman ever to hold the world titles at 60m, 100m, 200m and 4 x 100m relay simultaneously.
- She was IAAF World Athlete of the year in 2013.
- She was named as UNICEF National Goodwill Ambassador for Jamaica in 2010.
- She created the Pocket Rocket Foundation in Jamaica to support high school athletes from poorer backgrounds.

Shelley-Ann Fraser Pryce wins the 100 metre final at the IAAF World Athletics Championships in 2019, Doha, Qatar.

Profile

Merlene Ottey (born 10th May 1960)

- Sprinter who specialised in the 100 and 200 metres.
- Ranks at number four on the all-time list of 200 metres runners.
- Ottey is one of four athletes to win 20 or more medals at the Olympics and World Championships.
- She won 14 medals for Jamaica in six World Championships.
- She won three silver and six bronze medals for Jamaica in the Olympics.
- Ottey was the first female Caribbean athlete to win an Olympic medal.

Merlene Ottey.

Exercise

8 What sports are Jamaicans known to excel in?

9 What contribution did Shelly-Ann Fraser-Pryce and Merlene Ottey make to the cultural development of Jamaica? Write 100 words to explain.

10 Research two other examples of sportsmen or women who have made a contribution to Jamaica and explain how they have done this.

Profile

Nelson Christian Stokes (born 12th November 1963)

- He is the Chairman of the Jamaica Bobsleigh and Skeleton Federation.
- He has taken part in four Olympic games series.
- He was a member of the Jamaican bobsled team that made history, in the process stunning the world, when they appeared at the 1988 Calgary Winter Olympics.
- The movie, 'Cool Runnings' was inspired by the exploits of the team.
- James played an instrumental role in the creation of the world-famous MVP track club that is based at the University of Technology in Papine, St Andrew.
- He firmly believes that world-class athletes can be trained in Jamaica.

Winston Watts (C) and Marvin Dixon (L), Jamaica's 2-man bobsleigh team and Jamaican Bobsleigh Federation President Nelson Chris Stokes (R), address fans and media at a press conference in the at the Sochi 2014 Winter Olympics.

Profile

Michael Holding (born 16th February 1954)

- He played cricket for the West Indies in 60 Tests, taking 249 wickets.
- One of the best fast bowlers of all time. He was known as 'Whispering Death' as he had a very light footed run up to the wicket.
- In 1976, playing against England, he took 14 wickets for 149 runs – a West Indies test match record that still stands today.
- He played in 102 one-day games, and took 142 wickets.
- He was inducted in the International Cricket Council Hall of Fame in 2009.
- In 2020, he spoke out against racism he had encountered.

Michael Holding was one of the best cricketers ever to play for Jamaica.

Activity

1. Do some research on another present-day hero.
2. Write a biography of their life, explaining what contribution they have made to society.
3. Produce a poster or a PowerPoint on them, including video clips and images.

Exercise

11 Which film was made about the Jamaican bobsleigh team?

12 What contribution did Nelson Christian Stokes and Michael Holding make to the cultural development of Jamaica? Write 100 words to explain.

How should we value the contribution made by these individuals?

We are learning to:

- assess the way we value and remember Jamaican heroes
- suggest other ways that heroes may be honoured.

Each individual's contributions are different because of the different fields that they have been involved in. They have all helped to contribute to improving society, winning medals and trophies for their country, making artistic statements, helping ill people or making contributions to farming.

All these personalities have also had a positive economic effect on Jamaica, as well as helping to make people feel good about themselves and their country.

- Sportspersons like Shelly-Ann Fraser-Pryce and Usain Bolt were dedicated to being the best in their sports and gained worldwide recognition for doing so.
- Bob Marley became internationally recognised for his music, and today his records are still influential to new generations of Reggae fans.

How are Jamaican heroes honoured and remembered?

There are a number of ways in which the heroes of Jamaica are remembered, or their **legacies** are kept going.

For example:

- Heroes Day, a public holiday, as well as other important days set aside. For example, in 2012, the Jamaican government declared 17th August as Marcus Garvey Day.
- Some images of heroes have been put on currency notes or the side of a coin. For example, Nanny of the Maroons' image appears on the Jamaican $5 000 note, while Bogle's image appears on the Jamaican 10 cent coin.
- Roadways, buildings and institutions are sometimes named after heroes. For example, there is Marcus Garvey Drive and Bustamante Highway. The Paul Bogle High School in the parish of his birth is named after him.
- Musicians write songs about the heroes, for example, Reggae artists who have named and written songs in tribute to Paul Bogle include Lee Scratch Perry.

Discussion

Discuss as a class which of the personalities we have discussed has contributed the most to Jamaica and why you think this is. Remember, each personality has excelled in different areas, so this might affect your discussion.

Activity

In pairs, create a roleplay where one of you is a TV reporter and the other a famous Jamaican personality. Write a list of questions you would ask them about what they have achieved, and then act it out in front of the class.

The famous dancehall performer Gerald Levy's stage name was 'Bogle'.

- There are monuments built for the heroes. For example, Nanny of the Maroons has Nanny's Monument built in her memory, in Moore Town, Portland in Jamaica.
- Public gardens are built in memory of heroes, for example, Nannyville Gardens, located in Kingston, founded in 1977.
- Memorials are often used to remember the birthplace of heroes. For example, there is a memorial at Garvey's birthplace, 32 Market Street, St Ann's Bay in Jamaica. It is marked as a site of importance in the nation's history.

Monument to Nanny of the Maroons in Emancipation Park, New Kingston.

Exercise

1 Which personality has contributed globally to

    a) economics, **b)** sport, **c)** entertainment and **d)** medicine?

2 Choose one of these Jamaican personalities and write 100 words on how they have contributed both to Jamaica.

3 In groups, research text and photos, and any other relevant illustrations, about any two Jamaican personalities. Create a 'wall of fame' in your classroom.

4 Explain what is meant by a 'legacy'.

5 Imagine you are in government and you have been asked to pick a national hero to remember. Plan a suitable legacy for them, explaining why it is appropriate to them.

6 Why do you think it is important to remember heroes?

7 Can you think of any other ways that heroes might be remembered today?

Discussion

Do you think it should be the job of the government to decide who should be remembered?

Discuss in small groups and suggest other people who might want to be involved.

Research

Carry out some research into an unsung hero of Jamaica. Find out how they have been remembered, if at all. Write a letter to the government explaining why you think they should be remembered and suggest a suitable way of remembering them.

Key vocabulary

legacy

Questions

See how well you have understood the topics in this unit.

1. A _____ is a person who is admired for their courage, outstanding achievements or noble qualities.

   a) citizen

   b) hero

   c) legacy

   d) member of the public

2. _____ refers to acts that reflect brave or admirable qualities.

   a) Generosity

   b) Bravery

   c) Selflessness

   d) Herosim

3. A _____ is a hero who is female.

   a) heroine

   b) heroism

   c) governor

   d) peasant

4. Jamaica's awards system was introduced in:

   a) 1878

   b) 1943

   c) 1968

   d) 1990.

5. True or False? There are eight orders of awards that can be conferred upon Jamaicans.

6. Correct this statement: An unsung hero is someone whose life has been celebrated and remembered.

7. Outline three characteristics of a Jamaican hero.

8. Write a short definition of the following terms:

   Democracy
   Memorial
   Universal suffrage

9. Make a list of the different ways in which Jamaican heroes are remembered.

10. Which of the following individuals are automatically given a lifetime award, 'The Order of the Nation'?

    a) Governor Generals

    b) Teachers

    c) Scientists

    d) Mayors

    e) Police people

11. Give two examples of legacies of heroes in the arts.

12. Explain how heroes have changed Jamaican history in some way.

13. Give two reasons why a person might be given the Order of the National hero.

14. Find and read a blog or newspaper article about a contemporary sporting personality in Jamaica. Why do you think they were successful?

15. Imagine that you are part of a team identifying people who might be considered to receive an award. Write an essay of about 200 words justifying why you feel they should have an award.

Grade 7 Unit 2 Summary

National Heroes

In this chapter, you have learned about:

- What it means to be a national hero
- Who qualifies as a hero
- The characteristics of a hero
- The contributions of Mary Seacole.

How national heroes have contributed to Jamaica's development

In this chapter, you have learned about:

- The contributions of Nanny of the Maroons
- The contributions of Samuel Sharpe
- The contributions of Paul Bogle
- The contributions of George William Gordon
- The contributions of Norman Washington Manley
- The contributions of Marcus Garvey
- How the characteristics of Jamaica's national heroes compared to heroism criteria
- Jamaica's national heroes and their social and political contributions to national development
- How the actions of national heroes affect the quality of life of Jamaicans today.

Jamaican honours and awards

In this chapter, you have learned about:

- The different types of awards and honours that are conferred on deserving Jamaicans and foreign heads of state
- The significance of Heroes Day celebrations in Jamaica
- Why Jimmy Cliff was awarded the Honour of Merit
- The criteria used for different awards.

Outstanding Jamaicans and how we should value them

In this chapter, you have learned about:

- Some outstanding Jamaicans who have made cultural, social and economic contributions to national development
- How national heroes are honoured and remembered.

Checking your progress

To make good progress in understanding national heroes and their contributions to Jamaica's development, check that you understand these ideas.

Explain and use correctly the term *hero*.

Describe how a person becomes a hero of Jamaica.

Explain the differences and similarities between a hero and an unsung hero.

Explain and use correctly the term *unsung hero*.

Name the characteristics of a Jamaican hero.

Explain the role of the heroes in the development of Jamaica.

Explain and use correctly the term *heroine*.

Name three examples of heroes in Jamaica.

Explain the characteristics of a hero.

Explain and use correctly the term *development*.

Describe the system of awards for heroes and other important individuals.

Explain why it is important to remember heroes and ensure that there is a legacy for them.

Unit 3: Jamaica's Cultural Heritage

Objectives: You will be able to: ▸▸

Culture and cultural background

- understand definitions of the key terms
- use a variety of sources to identify the characteristics of culture
- understand different aspects of Jamaican culture
- classify aspects of culture as material and non-material.

What are the ethnic groups in Jamaica and what have been their contributions to Jamaica's culture and economy?

- assess the contributions made by different ethnic groups to Jamaica's culture and economy.

How have aspects of Jamaica's culture changed over time?

- understand which aspects of Jamaican culture should be preserved
- evaluate the ways used to preserve culture and heritage and suggest other methods that may be used.

How are culture and cultural heritage preserved?

- evaluate the ways used to preserve culture and heritage
- suggest other methods that can be used to preserve heritage and culture.

How effective are the institutions that currently help to preserve Jamaica's culture and heritage?

- evaluate the role of institutions that help in the preservation of Jamaica's culture and heritage.

Culture and cultural background

We are learning to:

- understand definitions of the key terms
- use a variety of sources to identify the characteristics of culture.

Culture is the customs, beliefs, arts and technology of a nation or people. A **cultural background** includes things that a group of people share, such as their religion, language, music, traditions, customs, art and history. Our **cultural heritage** consists of the cultural traditions that we have inherited from past generations. The culture of people from Jamaica is therefore rich and diverse.

People, for example, worship in different ways. Some Jamaicans are Seventh Day Adventists, while others are Pentecostal, Church of God, New Testament Church of God, Baptists, Jehovah's Witnesses, Rastafari or of other religions (Jewish, Muslim).

Everyone speaks English, but people also speak Jamaican Creole. Cuisine in Jamaica is very rich and diverse and people eat a wide variety of dishes, but in some families some meals are more popular based on their cultural background. Annually there are different festivals and celebrations linked to the various cultural groups.

Heritage refers to the features that belong to the culture of a particular society which were created in the past and have a continuing historical importance to that society. Examples include customs, traditions or languages. A person's culture is an important part of their identity. Identity is how you see yourself and how others see you.

Religions in Jamaica, 2011

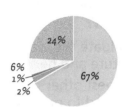

24%
6%
1%
2%
67%

▶ Protestant
▶ Roman Catholic
▶ Rastafarian
  Other religion/denomination
▶ No religion/denomination or not reported

Exercise

1 In pairs discuss, then write, your own definitions of the terms:

   a) multicultural   **b)** ancestor

   c) cultural background   **d)** culture

   e) heritage   **f)** cultural heritage.

2 In 100 words describe your own cultural background, giving examples of cultural practices you are involved with.

3 Write down three types of foods that you can eat in Jamaica that come from different types of cultural heritage.

Activity

Make a presentation about the cultural backgrounds of the students in your class. Find out about their religion, family customs and traditions and other information related to their cultural background. First, brainstorm your ideas as a class and decide who will do what. Then, work in groups and do your research. Use a computer to make your presentation. Include photographs or illustrations as well as music.

Our multicultural society

All countries in the Caribbean embrace many different cultures and people – Jamaica is therefore **multicultural**. Our **ancestors** are the people from whom we are descended. They are those members of our family and society who lived before us. Our ancestors came from many different countries. For example, some of the people who first lived in Jamaica came from South America, they are called Amerindians. Others are descended from people who came to live in Jamaica later on, as immigrants. This makes Jamaica a melting pot of different cultures, a mixture of people from different ethnic backgrounds.

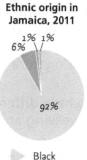

Ethnic origin in Jamaica, 2011

1% 1%
6%
92%

▶ Black
▶ Mixed
▶ East Indian
▶ Other

What are the characteristics of culture?

There are many different characteristics of culture. One of the main features of culture is that it is **learned**. We are not born with culture, instead we learn about culture from our parents and from interacting with each other. This means too that culture is **shared**. Another characteristic is that culture changes. It does not remain the same forever and so we say it is **dynamic**.

These characteristics can be applied to all cultures across the world but some cultures have features that are typical and noticeable about them. In some cases they have features that are unique.

For example, the Jamaican Creole or Patois is quite unique to the Jamaican culture. Your country's cultural heritage today is made up of many different things.

- There are different religions, such as Christianity, Islam, Hinduism, Judaism and Rastafarianism. The Christian religion has many denominations including Roman Catholic, Jehovah's Witnesses and others.

- There are different traditions and festivals, such as Jamaica Carnival, Accompong Maroon Festival, Easter, International Reggae Day, Independence Day Grand Gala, Christmas.

St Mary Parish Church in Port Maria, Jamaica.

- There are different types of cuisine (food), such as jerked chicken, ackee and saltfish, curried goat, oxtail, red peas soup, steamed callaloo, beef patty.

- There are different types of traditional dress, such as quadrille red and white plaid patterned dresses and shirts for men, bandannas for women.

Jamaica 50th Independence Grand Gala celebration at the National Stadium in Kingston.

Ackee and saltfish.

Traditional dress.

- People in Jamaica love music and dance. We listen to mento, ska, rocksteady, Reggae, dub music, dancehall, Reggae fusion.
- Folklore is also different. **Folklore** is the traditional stories and beliefs that are passed down in a society from generation to generation, mostly through word of mouth. Jamaican folklore includes characters such as Brother Anansi and stories about spirits (duppies) or mythical creatures (for example, rolling calf) that haunt people for various reasons.
  - We also have different arts and crafts including wood sculpture, ceramics, painting, basket weaving and bamboo craft.
- There are historical sites that are part of our cultural heritage, such as The Blue and John Crow Mountains (a UNESCO World Heritage Site), Port Royal, Accompong, The Rosehall Great House, Seville Heritage Park, Firefly Estate, Devon House.

Dancers in Falmouth, ahead of national labor day celebrations.

Traditional Jamaican wood carvings, Negril, Jamaica.

The Rosehall Great House in Montego Bay, Jamaica.

Case study

Folklore is the traditional stories and beliefs that are passed down from older family members to younger generations. Jamaican folklore includes many spirits or mythical creatures that haunt people for different reasons. Folklore is very important to our society, as it passes on important information about Jamaican culture, tells stories with moral messages or lessons to be learned and provides hours of imaginative fun.

Folklore like the Anansi stories originated in Ghana, West Africa, and came to Jamaica with the enslaved Ashanti people. Since then, various stories have been passed down from generation to generation. Many Jamaicans grew up hearing stories about the 'River Mumma', 'Pond Mother' or Mermaid. She is usually known to appear at midday.

How River Mumma might look.

Did you know...?

Jamaican Patois, known locally as Patois and called Jamaican Creole by linguists, is an English-based creole language with West African influences spoken primarily in Jamaica.

Case study

Arts and crafts in Jamaica have been influenced by the natural lanscape, plants and animals as well as the culture of the inhabitants living on the island. For example, the earliest inhabitants, the Taino Indians created zemis, carvings of their gods, which they used in religious ceremonies. Once Europeans arrived, the arts and crafts changed again. Today the arts and crafts reflect the wide range of different cultures living on the island.

Taino deity figure in wooden carving.

Activity

Patois Poetry

Tenky Miss Lou, Tenky

Mi is a born Jamaican, an mi proud

An yuh fi feel proud to

Fi walk roun an big up yuh chest

An say tanks to Miss Lou

When she did start, she neva know

A ow it woulda go

An nuff nuff people wen da laugh

An a call her poppyshow

1. What do you think this extract of a poem means?

2. Why do you think it is important poems are written in patois?

3. Write the third verse.

Exercise

4 Give at least one example of cultural influence the following groups have had on Jamaica today:

    a) Chinese   **b)** Indians   **c)** Africans   **d)** Spanish.

5 What are the cultural characteristics of your family?

6 Carry out some research into Patois, finding out when it emerged.

Research

Find out about the many different types of music and dance there are in Jamaica. You are to look at both traditional and modern forms. Write 250 words on the topic.

Key vocabulary

culture

cultural background

cultural heritage

heritage

multicultural

ancestor

learned

shared

dynamic

folklore

Jamaican national identity

We are learning to:

- understand different aspects of Jamaican culture.

As well as having a range of different cultural **practices** and objects, Jamaica also has a range of national symbols and practices, that contribute to our **national identity**. Here are some examples of the main national symbols.

Flag

The colours of the national **flag** symbolise different aspects of the island and the people of Jamaica. Gold represents the country's wealth and sunshine. Green represents hope and the island's rich vegetation, and black stands for the creativity and strength of the people.

National flag.

Coat of arms

Jamaica's history and natural wealth are symbolised in each part of the **coat of arms**. The two figures on either side of the shield represent the first inhabitants of Jamaica, the Taino tribe. The crocodile on top of the royal helmet of the British Monarchy and the pineapples on the shield represent the animals and fruits of the island. The motto 'Out of many, One people' is a tribute to the unity of the different cultural groups making up the society.

Jamaican coat of arms.

Anthem

Eternal Father bless our land,
Guard us with Thy Mighty Hand,
Keep us free from evil powers,
Be our light through countless hours.
To our Leaders, Great Defender,
Grant true wisdom from above.
Justice, Truth be ours forever,
Jamaica, Land we love.
Jamaica, Jamaica, Jamaica land we love.

Teach us true respect for all,
Stir response to duty's call, strengthen us the weak to cherish,
Give us vision lest we perish.
Knowledge send us Heavenly Father,
Grant true wisdom from above.
Justice, Truth be ours forever,
Jamaica, land we love.
Jamaica, Jamaica, Jamaica land we love.

The National Bird

The national bird is the Red-Billed Streamertail. It is also called the Swallowtail Hummingbird or Doctorbird, a species of hummingbird, which lives only in Jamaica and is endangered.

Tree

The national tree is the indigenous Blue Mahoe which grows rapidly and is often used for reforestation. Due to the beauty and durability of the wood it is often used in cabinet making and for carving decorative objects.

Red-Billed Streamertail in the Blue Mountains.

Fruit

The national fruit, the ackee, was originally from West Africa and was probably brought over on a ship carrying enslaved people. The ackee tree now grows abundantly on the island and produces large quantities of fruit.

The Blue Mahoe is a flowering tree in the mallow family.

Ackee, the national fruit.

Flower of Lignum Vitae.

Flower

The national flower is the attractive blue blossom of the Lignum Vitae, or the 'Wood of Life'. Various parts of the plant are used for a variety of purposes including medicinal remedies.

Exercise

1 Draw an image of the flag with arrows and labels to explain what the different colours mean.

2 Name three other plants and three other animals that are indigenous to Jamaica.

3 Why is national identity important?

Key vocabulary

practice

national identity

flag

coat of arms

What are the material and non-material aspects of culture?

We are learning to:

- classify aspects of culture as material and non-material.

Culture, or the way of life of a group of people is expressed in two main ways:

1. **Material culture** is physical. It can be touched, it is tangible and includes symbols, cultural buildings, heritage sites and objects used in traditions. Other examples include, food, clothing, sculptures or national heritage sites.

2. **Non-material culture** is not physical, it is intangible. It must be learnt and practised and has to do with how people in a culture think about the world around them, others and themselves. These include proverbs, customs, norms, values. Non-material culture also includes language, such as the Patois spoken by Jamaicans.

Material culture

Examples of material culture

Examples of material culture	
The ackee is the national fruit of Jamaica and is one of the main ingredients in the Jamaican national dish. Ackee is eaten with roasted breadfruit, fried dumpling and plain rice. It is highly nutritious and rich in protein, vitamin C, calcium and sodium.	
Jonkonnu is one of the oldest forms of dance in Jamaica. Jonkonnu is a band of masquerades usually performed in towns and villages on Christmas Day, Boxing Day and New Year's Day. The dancers would dress in costumes and wear masks representing different animals or figures such as a "horse head", "cow head" or "pitchy-patchy".	

Non material culture refers to part of the way of life that is **intangible**. This means you cannot touch it but it exists. Examples of non material culture include:

- greetings and body language used in Jamaica
- Jamaican folklore
- the sayings, or proverbs that are used in Jamaica
- unspoken rules or ideas about how to dress or dance
- attitudes and values
- customs and practices in Jamaica.

Proverbs are a good example of non-material culture.

Jamaican proverbs:

- Finger neber say "look here," him say "look yonder." (Finger never says, "look here," he says, "look yonder.")
- "When chubble tek yu, pikney shut fit yu". (When you're in trouble, a child's shirt will fit you.)
- No wait till drum beat before you grine you axe. (Do not wait until the drum beats before you grind your axe.)
- Cowad man kip soun' bone. (A cowardly man keeps sound bones.)

Exercise

1 What do you think each proverb means?

2 Why do you think proverbs are important?

3 How do these proverbs show Jamaican values?

Activity

Think about the non material aspects of your culture:

a) How do you greet different people? How do you say goodbye?

b) Make a list of the folklore stories you were told. What messages did they give you about Jamaican morals?

c) State two important values in Jamaican culture and explain why these are important.

d) Can you think of any customs you have in your family that involve non-material aspects of culture such as prayer or singing or dancing?

Activity

Create a culture club. Design and make a community board in your school and feature aspects of our material culture or non-material culture each week, with details on these are significant to Jamaican culture.

Key vocabulary

material culture

non-material culture

intangible

What are the ethnic groups in Jamaica?

We are learning to:

- assess the contributions made by different ethnic groups to Jamaica's culture and economy.

An **ethnic group** is a group of people who have common cultural backgrounds. They belong to an ethnic group because of their ancestors, their language or religion, or because of where they live. Jamaica is a multi-ethnic region because there are many different ethnic groups living in the region. Each ethnic group has different cultural traditions. They may eat certain foods or wear certain clothes. They may speak English in a certain way because of the language that they speak at home.

Our ancestors are the people from whom we are descended. They are members of our family who lived before us. The ancestors of people who live in your country today come from many different ethnic groups.

For example, in Jamaica some people are descended from the Tainos who first lived on the islands. Others are descended from people who later came as immigrants. These immigrants came from other Caribbean countries and from countries in Africa, India, China and European countries such as Britain, Germany and Ireland. Each group had different reasons for coming and each has made significant contributions to our rich and diverse culture.

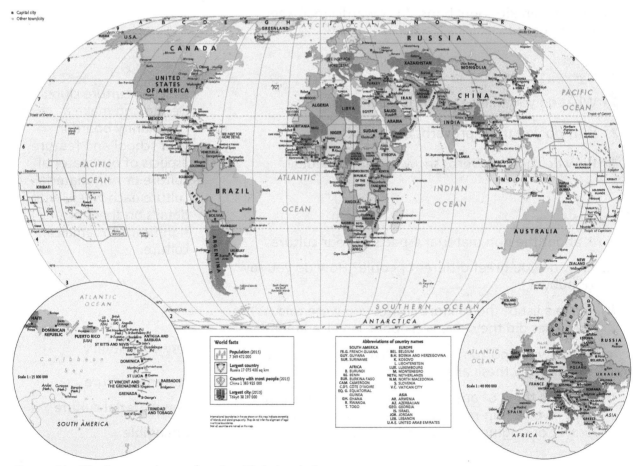

Can you identify where people came from to settle in Jamaica?

The first inhabitants ›››

The first people to live in Jamaica, known as the **indigenous** people of Jamaica, are believed to be the Tainos. They came from South America around 2 500 years ago. They named the island Xaymaca, which meant "land of wood and water". The Tainos were a group of people who lived peacefully. Each Taino village was headed by a chief called the cacique. He was responsible for organising all activities in the village including religious ceremonies. The position of the cacique was hereditary and included many privileges. The Tainos did mainly farming but also did hunting and fishing. The main plants grown included cassava, sweet potatoes, maize (corn), fruits, vegetables, cotton and tobacco.

These indigenous people settled in villages that they built all over the island. However, the majority of Taino people settled on the coasts and near rivers. This was partly because fish were an important part of their diet.

The Tainos lived in Jamaica without conflict until the Spaniards arrived after Christopher Columbus came to the island in 1494. The Tainos were painters, leaving paintings on cave walls. They were also master carvers, producing many exquisitely carved objects, including utensils, zemis and wooden stools used in ceremonies.

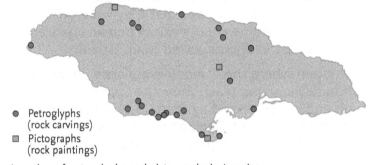

● Petroglyphs
(rock carvings)
□ Pictographs
(rock paintings)

Location of petroglyphs and pictographs in Jamaica.

Exercise

1 Which cultural group does your family belong to? Can you identify other cultural groups in your community?

2 Name six countries from which our Jamaican ancestors came. Use your atlas to find these places on a map of the world.

3 What other information can you find about these places from your atlas? (For example, neighbouring countries, rivers, mountains.)

4 How did the Tainos organise and govern themselves?

5 What were their religious beliefs?

6 What were their farming practices like and what other economic activities did they engage in?

7 What legacy did the Tainos leave in our country?

> **Did you know...?**
>
> For decades it was believed that the Tainos in Jamaica were extinct. In 2014, descendants of Tainos living in Jamaica came forward to declare their Taino ancestry.

> **Did you know...?**
>
> Words commonly used in both the English and Spanish languages such as barbacoa/barbecue, canoas/canoes, hamaca/hammock, and jurakan/hurricane are words invented by the Taínos.

The Spanish settlers

In 1494 a European explorer named Christopher Columbus landed in Jamaica. Columbus had heard rumours about Jamaica as "the land of blessed gold," even though he later discovered that there is no gold in Jamaica.

When he arrived in St Ann's Bay, Columbus discovered Tainos living in Jamaica. Columbus also needed a place to stay while his ship was repaired and to stock up on water and food supplies. After some violence between the Taino people and Columbus' men, Columbus claimed Jamaica as Spanish.

Fifteen years after Columbus discovered Jamaica, in 1509, the first Spanish colonists arrived under the Spanish Governor Juan de Esquivel. They first settled in the St Ann's Bay area. The first town was called New Seville or Sevilla la Nueva.

The Spanish mainly established small settlements. The only town that was developed was Spanish Town, the old capital of Jamaica, then called St Jago de la Vega. It was the centre of government and trade and had many churches and convents. In the following few years Jamaica was used mainly as a storage base for food, horses and goods. Very few Spanish people actually settled there. **Colonists** are people who seek to take control of a place and its people, often by force.

The arrival of the Spanish in Jamaica had a significant impact on the Taino population on the island. The Spaniards' impression of the indigenous people was that they were ignorant of many things and so their attitude towards them was one of superiority and arrogance. They were believed to be of no religion and could be easily converted to Christianity.

The Spaniards established the **Encomienda** system where the Tainos were placed under the rule of a Spanish master who would Christianise them and teach them the Spanish culture, and the Tainos would in turn work for them and be 'protected by them'. The Tainos were severely abused under the system and many died as a result. The Spaniards later turned to the continent of Africa for labourers and introduced the first group of enslaved Africans to the island in 1513.

Jamaica under Spanish rule.

The arrival of the British

The Spanish were living in Jamaica for approximately 150 years after Columbus first arrived but they lost control on 10th May 1655. The British led a successful attack on the island. The attack was led by Admiral William Penn and General Robert Venables. The island was not well defended and so it was easy for the British to capture it. The Spaniards surrendered to the British, freed the enslaved Africans and then left. It was this set of freed enslaved Africans and their descendants who became known as the **Maroons**.

The British settlers focused on growing crops that could easily be sold in England. Tobacco, indigo and cocoa soon gave way to sugar cane which became the main crop for the island due to the demand for sugar in England. The sugar industry grew so rapidly that by 1739 the number of sugar estates on the island grew from 57 to nearly 430. The growth of the industry led to increase in demand for labour and this influenced the growth of the Transatlantic Slave Trade. Millions of Africans were brought to the Caribbean to work on the sugar estates as enslaved persons.

From the 1750s until the 1850s, British-style buildings were the most popular style in the country. These were also made to withstand the tropical climate, heat, earthquakes, humidity, hurricanes and insects. Much of Jamaica's important building work from this period is found in Kingston, including public buildings such as Falmouth Court House.

Africans 》》》

Most of the African people who moved to the Caribbean came as enslaved people to provide labour for the sugar plantations. Millions of Africans were taken into enslavement and were shipped across the Atlantic during the 18th and 19th centuries to work on the sugar plantations and in the sugar factories. The majority of Africans who arrived as enslaved people in the Caribbean came between 1700 and 1810, the time period during which Jamaica became known for its high levels of sugar production.

The enslaved Africans came mainly from Central and West Africa. They came from the Asante, Hausa, Yoruba, Congolese, Igbo and Malinké communities. Many were kidnapped while others were sold to European traders. They were transported across the Atlantic Ocean on ships which were often tightly packed.

The journey between West Africa and the Caribbean was called the Middle Passage, the second leg of a larger system of trade called the Triangular Trade. Many Africans died on the journey to the Caribbean due to the horrible conditions on the ships, and many jumped overboard to escape enslavement.

Enslaved Africans filled the large labour force required for the sugar industry. They worked long hours on the sugar plantations and were often abused as they had little or no rights. Many would run away to escape the harsh treatment and conditions they faced. Those who were successful in running away joined the Maroons in the mountains. Those who were unsuccessful often faced severe punishment when they were caught.

Activity

The English/British maintained control of Jamaica for over 300 years until 1962 when it gained its independence. Work in pairs to find out more about the British in Jamaica.

1. What type of government did they establish in Jamaica?

2. What was their social life like?

Activity

Find out more about life on the sugar plantations for the enslaved Africans.

1. How were they organised for work on the plantations?

2. What were their living conditions like?

3. What were some of their pastime activities?

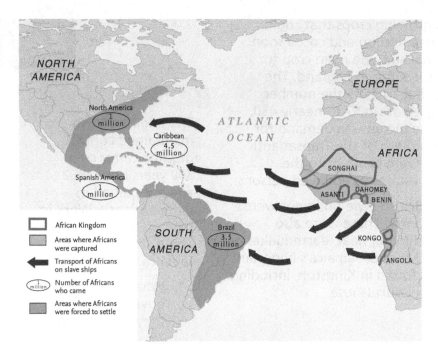

Asians (East Indians and Chinese)

When enslavement was abolished in 1838 in the British colonies, most of the former enslaved persons left the plantations to set up their own small farms and industries. This meant that there were not enough people to work on the big plantations, and this affected the economy of the island. Plans were drawn up to bring labourers from India under the **indentured labour system**. Indentured labourers are workers who are bound or obliged to work for somebody for a period of time at an agreed salary. The East Indians are the largest ethnic minority in Jamaica. The first group arrived in 1845. Most came from areas in north-eastern India and many came to escape poverty and for a chance to improve their lives.

Most Indian immigrants decided to stay and make the Caribbean their permanent home after they had completed their indenture. They brought their families to the islands, bought land and started their own businesses. Their cultural legacy is evident in the religious practices, foods, music and festivals of Jamaica.

The Chinese also came to Jamaica to work as indentured labourers on the sugar plantations after the end of enslavement. The first group came in 1854 and then others followed up to 1886 and then later, between 1900 and the 1940s, introducing a large number of businesses into Jamaica. The Chinese were experiencing difficult living conditions in China and saw Jamaica as a place of peace and a chance to build a new life.

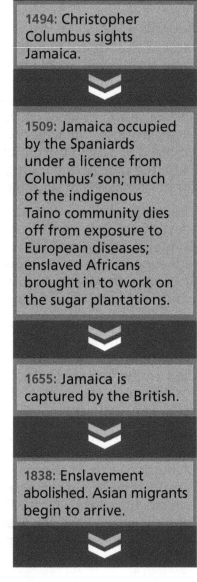

1494: Christopher Columbus sights Jamaica.

1509: Jamaica occupied by the Spaniards under a licence from Columbus' son; much of the indigenous Taino community dies off from exposure to European diseases; enslaved Africans brought in to work on the sugar plantations.

1655: Jamaica is captured by the British.

1838: Enslavement abolished. Asian migrants begin to arrive.

Jewish people

The first Jews came to Jamaica during the Spanish occupation of the island 1494–1655, mainly from Spain and Portugal. Jewish people were given citizenship by the British and then awarded full rights in 1831.

Syrian and Lebanese immigrants

In the last decade of the 19th century, immigrants from the Middle East began arriving in Jamaica. Those that came were the Syrians and Lebanese who wanted to escape Turkish oppression. When these immigrants arrived in Jamaica, many of them went into cultivating bananas or buying and selling. Many eventually gave up the banana business and went into retail trading since hurricanes often upset the banana industry.

Despite being a small percentage of the Jamaican population, this group has played a significant role in the commercial and industrial development of the economy. Through their influence as well, Syrian food has become very popular among Jamaicans.

Activity

Work in small groups.

Each group should choose one of the following and find out more about their history in Jamaica: Spanish, British, African. Find out when they arrived and how they influenced the culture and life in your country.

Exercise

8   Look at the map on page 68. From which parts of Africa did people come from?

9   Why was the indentured labour system set up?

10   Research why the Chinese came to Jamaica. Give two reasons.

1865: The British ruthlessly stopped the Morant Bay rebellion, which was organised by freed Africans in response to exploitation, and tried to force the local law keepers to give up their powers; Jamaica becomes a Crown colony.

1884: New constitution marks the beginning of steps towards Jamaican independence.

1961: Jamaica withdraws from the Federation of the West Indies.

1962: Jamaica becomes independent within the British Commonwealth.

Key vocabulary

ethnic group

indigenous

colonist

Encomienda

Maroons

indentured labour system

How has each ethnic group contributed to Jamaica's culture and economy?

We are learning to:

- assess the contributions made by the different ethnic groups to Jamaica's culture and economy.

In this unit you have learned about a range of ethnic groups that make up Jamaica's unique cultural heritage. In this section we explore the contribution each of these ethnic groups makes to Jamaica's culture and economy. The word **economy** means the system of how money is made and used within a particular country or region.

Taino

Contribution	Examples
Food and crops	Mammee apple, pineapple, star apples, naseberries, guavas, cashews, maize, cassava, sweet potatoes, ground nuts, peanuts
Cooking skills	Bammy – The cassava root was a primary root crop that was cultivated by the Tainos and baked into a flat cassava bread. The dish was prepared by first cutting the cassava into small pieces, and squeezing out the poisonous juice from the cassava pieces. When this was done, they would shape the juiced cassava and thrash into slab-like bread and bake them. Today, this cassava bread is known as "bammy" and has become a popular Jamaican dish. It is usually coupled with Escovitch fish (a cuisine from the Spaniards). Fried bammy, fried plantain, ackee and saltfish.
Place names	Guanaboavale, Xamayca
Carvings, artistry and other craftsmanship	The Tainos made carvings of their gods, called zemis, out of wood, bone, clay and stone for religious purposes. They also made clay cups and bowls. Taino clay bowl.

Exercise

1. What is cassava bread known as today?

2. What was the name of the Taino gods?

3. Describe how Taino culture has influenced Jamaica today.

Key vocabulary

economy

Contribution	Examples
Flora and fauna	The Spanish brought crops from the Mediterranean, including tamarind, sweet and sour oranges, lemons and limes, sugarcane, plantains, bananas, ginger, indigo, avocado and chocho. Later, sugarcane, bananas and citrus were to become important commercial crops. The Spanish also introduced almost all of the most common animals in Jamaica today, including pigs, horses, sheep, cows, goats, dogs, cats, rats and mice, as well as chickens.
Place names and names of features	Ochos Rios and Port Antonio are two place names associated with the Spanish. The names of some rivers are also linked to the Spanish, for example, Rio Minho, Rio Cobre, Rio Grande.
Cooking ideas and skills	Escovitch fish – this dish is usually enjoyed during the Easter season. The Spanish Jews who settled in Jamaica brought the Escovitch style of cooking to Jamaica, which includes a fried red snapper marinated with vinegar and covered with Scotch bonnet peppers, carrots, sweet peppers, onions and Jamaican all-spices.  Escovitch fish.
Religion	Among the many Christian denominations that exist in Jamaica, the Roman Catholic denomination was the first to be introduced by the Spanish. Although the Spanish first came to Jamaica in 1494, the first set of Spanish settlers came in 1509. The Spaniards who came were baptised Roman Catholics. Their arrival brought about the introduction of the Roman Catholic faith to the Caribbean and indoctrination of all those who were under their rule. However, in 1655 when the British defeated the Spaniards and captured Jamaica, they introduced the Anglican faith and banned Catholicism. As a result, today less than 3% of Jamaicans are Roman Catholics.

Exercise

4 Name three crops that were brought to Jamaica by the Spanish.

5 What does 'rio' mean in Spanish?

6 Describe the influence of Spanish culture in the area where you live.

Spanish names	Current names
Caguaya	Passage Fort
Esquivel	Old Harbour
Oristan	Bluefields
Los Chorreras	Las Chorreras
Savanna-la-mar	Savanna-la-mar
Puerto Antan	Port Antonio

The British have contributed significantly to the Jamaican culture due to the long period over which they controlled the island. Along with the areas outlined in the table below, their influence is seen in our political system, legal system, education system along with many practices and traditions related to social graces, etiquette and celebrations. Their legacy is widely seen in historical buildings and architectural styles.

Contribution	Examples	
Language	Officially spoken language, English	
Religion	Protestant Christianity – Anglican, Methodists, Baptists, Moravians	Anglican church.
Food and cooking skills	Rose apples and otaheiti apples, black pepper, tumeric and coffee, ackee, breadfruit, easter buns, sponge cakes, pies, pancakes, puddings. The British introduced the practice of having three course meals and methods of preparing foods through baking and steaming.	Hot-crossed buns.
Place names and surnames	Many places in Jamaica, such as the counties and parishes are named after places in Britain or people of British descent. The surnames of most Jamaicans are also British in origin. In particular, surnames such as McKenzie and McLean are directly associated with the Scots.	
Festivals and celebrations	Easter, Christmas, Boxing Day	
Political system	Parliamentary system of government, called the Westminster System. This is how the government is structured and its functions, which is modelled off the British Parliamentary system.	

Exercise

7 What types of religion did the British bring to Jamaica?

8 What cooking methods did the English introduce?

9 Which British festivals and celebrations do you celebrate, if any? Describe what happens.

Africans have had significant impact on the Jamaican culture. Their impact is widely seen in our non-material culture in terms of values, beliefs, traditions, customs, rituals, music, dance and folklore. In terms of material culture, their influence is evident in our art, craft, musical instruments, styles of clothing and accessories.

Contribution	Examples
Language	The Jamaican Creole developed from our African ancestors despite having strong links to the English language.
Religious forms	Ancestral worship, myal, Revivalism (Christianity and myalism), Rastafari
Food and cooking styles	Okra, coco, yam and ackee came from Africa even though they may not have been brought by the Africans themselves. Some methods of preparing foods are traditionally from West Africa while other methods developed while they worked on the plantations and had to find creative ways to survive. They cooked a lot of one-pot dishes and came up with creative dishes using what was available to them. Some of these include manish water or goat belly soup, mackerel rundown, duckunno or blue draws.
Music and dance	Use of the drums and the rhythms of Jamaican music are influenced by the Africans.
Folklore and folk medicine	Storytelling, especially about Anansi, stem from the Africans. Also the use of traditional herbs for different ailments.
Myths and superstitions	Belief in spiritual healing, spirits (duppies)

Okra.

Exercise

10 a) Name two material forms of Jamaican culture that come from Africa.

b) Name two forms of non-material Jamaican culture that come from Africa.

11 Describe your favourite Jamaican dish that originates from Africa.

12 Carry out some research on a religion in Jamaica which is influenced by African culture and describe it in a paragraph.

Contribution	Examples
Food	Curried food, lettuce, green beans, scallion, cucumber, cabbage, roti, wheat flour, egg plant
Farming techniques	Innovative methods of farming, including rice cultivation
Skills	Skilled metalsmiths and jewellery workers who created brass, silver and gold ornaments Metalsmiths can create beautiful designs.
Music, dance and traditional dress	Distinctive music, dance and traditional dress that were incorporated into Jamaica's culture Rajasthani folk dancers performing Chakri dance.
Religion	Influence of Indian belief systems, such as Hinduism incorporated into Jamaica's religious practices

Chinese >>>>

Contribution	Examples
Food	The salting of fish (particularly the angel fish) and hanging in the sun to dry for weeks was inherited from the Chinese. Stir fried recipes Steamed recipes Sweet and Sour recipes The extensive use of the vegetable Pak Choy
Business	By 1954, there were over one thousand commercial establishments owned by the Chinese. The Chinese were noted for their business skills and for the caring and nurturing of their children, placing great emphasis on education and family life. These characteristics have positively impacted Jamaican society. Over the years the Chinese became integrated in many professions such as law, medicine, business, retailers, civil servants and teachers, while others remained in the banking and manufacturing sectors.

Contribution	Examples	
Festivals and celebrations	During Christmas and other special occasions one can always look forward to performances of the Dragon Dance in the floats in the city.	Dragon dance.

Exercise

13 Which continent are India and China found on?

14 Draw a map of your local area, labelling the Indian and Chinese restaurants.

15 Do some research on Hinduism, and write three facts about the religion.

Activity

Aspects of our culture

Work in groups. You are going to prepare a presentation for a cultural or heritage day at your school. Each group will research and make a presentation about the contribution made by one ethnic group to the culture of Jamaica, such as the Europeans, the Africans, the East Indians, or the Chinese. Your teacher will help you to choose one of the groups and will organise a field trip to a local museum or library to help you collect information.

Spicy grilled jerk chicken with lime.

Here are some suggestions about steps you could follow or things you could do.

- Discuss how you are going to go about this project. How will you collect information?
- Make a list of categories into which you can organise the information: languages, religion, traditions, music, cuisine (food), dress. Allocate one category to each person in the group.
- Collect information. Make notes as you work. If you find out something interesting about another category, pass on the information to the person in your group who is dealing with that category.
- Collect or draw pictures. Collect real items too (such as clothes or food) and make a display.
- Draft three paragraphs about each category.
- Make posters or a presentation on your computer.
- Check and edit your presentation.

Discussion

In groups, discuss the contributions made by the different ethnic groups to our modern society. Collect photographs and make a collage to display all the characteristics discussed.

How have aspects of Jamaica's culture changed over time?

We are learning to:

- understand which aspects of Jamaican culture should be preserved
- evaluate the ways used to preserve culture and heritage and suggest other methods that may be used.

Jamaican beliefs: Rastafarianism 》

Culture and cultural practices change over time. This section explores examples of Jamaican culture that have changed and continue to change over time, such as **Rastafarianism**.

In 1973 Joseph Owens published a modern approach to Rastafari beliefs.

This approach includes:

- Haile Selassie is seen by Rastafarians as a living God
- The idea that God is found within every man
- Salvation for Rastafarians is an earthly idea, rather than heavenly
- Human nature is very important to Rastafarians and they should preserve and protect it
- Rastafarians have enormous respect for animals and the environment, as seen in their food laws
- Speech is very important to Rastafarians, as it allows the presence and power of God to be felt.

Exercise

1 Name some of the beliefs of Rastafari.

2 Carry out some research into how many Rastafari there are in Jamaica today, and around the world.

Jamaican culture: Food, dress and recreation 》》

New dishes have been embraced from other countries and some traditional recipes have been modified in terms of their ingredients and how they are prepared. It is common now, for example, to use coconut milk powder to prepare rice and peas. It is also common to find people eating Mediterranean-influenced meals.

Activity

Work in pairs and do your own research into the different religions that are practised in your own community. Find out about different denominations associated with Christianity.

A Rastafarian man with dreadlocks.

Did you know...?

The wearing of hair in dreadlocks by Rastafarians is believed to be spiritual; some trace this back to a quote in the Bible that says: 'They shall not make baldness upon their head.'

Significant changes have been seen in fashion in terms of clothes, hairstyles and accessories. These changes have been influenced mainly by North American and European styles.

With the advances in technology and the influence of the internet, significant changes are seen in the recreational activities for both children and adults. Ring games and storytelling are no longer as common as before.

Jamaican culture: Reggae music

The term **Reggae** was derived from rege-rege, a Jamaican phrase which means "rags or ragged clothing," in other words a raggedy style of music. The Reggae genre began in the 1960s evolving from Rocksteady and Ska musical styles. Reggae music is known to expresses the pain, struggle, hope and emotion felt by people.

What makes Reggae music distinctive is its distinctive rhythm, chanting and beat. In the 1970s Reggae became famous beyond Jamaica. This was partly due to the music of Bob Marley.

Marley was both a Reggae singer and also a committed Rastafarian and a political activist. Through his music, his words and his actions, he helped show the rest of the world Reggae and Jamaican culture. Since the 1960s and 1970s, Reggae music has spread and developed in many different ways around the world.

Research

Carry out a survey with other students in your school to find out which Reggae song is the most popular. Listen to the winning song in your class and then list some adjectives to say how the song makes you feel.

Research

1. Find out more about the musical forms that came before Reggae. How different were these from Reggae? What is Reggae music like today?

2. Take a tour of the Bob Marley museum. The museum is the former home of the Reggae legend. Marley's home is filled with rich memories and treasured mementos, which preserve the life and accomplishment of this great Jamaican musician.

3. Find out about two other Reggae icons and their contributions to the musical form.

4. Research the Sumfest Reggae Festival. How does it aim to preserve the cultural importance of Reggae?

Research

Create a presentation of three artefacts or examples of material culture and two non-material cultural characteristics. Describe how they have changed over time. On Jamaica Day do a presentation of your collection of artefacts using pictures, videos and PowerPoint.

Maintaining cultural practices in Jamaica today ➤➤

As we have seen, aspects of Jamaican culture tell us a lot about the history of Jamaica as well as about the importance of understanding what it means to be a Jamaican citizen. Culture changes all the time, for the following reasons:

- the spread of ideas from other countries through the internet
- people visiting Jamaica or Jamaicans visiting other countries bringing different cultural ideas with them.

In the process of culture changing, it is important to decide which parts of our culture we see as important to keep and which parts of our culture are no longer as important.

In some cases, there may be aspects of culture that are negative and should be abandoned.

In addition, changes in technology and new inventions result in new tools and new ways of doing some things.

Which cultural practices should be maintained? ➤➤➤

There are many cultural practices which are seen as important for Jamaica today, including folklore, Reggae, Jamaican recipes, traditional dress and dance as well as religious practices. There are also newer forms of cultural practices such as participating in sporting events like the Boys and Girls Athletic Championships (Champs). Festivals play a big part in celebrating Jamaican culture.

Case study

Carnival is an important festival in Jamaica, which attracts people from all over the world, to take part in a cultural celebration of music, dance and national pride. In Jamaica, carnival began at the University of the West Indies Mona campus in the 1950s. This became known as the "UWI Carnival", an annual event which still exists today. Carnival, however, did not properly begin on the island until Byron Lee, a Jamaican musician, decided to start it formally in 1990, and it has grown ever since.

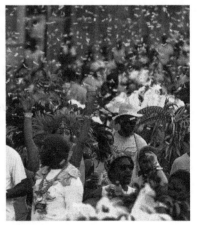

Celebrating in the street, Carnival, Kingston.

Discussion

In small groups, discuss what you have learnt so far about Jamaican culture and the different elements of Jamaican culture you are proud of and believe should be preserved and maintained. Be ready to explain, or justify your answer.

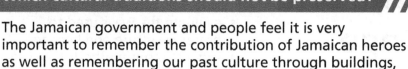
The Jamaican government and people feel it is very important to remember the contribution of Jamaican heroes as well as remembering our past culture through buildings, festivals, and religious practices. There are some cultural practices which are now seen as out of date, for example practices that represent old outlooks, such as men and women not being equal.

If a cultural tradition or practice involves treating someone badly, or harming them, if it is discriminatory, unhealthy, or damages the environment, it should not be allowed.

Discussion

Have a class discussion about family practices and other cultural practices in our society that you believe are harmful and should not be preserved. From your discussion create a list of criteria that could be used to select which traditions, beliefs, practices and values which should be kept and which should not.

Exercise

3 **a)** Name three cultural traditions which continue to be important in Jamaica today.

 b) Explain why each is important in preserving what it means to be Jamaican.

4 Why should some cultural traditions not be preserved?

5 Research one cultural tradition which is no longer preserved in Jamaica and write 150 words explaining why.

Key vocabulary

Rastafarian / Rastafarianism

Reggae

How are culture and cultural heritage preserved?

We are learning to:

- evaluate the ways used to preserve culture and heritage
- suggest other methods that can be used to preserve heritage and culture.

Preserving our culture

Preserving culture does not just involve human made objects or non-material cultural practices such as dance. Some parts of our cultural heritage are natural, and these need to be protected and preserved as well.

Preservation and conservation

If we preserve something, we try to keep it in its original state. So, for example, we can preserve food or we can preserve a building. But we can also preserve a tradition. The terms '**preservation**' and '**conservation**' have similar meanings. If we conserve something, we try to protect something from harm or from being damaged.

Case study 1

The Jamaica Conservation and Development Trust

The Jamaica Conservation and Development Trust runs a cultural conservation programme. One of its goals is to preserve the tangible and intangible cultural heritage associated with the Blue and John Crow Mountains, and in particular that of the Winward Maroons. Their work involves:

1. developing guidelines for conservation of natural and cultural heritage on nature trails

2. developing an education programme for schools

3. helping create guidelines for archaeologists working in the region

4. helping research to take place on the sites.

Blue and John Crow Mountains.

Case study 2

The Jamaica National Heritage Trust

This is an organisation responsible for making sure that Jamaica's cultural heritage continues and is developed. This includes buildings, monuments and bridges for example.

Their mission

To inspire a sense of national pride through the promotion, preservation and development of our material cultural heritage, using a highly motivated and qualified team with partners.

Our vision

To be the primary organisation that actively promotes and sustains Jamaica's rich heritage.

Their objectives

- To foster a sense of national pride and identity through heritage education;
- To identify, research, record, interpret, regulate, protect and preserve the material cultural heritage resources of the Jamaican people;
- To promote the sustainable utilisation and management of our material cultural heritage resources.

Functions

The primary functions of the Jamaica National Heritage Trust are:

- to promote the preservation of national monuments and anything designated as protected national heritage for the benefit of the island
- to conduct such research as it thinks necessary or desirable for the purposes of the performance of its functions under the Jamaica National Heritage Act
- to carry out such development as it considers necessary for the preservation of any national monuments or anything designated as protected national heritage
- to record any precious objects or works of art to be preserved and to identify and record any species of botanical or animal life to be protected.

Headquarters House, Jamaica National Trust.

Exercise

1 Visit a historic site, gallery, museum and find out how the site is preserved, take notes on your visit and then write a report on the findings. Include diagrams.

2 How important is the site? Evaluate reasons for and against its importance and draw conclusions.

3 Summarise the work of both organisations described above.

Why do we need to conserve our heritage? ▶▶▶

Our cultural heritage is in the food we eat, the clothes we wear, the music we listen to, the buildings we enjoy and the religions we practise. It is something we have inherited from the past, that we live with now and that we will pass on to future generations.

Our culture: ▶▶

- gives us a sense of belonging to a country
- helps us to develop an identity
- inspires us to carry on traditions
- connects us to other people
- helps us to understand the past
- connects us to the past
- gives us support when we have to face difficult situations
- helps us to understand who we are.

If we do not preserve our heritage, future generations will not understand what it means to be Jamaican. Without this knowledge and understanding of where we come from, people could lose their identity and lose respect for each other, which could result in conflict and unrest in our country.

Research

Carry out research into the cultural heritage of another Caribbean Island. Explore:

a) the flag

b) the customs

c) the traditional food

d) the celebrations.

Produce a PowerPoint describing all of the different cultural practices and heritage found in your chosen location.

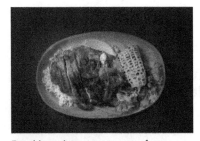

Food is an important part of our culture.

Our flag is part of our identity.

Chronixx has taken Jamaican Reggae music across the world.

Discussion

Have a class discussion about why it is necessary to conserve and preserve our cultural heritage. Your teacher may also invite a speaker to the class to talk about cultural heritage.

Exercise

4   Give two reasons why we need to conserve our cultural heritage.

5   Give one example of what could happen if we did not conserve this heritage.

6   Imagine that you leave your country and you go to live in another country for 10 years. The other country has a different culture. What would you miss about your country? What would you want to see and do when you returned to Jamaica on a visit?

7   Write an essay in which you explain the cultural heritage that you would like to experience on your return to the country.

Key vocabulary
....

preservation

conservation

The Jamaica National Heritage Trust

How effective are the institutions that currently help to preserve Jamaica's culture and heritage?

We are learning to:

- evaluate the role of institutions that help in the preservation of Jamaica's culture and heritage.

Culture and heritage are preserved through various means. These include teaching about them in schools, and ensuring students at all levels of the education system learn about and engage in activities that celebrate and preserve our cultural heritage. These activities include **Heritage Week** activities and **Jamaica Day**. Some aspects of culture and heritage have to be protected and so laws are passed to do so, for example, **The Jamaica National Heritage Trust Act** speaks to how historical sites can be used and should be treated.

Cultural preservation is also done through commemorating events and restoring historical sites.

Commemorating events ⟩⟩

We remember and learn to understand our history by commemorating important events. These celebrations help to conserve and preserve our cultural heritage. For example, we commemorate the time when enslaved Africans were freed and the arrival of our ancestors from other countries.

Study the table below. It provides some information about a few of the festivals and celebrations held in Jamaica each year.

Festival	What it commemorates	When it takes place
Jamaica Independence Day	This is a national holiday. On 6th August, Jamaica celebrates its independence from the United Kingdom in 1962. Street performers in Falmouth on this national holiday.	August

Festival	What it commemorates	When it takes place
Accompong Maroon Festival	An important annual festival, celebrating over 200 years since the signing of the peace treaty between the Maroon and the British.	January
Taino Day	This day commemorates the encounter of cultures between the Tainos and the Europeans (Spanish). An actress dressed in Taino dress.	May
Heroes Day	A day to celebrate the contribution of those who have made a significant contribution to Jamaica, as well as to confer awards.	October

Exercise

1 Why is Independence Day so important for Jamaicans?

2 Do you think that Indian Arrival Day should be a public holiday? Support your answer.

3 Find out about three other festivals that take place in Jamaica. Research what they celebrate.

Religious organisations in Jamaica also have several festivals that commemorate events in different religions. The table on the next page summarises some of these events. Religious events do not always take place on exactly the same date every year, because events are based on religious calendars rather than the January to December calendar we use every day in Jamaica.

Activity

Work as a class and create a cultural calendar for your classroom. The calendar should have pictures and information about all the main religious and non-religious festivals celebrated by different ethnic groups in the Caribbean.

- Brainstorm a list of festivals.
- Make a list of festivals according to the month in which they take place.
- Decide who will write and collect pictures about each event.
- Compile your calendar and display it in the classroom.

Festival/ Celebration	What it commemorates	When it takes place
Christmas	The birth of Jesus. This involves traditional food, gift giving and family and community celebrations. Celebrated by Christians and Rastafari.	25th December
Easter	Commemorates the death and resurrection of Christ, celebrated by Christians.	March or April
Hosay	A traditional Shia Muslim festival that arrived with the indentured Indians brought to Jamaica in the years following emancipation. Hosay (often pronounced Hussay) used to be held in communities of significant East Indian populations across the island, including Kingston, Spanish Town, Sav-la-Mar, and Port Maria.	Four days either in April, May or June in line with the Islamic lunar calendar.
Diwali	Hindu 'festival of lights'. It celebrates the victory of light over darkness.	On Amavasya, that is, the fifteenth night of the dark fortnight of the month of Kartik (October/ November).
Eid al-Fitr	This Muslim holiday, which is also called the 'Feast of Breaking the Fast'. It celebrates the end of the 29 or 30 days of dawn-to-sunset fasting during the entire month of Ramadan.	Varies each year, at the end of Ramadan.
Krishna Janmashtami	An annual Hindu festival that celebrates the birth of Krishna.	The date varies.

Exercise

4 Which religion celebrates Diwali? What does Diwali mean?

5 What does Easter commemorate? Is Easter a public holiday in Jamaica?

6 Do you know of any other religious celebrations not discussed here? Make a list.

Project

Interview a friend or family member to find out which festival means the most to them and how they celebrate it.

Share your findings with the rest of the class.

Restoring historical sites >>>

Historical sites are sites that served various political, military, cultural or social purposes in the past. A site can be a house, a military fort, a government building, a factory, a battlefield or a garden, for example. Historical sites are social and economic assets. They need to be maintained and restored to their original state if they are to be preserved for future generations.

Restoration of a building involves understanding the significance of a building and then repairing damage caused by use of the building and by the weather. Restoration sometimes involves removing structures added to the building that are not in keeping with the original style. The grounds around the building also need to be maintained.

Other parts of a site, such as a library inside a building, need to be preserved as well. Restoration of a field or a garden requires knowledge of how the area was used in the past. Was it a working farm? Was it a battlefield or the scene of social protest?

Restoration requires expert knowledge >>>

It is expensive and time-consuming. Allowing people to visit historic buildings and making them pay a fee to do so helps to pay for the restoration and conservation of a site. There are several organisations that are involved with restoration projects, including:

- Institute of Jamaica
- Jamaica Cultural Development Commission
- Jamaica National Heritage Trust.

Exercise

7 Explain what you understand by the term 'restoration'.

8 Research a historical site in your country and create a timeline from when it was first established to today. Has it had restoration work done on it?

9 Explain why you think the old buildings were preserved. What is the value of this site?

Key vocabulary

Heritage Week

Jamaica Day

Jamaica National Heritage Trust Act

restoration

Questions

See how well you have understood the topics in this unit.

1. A _____ is a way of life of a group of people.

    a) citizen

    b) culture

    c) melting pot

    d) heritage

2. A melting pot refers to:

    a) a mixture of people in a society, from a range of different ethnic groups

    b) something you cook with

    c) a society which is made up of only one ethnic group

    d) a country which has very high temperatures.

3. A/An _____ person is someone who is considered the 'original' individual or group living somewhere.

    a) immigrant

    b) emigrant

    c) indigenous

    d) tourist

4. Fill in the gaps.

_____ refers to objects that have a special symbolic meaning. They are tangible, whereas _____ refers to the practices, values and beliefs of a group. Examples of such touchable artefacts or objects include _____ and _____. Jamaica has a number of symbols for example, its flag, _____ and _____.

5. True or False? Chinese people came to Jamaica before African people.

6. Correct this statement: The indigenous group living in Jamaica were the Spanish.

7. Outline three characteristics of culture.

8. Write a short definition of the following terms:

    Heritage
    Economy
    Preservation

9. Make a list of three festivals or celebrations that take place in Jamaica.

10. Which of the following are Jamaican place names that have a Spanish origin?

   a) Port Antonio

   b) Kingston

   c) Bridgetown

   d) Savana-la-mar

11. Give two examples of legacies of heroes in the arts.

12. Explain how African cultures and practices have contributed to Jamaica in some way.

13. Give two reasons why some cultural practices should not be continued.

14. Identify two organisations in Jamaica involved with cultural preservation and explain what they do.

15. Identify two heritage sites in Jamaica. Write 100 words describing the importance of each sites.

Grade 7 Unit 3 Summary

Culture and cultural background

In this chapter, you have learned about:

- What culture, heritage, cultural background and cultural heritage mean
- Why Jamaica is considered a multicultural society
- The characteristics of culture
- Jamaica's national symbols and their contribution to national identity
- Classifying aspects of Jamaican culture as material and non-material.

Ethnic groups and their contributions to Jamaica

In this chapter, you have learned about:

- The contributions of the indigenous people to Jamaican culture
- What the Spanish and British contributed to the culture of Jamaica
- The influences of Africans on Jamaica's culture
- The contributions of Asian, Jewish people, Syrian and Lebanese immigrants to the culture
- The aspects of Jamaican culture, such as food and art, contributed by the ethnic groups.

How Jamaican culture has changed over time

In this chapter, you have learned about:

- How Rastafarianism has evolved as a part of Jamaica's culture
- How food, dress and recreation are impacted and changed over time
- Reggae music and how it became what it is today
- The importance of maintaining cultural practices in present-day Jamaica.

Preserving cultural heritage

In this chapter, you have learned about:

- The views on which parts of Jamaican culture should be preserved
- The cultural traditions and icons, and heritage sites in Jamaica
- Why we need to conserve our heritage
- The effectiveness of the methods used to preserve the culture and heritage in Jamaica
- The work of institutions that preserve Jamaica's culture and heritage.

Checking your progress

To make good progress in understanding Jamaica's cultural heritage, check that you understand these ideas.

Explain and use correctly the term *culture*.

Describe how different cultural groups contributed to Jamaican culture.

Explain the differences and similarities between different ethnic groups in Jamaica.

Explain and use correctly the term *cultural heritage*.

Name the main cultural groups in Jamaica and give examples of their way of life.

Explain the role of different ethnic groups in the development of Jamaica's society.

Explain and use correctly the term *cultural preservation*.

Name three examples of cultural preservation in Jamaica.

Explain why some cultural practices should be maintained and others should not.

Explain and use correctly the term *melting pot*.

Describe the main festivals in Jamaica.

Explain why cultural preservation is important.

End-of-term questions

See how well you have understood ideas in Unit 1.

1. Explain why it is important to become a good citizen of Jamaica.

2. Describe the characteristics of the ideal Jamaican.

3. Make a list of four freedoms that you enjoy as a citizen of your country.

4. Match these definitions to the correct terms:

    a) citizen

    b) naturalisation

    c) economic citizenship

    d) rights

    i) Something to which you are entitled

    ii) Someone who becomes a citizen of a country because they have invested money into that country in some way

    iii) Someone who belongs to a nation, or country

    iv) The process where a foreign person becomes accepted as a citizen of another country.

5. Briefly describe the Charter of Fundamental Rights and Freedoms.

6. Write about which organisations in Jamaica that you can go to get help if a citizen's rights are violated in some way. Explain how they can help.

7. Are children's human rights always respected? Give an example.

8. Explain what is meant by citizen action, and give an example of a citizen action group in Jamaica.

9. Explain what the aims of UNICEF are and give an example how they can help someone.

See how well you have understood ideas in Unit 2.

10. Explain what is meant by heroism and give examples.

11. Provide two examples of national heroes of Jamaica, explaining why they are seen as heroes.

12. Give two examples of the contribution national heroes have made to the development of Jamaica.

13. Make a list of the characteristics of heroes.

14. Match these characteristics of a hero, with their definitions.

    a) bravery

    b) self-sacrifice

    c) honesty

    d) helpful

    e) courage

    f) moral integrity

    i) A hero is truthful to themselves and others even if it costs them personally as a result.

    ii) A hero is someone who thinks about how they can help other people, rather than always putting their own needs first.

    iii) A hero will stick to what they personally believe in, their morals and values, regardless of what is happening around them.

    iv) Heroes often put their lives, jobs and families at risk in the actions that they take.

    v) Heroes are willing to give up their own needs and wishes in order to help others.

    vi) A hero is brave even in very difficult circumstances.

15. Give two examples of the ways that heroes are remembered in Jamaica today.

Questions 16–21 〉〉

See how well you have understood ideas in Unit 3.

16. Write about 200 words, explaining what the terms culture, cultural background, cultural heritage and identity mean in relation to the people living in Jamaica. Give examples of each.

17. Explain how Jamaica became a multicultural society.

18. Why is it important to accept and understand that people have different cultural backgrounds? Write a short paragraph to explain.

19. Write a short essay of six paragraphs in which you mention at least four cultural celebrations that are held in Jamaica. You should explain why there is a need for these celebrations and what each celebration commemorates.

20. Explain why you think it is important to preserve our national heritage. Give at least three examples in your answer of things that you think need to be preserved.

21. Create a timeline showing:

    a) The first settlers in Jamaica

    b) European settlers

    c) African settlers

    d) Asian settlers, and any key events in the development of Jamaica.

Unit 4: Utilising Our Resources: Natural Resources

Objectives: You will be able to: ❯❯❯

Physical resources and our environment

- understand key concepts
- understand the value of natural resources.

The overuse of natural resources

- justify the more frequent use of some resources over others
- advocate for the proper use of natural resources.

The importance of forests

- examine and analyse evidence from a variety of sources about the benefits of the forests for human beings and the physical environment.

Effects of misuse of the forest by humans

- assess the immediate and long term multiple effects of the misuse of forests on human beings and the physical environment
- put forward solutions for the problems created by misuse of the forest by humans.

The natural resources of Jamaica

- locate on a map of Jamaica areas that are rich in mineral/ore deposits and analyse the relationship between the exploitation of the resource and the growth and development of surrounding communities

- recognise how natural resources contribute to community development.

Economic policies and natural resources in Jamaica

- draw conclusions about the relationship between government's economic policies concerning Earth's resources and wealth creation and distribution.

Physical resources and our environment

We are learning to:

- understand key concepts
- understand the value of natural resources.

What are natural resources? Why are they important? >>

A **resource** is anything natural or physical that people can use to improve their standard of living or create wealth. **Natural resources** are materials that form naturally in or on the Earth. These include substances such as coal, oil and gas. Natural resources are considered very valuable and are sold between countries.

Many natural resources have to be **extracted** (taken out) from the Earth. Mining is a common way of extracting natural resources like coal, gold and tin.

Natural resources can be used as **raw materials** – that is, they are used to make something else. For example, trees are an example of a natural resource as they form naturally. Trees are also raw materials, because we can make paper, furniture and houses from them.

Renewable and non-renewable resources >>

Natural resources can be both renewable and non-renewable.

- **Renewable resources** can be constantly replaced and will never be used up – for example, water and trees.
- **Non-renewable resources** cannot be replaced. Once they have been used up, they are gone for good – for example, fossil fuels such as coal, oil and gas. Non-renewable resources are often considered more valuable, because they cannot be replaced.

Renewable resources: Dyewood cut and ready to be exported.

Non-renewable resources: coal being processed in a coal power plant.

Many of the Earth's natural resources are finite, which means that they will run out at some point. This means that we have to find alternative, more sustainable forms of energy and utilise other resources sustainably. **Sustainable** means using a resource in such a way that it can last for ever or carrying out an activity in such a way that it does not have damaging consequences that might limit that activity in the future.

Sorting activity

Which of the following resources are renewable? Which are non-renewable?

- Coal
- Wind
- Oil
- Natural gas
- Water, also called hydro
- Nuclear
- Gas
- Biomass, or organic material from plants and animals
- Geothermal energy, which is naturally occurring heat from the Earth.

Discussion

In groups, discuss why is it better for the environment to use renewable forms of energy?

The Sun 〉〉

We cannot live on Earth without the Sun:

- The Sun is crucial in providing heat and light.
- The Sun helps plants to make their own food by the photosynthesis process.
- The Sun is used in heating water and warming houses by the solar heater which changes the solar energy of the Sun into the heat energy.
- The Sun is very important in the formation of the clouds, the rain and the winds.
- When the Sun evaporates the water in the seas, the lakes and the oceans, water vapour is formed and the clouds are formed. When the water vapour rises in the sky, it cools and condenses forming the clouds. From this we may get rain.
- The Sun is important in the formation of vitamin D that is necessary for bones to grow.

The Sun is our most crucial source of heat and light.

Land and soil 〉〉〉

Humans could not survive without soil. It is an essential resource:

- Soil provides the nutrients for growing plants for humans and other animals.
- Soil absorbs carbon and carbon dioxide.
- Water is purified by soil. Water that flows onto soil is purified by a natural filtering processes, making runoff water far less toxic when it eventually reaches whatever destination, such as a river, or the ocean, it is diverted to.
- Nutrients like calcium, magnesium and potassium are absorbed by the soil and removed from the water supply.
- The soil provides lots of antibiotics and bacteria which are necessary to fight infections and illnesses.
- Land is an important resource as it provides the foundation for building, roadways and other infrastructure.
- Land is important for agricultural activities including both planting of crops and rearing of animals.

Soil is full of nutrients for growing plants.

Water

We cannot survive on Earth without water.

Water is another essential resource on Earth. Humans cannot survive without it:

- Water is a valuable resource. Every living thing needs water to survive. It should be used as efficiently as possible.

- Water is important for domestic purposes as well as industry and is very important in maintaining clean and healthy environments. In Jamaica our water resources play a large part in the tourist industry, which generates income for a thousands of people and contributes to the growth of the economy.

- As the human population increases, water use increases; yet water is a limited resource. Fortunately, it is also a renewable resource.

- The water cycle brings water to the Earth in the form of precipitation (rain, snow, for example.). It falls on impermeable surfaces – such as roofs and pavement – and on porous surfaces – such as lawns – as well as into oceans, lakes and rivers. It filters through porous surfaces into underground aquifers. Throughout this process, it provides water for use by plants and animals.

- Water evaporates from land and water surfaces, from animals, and, via transpiration, from plants to form water vapour. This water vapour then condenses and returns to the earth as precipitation.

Exploitation of our natural resources

Countries and companies can make a lot of money through the exploitation of natural resources. For example, countries such as Brazil have exploited their natural rainforests in order to make money. Exploitation means to make use of something. However, we have to ensure we do not overuse or over exploit our resources.

Over exploitation of our resources has come at the expense of the environment. For example, much of our land resources have been degraded due to over exploitation through deforestation. Soil in many areas is of very poor quality now, and is therefore unsuitable for other activities, such as farming.

Research

In small groups, you are going to carry out detailed research on one natural resource (Sun, land or water). Find out:

1. What sort of energy it produces for humans, animals and plants.

2. The advantages and disadvantages of the natural resources.

3. How important is this natural resources to Jamaica?

4. What is being done to protect and conserve this natural energy in Jamaica?

Put your findings together in a video or PowerPoint presentation, with examples and present to the rest of your class, with a handout.

The use and overuse of natural resources has many negative effects on the environment:

Natural resource	Impact on the environment
Coal	• Burning coal creates thick smoke that can pollute towns and cities. • Burning coal releases many dangerous gases into the atmosphere, such as sulphur dioxide. Large amounts of these gases in the atmosphere can be very harmful, as they trap heat energy and can lead to climate change and global warming.
Oil	• Oil that is used to fuel vehicles, planes and to heat homes releases dangerous gases into the atmosphere such as carbon dioxide and carbon monoxide. These gases can lead to climate change and global warming. • Oil that is extracted from the Earth often results in oil spills where oil leaks out into the sea. This can result in a significant loss of wildlife.
Gas	• Gas used to heat homes and create electricity causes air pollution by releasing dangerous gases into the atmosphere. This can lead to climate change and global warming.
Wood (forests/trees)	• Destroying forests can lead to global warming, as there are fewer trees to absorb carbon dioxide and release oxygen. • Deforestation can affect the global hydrological cycle (or water cycle), the continuous movement of water around the world. As there are lots of trees in rainforests, these areas contribute a lot of moisture to the atmosphere. • Trees are also able to intercept and store water, which is useful to prevent flooding. When large areas of trees are cut down, less moisture is put back into the atmosphere through transpiration, and flooding increases, as rainwater is not intercepted by the vegetation. • Deforestation can lead to soil erosion and loss of habitat and wildlife.

Exercise

1 Define the term natural resources and give examples.

2 Explain the difference between natural resources and raw materials.

3 Explain the terms renewable resources, non-renewable resources and exploitation.

4 Choose two natural resources and explain how their use impacts the environment.

5 Can you think of any other natural resources that are exploited?

Key vocabulary

resource

natural resources

extracted

raw material

renewable resources

non-renewable resources

sustainable

The overuse of natural resources

We are learning to:

- justify the more frequent use of some resources over others
- advocate for the proper use of natural resources.

The overuse and burning of fossil fuels such as coal, oil and gas, as well as the destruction of rainforests, can lead to global warming.

- Coal has been used for many centuries and continues to be important today. Coal is mainly used for power and heating homes.
- Oil is used as a fuel, to power vehicles and planes. It is also used to heat homes.
- One of the main uses of gas is to create electricity.

When all of these fuels are burned, they release dangerous gases into the atmosphere. One of the most dangerous of these is carbon dioxide.

Discussion

In groups, discuss different ways that you can think of for using less energy in the home. Share your ideas with the rest of the class.

Greenhouse gases 》

Carbon dioxide is a greenhouse gas. This means that it is a gas that forms naturally in the atmosphere.

Small amounts of greenhouse gases in the atmosphere are a good thing, as they keep the temperatures in the atmosphere warm enough to sustain human life. However, an increase in quantity of the different greenhouse gases is dangerous.

Too much carbon dioxide, methane, nitrous oxide and the other greenhouse gases in the atmosphere leads to an increase in global temperatures, otherwise known as global warming. Global warming can have very negative impacts on the environment such as melting of glaciers, increase in sea levels, higher, temperatures, drought and an increase in hurricanes.

Did you know...?

In 2014, Jamaica was ranked 94th out of 192 countries in terms of its greenhouse gas emissions.

Exercise

1 Give two examples of activities that may lead to global warming.

2 In your own words, define greenhouse gas and global warming.

3 Give three examples of how energy is used in the home.

4 Where in the world is very rich in copper?

5 What is copper used for? Use the internet to do some research.

Key vocabulary

carbon dioxide

The Earth's natural resources

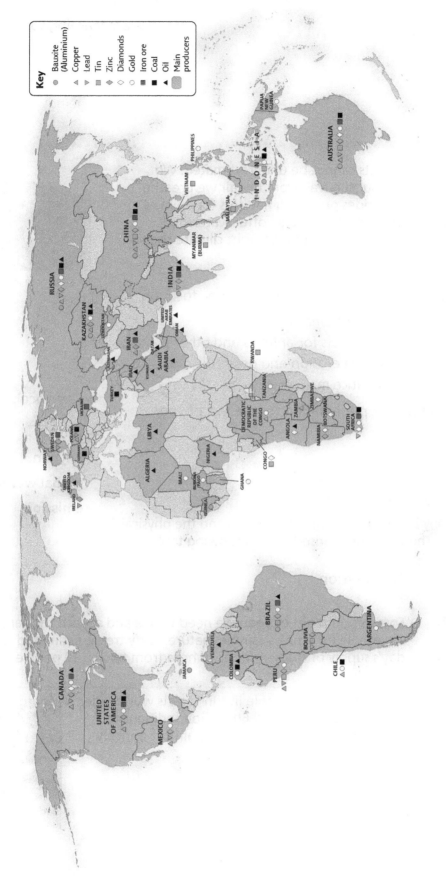

Key

- ● Bauxite (Aluminium)
- ◂ Copper
- ▾ Lead
- ▪ Tin
- ◆ Zinc
- ◇ Diamonds
- ○ Gold
- ▪ Iron ore
- ■ Coal
- ▲ Oil
- ▨ Main producers

The importance of forests

We are learning to:

- examine and analyse evidence from a variety of sources about the benefits of the forests for human beings and the physical environment.

The importance of forests cannot be underestimated. We depend on **forests** for our survival, from the air we breathe to the wood we use. Besides providing habitats for animals and livelihoods for humans, forests also offer watershed protection, prevent soil erosion and help fight climate change.

Forested area in Jamaica.

Research

Carry out research on the importance of forests, focus on:

- the role of forests for humans
- the importance of forests for animals and other plants
- how they prevent soil erosion and desertification
- how they help produce medicines.

Produce a PowerPoint presentation for the rest of your class, use images.

Key vocabulary

forest

oxygen

global warming

emission

The benefits of forests for humans and the physical environment

There are many benefits of forests for humans and the physical environment. These are summarised in the following tables:

Benefit for humans	Explanation
They supply oxygen and help us breathe.	Forests pump out **oxygen** we need to live and absorb the carbon dioxide we exhale (or emit). A single mature, leafy tree is estimated to produce a day's supply of oxygen for anywhere from two to 10 people.
They provide people with a place to live.	Some 300 million people live in forests worldwide, including an estimated 60 million indigenous people whose survival depends almost entirely on native woodlands. Block home on the side of a jungle covered mountain.

Benefit for humans	Explanation	
They keep us cool.	By growing a canopy to protect against sunlight, trees also create vital shaded areas on the ground. Trees in urban areas help buildings stay cool, reducing the need for electric fans or air conditioners, while large forests can regulate temperatures.	Apartment buildings in Milan, built with trees in the design to keep temperatures down in summer.
They provide food for us and the animals we eat.	Vast amounts of foods are produced by trees. Not only do trees produce fruits, nuts, seeds and sap, but they also enable a mixture of food near the forest floor, from edible mushrooms, berries and beetles to larger game like deer, turkeys, rabbits and fish.	Mushrooms on the forest floor.
They provide the materials needed for medicines.	Forests give us many natural medications, and increasingly create ideas for creating man-made chemicals. For example, the asthma drug theophylline comes from cacao trees, while a compound in eastern red cedar needles fights drug-resistant bacteria.	Eastern red cedar.
We use trees to build things.	Humans have long used trees as renewable resources to make everything from paper and furniture to homes and clothing, but we also have a history of overuse and deforestation. Thanks to the growth of tree farming and sustainable forestry, it is becoming easier to find responsibly sourced tree products. This also provide jobs for people.	Natural clothing is becoming more and more popular.

Benefit for the physical environment	Explanation
They keep Earth cool.	Trees keep the earth cool: they absorb carbon dioxide (CO_2) that fuels **global warming**. Plants always need some CO_2 for photosynthesis, but Earth's air is now so thick with extra **emissions** that forests help fight global warming just by breathing. CO_2 is stored in wood, leaves and soil, often for centuries.
They help in the rain cycle.	Large forests can influence regional weather patterns and even create their own microclimates. The Amazon rainforest, for example, generates atmospheric conditions that not only promote regular rainfall there and in nearby farmland, but potentially as far away as the Great Plains of North America.
They help to reduce flooding.	Tree roots are really important in heavy rain, especially for low-lying areas like river plains. They help the ground absorb more of a flash flood, reducing soil loss and property damage by slowing the flow. Here we can see the depth of these tree routes descending into a cave.
They help prevent wind damage.	Farming near a forest has lots of benefits. Groups of trees can serve as a windbreak, providing a buffer for wind-sensitive crops. And beyond protecting those plants, less wind also makes it easier for bees to pollinate them.
They prevent soil from blowing away.	A forest's root network stabilises huge amounts of soil, bracing the entire ecosystem's foundation against erosion by wind or water. Not only does deforestation disrupt all that, but the ensuing soil erosion can trigger new, life-threatening problems like landslides and dust storms.
They clean the air.	They can clean the air pollutants, not just CO_2. Trees absorb a wide range of airborne pollutants, including carbon monoxide, sulphur dioxide and nitrogen dioxide.

Research

Carry out some research into the trees and forests in your area.

a) Draw a map of your neighbourhood, including any trees or any forest areas

b) Make a list of the benefits of those trees on humans and the environment

c) Imagine you are given the task of proposing more trees to be planted. Which trees would you pick, and where would you plant these in your neighbourhood. Explain your reasons.

Trees planted in an urban area.

A mahogany tree.

A rosewood tree.

Palmetto palm.

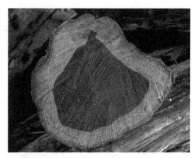

A cross-section of an ebony tree.

Leaves of the allspice tree.

The Jamaican dogwood tree has brightly coloured flowers.

Coconut palms are found all over the island.

Exercise

1 What chemicals do trees absorb? How does this help humans and other living species?

2 How do trees regulate the temperature and the weather?

3 Explain how forests keep the earth cool. Carry out some research to find examples.

Effects of misuse of the forest by humans

We are learning to:

- assess the immediate and long term multiple effects of the misuse of forests on human beings and the physical environment
- put forward solutions for the problems created by misuse of the forest by humans.

Deforestation

Deforestation refers to the removal of forests or trees. Between 1990 and 2010, Jamaica lost about 8 000 hectares of forest, 2.3% of its total forest cover. Although there has been an increase recently in total forest area, from 337 100 hectares in 2010 to 438 800 hectares in 2014, deforestation is a major issue with pressure from mining, illegal logging, clearance from crop cultivation and expansion of urban areas for housing and tourism.

Forest area, 2009–2014

Thousand hectares

500 400 300 200 100 0

2009 2010 2011 2012 2013 2014

Forestry cover, 2014

- Protected forest area
- Other forest area
- Other land

11%
29%
60%

Land cover

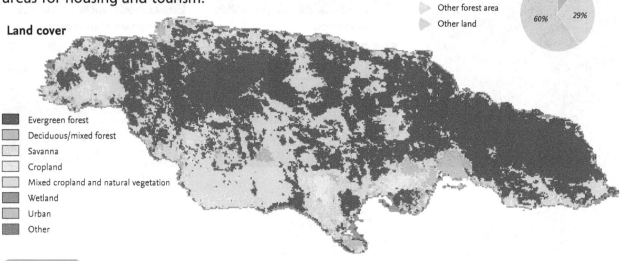

- Evergreen forest
- Deciduous/mixed forest
- Savanna
- Cropland
- Mixed cropland and natural vegetation
- Wetland
- Urban
- Other

Exercise

1 What has happened to the amount of forest area since 2009?

2 What does 'protected forest area' mean?

3 Look at the pie chart. What percentage of land in Jamaica is covered by trees?

4 Describe the land cover in Jamaica – describe:
   - where does most evergreen forest exist
   - where are the urban areas
   - where are the wetlands, and why are these important for wildlife?

5 Looking at the map, what would you say is the most important priority for the Jamaican government in terms of protecting the environment?

The impacts of deforestation include:

- loss of plant and animal species
- landslides on steep slopes, which may cause loss of crops, homes and lives
- soil erosion which leads to loss of farm lands and build-up of silt in rivers
- increased run-off which leads to flooding and decline in ground water supplies.

What are the solutions to the problems created by deforestation?

As we have seen, trees and forests are absolutely vital to life on Earth, but they are also being destroyed at an alarming rate. Trees are cut and burned down for a number of reasons. Forests are logged to supply timber for wood and paper products, and to clear land for crops, cattle, and housing. Other causes of deforestation include mining and oil exploitation, urbanisation, acid rain and wildfires. Deforestation also contributes to air and water pollution, a loss of different animals and plants, erosion, and climatic disruption.

Here are some solutions to the problems created by deforestation.

1. Plant a tree.

2. Go paperless, try to avoid using paper wherever possible.

3. Recycle and buy recycled products.

4. Look for the Forest Stewardship Council (FSC) certification on wood and wood products.

5. Eat less meat. Trees are often cleared so that cattle can graze for meat products.

Recycling your paper products is very important.

Discussion

In small groups think about how many of the above actions you can improve in your school. Create an action group in your school to raise awareness of the solutions above. Create a noticeboard and plan some actions, for example a tree planting in your school grounds.

Key vocabulary
....

deforestation

Activity

Look at the symbols below and explain what each means. Explain how each of these symbols help reduce deforestation.

The natural resources of Jamaica

We are learning to:

- locate on a map of Jamaica areas that are rich in mineral/ore deposits and analyse the relationship between the exploitation of the resource and the growth and development of surrounding communities
- recognise how natural resources contribute to community development.

What are the natural resources of Jamaica and the wider Caribbean?

Some of the most valuable minerals in the world are found in Cuba, Jamaica, and Trinidad and Tobago. Several Caribbean nations are rich in natural resources; including Trinidad's natural gas reserves, Jamaica's bauxite and most recently, a large oil field discovered in Guyana. The resources that make major contributions to the economy and the creation of jobs are: fisheries, land and water resources , forests, oil and gas, bauxite, iron, nickel, petroleum and timber.

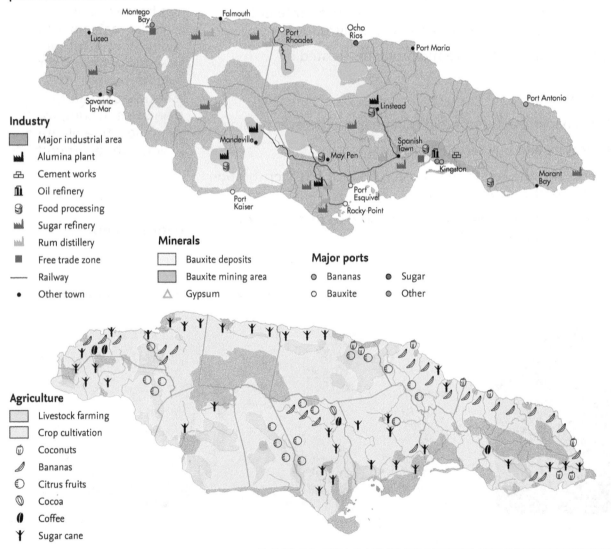

Industry

- Major industrial area
- Alumina plant
- Cement works
- Oil refinery
- Food processing
- Sugar refinery
- Rum distillery
- Free trade zone
- —— Railway
- • Other town

Minerals

- Bauxite deposits
- Bauxite mining area
- △ Gypsum

Major ports

- ○ Bananas
- ● Sugar
- ○ Bauxite
- ● Other

Agriculture

- Livestock farming
- Crop cultivation
- Coconuts
- Bananas
- Citrus fruits
- Cocoa
- Coffee
- Sugar cane

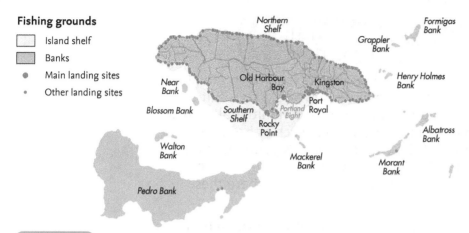

Fishing grounds

- ☐ Island shelf
- ▨ Banks
- ● Main landing sites
- · Other landing sites

Exercise

1 According to the map opposite, what is the mineral that is most commonly extracted in Jamaica?

2 Where are the most industrial areas?

Have a look at the pie chart.

3 What do you think is meant by 'services?' Give examples.

4 What is more common in Jamaica, livestock farming or agriculture?

5 Identify three foods commonly grown for export in Jamaica.

6 What are the benefits of farming for Jamaican people?

Economic activity, 2017

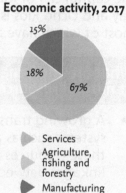

15%
18%
67%

- ▸ Services
- ▸ Agriculture, fishing and forestry
- ▸ Manufacturing

Resource	Changes in resource
Fisheries	Fish resources have changed due to overfishing and other issues such as habitat loss and pollution. The National Environment and Planning Agency has reported that the quantity of fish from our reefs has declined and that most of those caught are juvenile fish or young adults. Some species of fish such as snapper, parrot and grouper have declined significantly. Other forms such as aquaculture (freshwater fish) and ornamental fish have increased over the years.
Forests	Forest resources have been an important source for Jamaicans. However, in recent years these forests have been increasingly protected for environmental reasons. Therefore many areas of forestry are now in natural parks, or protected by law to ensure that deforestation does not occur.
Bauxite	Jamaica's bauxite occurs in a series of deposits across the middle of the island, east to west. The largest deposits are in the parishes of St Ann, Manchester, St Elizabeth, and Trelawny, with smaller deposits in Clarendon and St Catherine. Jamaica in the 1950s was world leader in bauxite production, producing about 5 million tonnes of bauxite each year. In the 1970s, Jamaica's bauxite production declined as Australia, Brazil and other countries started producing bauxite. By 2018, Jamaica's share of world bauxite output dropped from 8% in the 1970s to about 2% of total world production.

The growth of mining, extraction of minerals and farming in Jamaica over the past 200 years or so has led to more jobs and, as a result a growing population. As the population grows, communities also grow as there is a greater need for community services such as hospitals, schools and shops. Like much of the world, Jamaica's population has gone through a process known as **urbanisation**, where there is an increasing number of people living in towns and cities where these services are more likely to exist.

Over two-thirds of Jamaica's land consists of a central range of hills and mountains. This means that urban development in areas such as the capital city of Kingston and other principal towns such as Montego Bay and Ocho Rios is limited to the relatively small amount of flat lands most of which have a coastal location.

What are the benefits of utilising the range of natural resources in Jamaica?

- A growing transport infrastructure – which means better transport systems such as a rail and road network, not only to transport these resources after they have been extracted, but to create linkages between communities and facilitate the movement of people.

- A wider range of community services, such as schools, hospitals and other medical services have developed. As these resources are utilised, more people are attracted to the areas where they are in search of jobs and other opportunities. Services are developed to facilitate the growth in population.

- More jobs are created not only from the use of the resources themselves but also through the increasing services infrastructures such as jobs in shops, offices and a variety of other businesses.

Case study

Ocho Rios

The town of Ocho Rios in St Ann is described as a resort town. A resort town is one in which the main activities taking place there are related to tourism and vacationing. Ocho Rios started out as a small fishing village where fishermen and other informal workers made their living on the beaches. Its location along the coast and the natural resources in the area such as beaches, rivers and waterfalls made it ideal for development as a tourist area and so, transformation of the town for tourist activities started in the 1950s.

The tourist industry in Ocho Rios started out as a small industry but it eventually grew as more hotels were built and different attractions emerged. This spurred a growth in the town's population as people migrated from other parishes in search of jobs in the hotels and other businesses. By the 1970s, several residential neighbourhoods had been established and many returning residents purchased land in the area. The number and size of hotels grew and services available in the town also increased. Restaurants, shopping malls and entertainment areas were built to meet the needs of both tourists and residents. This also caused the town to grow in size, extending from the coastline to further inland. By the 1970s, the town's population had grown to almost 6 000 persons and to more than 8 000 in the 1990s. Today, the population has more than doubled with over 16 671 (2011 Census data) living there.

Ocho Richos, 1892.

Ochos Richos, today.

Activity

Read the case study above. Explain the reasons why Ocho Rios has grown into the town it is today.

What are the potential problems of the use of natural resources for communities in Jamaica?

- Urbanisation can lead to overcrowding in cities. This can lead to pollution and a lack of decent infrastructure such as sanitation and school places.

- Environmental damage may occur, for example, people cutting down trees and forests on the edges of towns and cities to make new houses for people moving into the area.

- Rapid, poor quality building into areas where there are hills on the edges of towns and cities can lead to mudslides or landslides.

- Where urbanisation occurs, there may be a lack of proper waste disposal systems meaning there is pollution of natural areas by rubbish and waste.

- Where mining and other related activities take place pollution of water and air may occur as result of waste generated and dust.

- Where land is being used for mining, cash crops or logging (where forests are being cut down for sale) and other uses, the natural habitat of some plant and animal species is being destroyed. Endangered species include the Jamaican Iguana, the Blue Mountain Vireo and the Golden Swallow.

Did you know...?

56% of the population of Jamaica lives in urban areas.

Research

Carry out a school survey to find out how students feel about the environment they live in, and what they would like to change if they could. Share your findings with the rest of the class.

Windalco bauxite plant

In 2019, effluent (liquid waste) released from the Windalco bauxite plant contaminated Rio Cobre river and caused a massive fish kill in the river. Residents from nearby reported seeing large quantities of dead fish floating in the river. Investigations carried out by the National Environment and Planning Agency confirmed that it was caused by waste from the bauxite plant. More than 40 fishermen who operate along the Rio Cobre have had their livelihood disrupted because of the contamination of the river.

Discussion

In small groups, discuss the advantages and disadvantages of having rich natural resources. Decide if there are more advantages or disadvantages and why?

Population density, 2016

Water pollution

Water pollution is a major environmental problem. Coastal areas are polluted by industrial waste, sewage and oil spills. The mining and refining of bauxite has led to the contamination of ground water. In Jamaica's urban areas such as Kingston and Montego Bay, waterways are polluted by sewage and trash, particularly plastics which do not biodegrade.

Exercise

7 Look at the population density map above. What does 'population density' mean?

8 Where is the population most dense?

9 Explain why more people may live near bauxite deposits.

What are the problems in mining communities?

Where people live close to a mining site, for work, there are often concerns about how mining communities force farmers to give up their land, which means they lose their way of life and income.

Mining damage

After the excavation of bauxite, red sludge waste is produced during the refining process; red mud lakes now cover many areas of Jamaica where alumina refining has taken place.

Residents of an area near St Ann, are nervous that the bauxite mining currently taking place in their community will not only displace farmers, but could possibly force them to leave the area altogether.

Having witnessed the aftermath of mining in the neighbouring communities, where they say the majority of persons had to migrate to nearby town centres, residents are worried that this too could be their fate. "We are now a practically dead community, and it is because of the mining. If you look at most of the buildings, you see that they are empty — just a few persons left," one resident reported.

"The nearby town used to be a big community, and then since the mining started there most of the persons who lived there migrated. The school population has fallen," said another resident. One active community organiser, told how, in previous years of mining, private landowners sold their property to a Bauxite Company and had long migrated, leaving the remains of a once thriving farming district.

One retired principal said that most of the residents have resettled primarily in the nearby town centre: "Right now this is a very small community because all of us have been mined out. If they come and mine out the land, where are we going to live? The people have to move to the local town to look for work because as you see, this is a rural community and it is basically farming that the people do, and if their livelihood is gone, they have to migrate to look after their family".

Exercise

10 What is meant by 'aftermath?'

11 What are the possible effects of mining companies on existing small communities?

12 What could the Bauxite companies do to help protect local communities? Make two suggestions.

13 Write a 100 word report on the advantages and disadvantages of mining.

Key vocabulary

urbanisation

Economic policies and natural resources in Jamaica

We are learning to:

- draw conclusions about the relationship between government's economic policies concerning Earth's resources and wealth creation and distribution
- propose alternative policies, practices and actions relating to how natural resources can be used to foster economic development in Jamaica and the wider Caribbean.

An **economic policy** is a set of aims or goals or laws set out by the government to grow the country's economy by creating jobs and earning revenue. For example, an economic policy may focus on building the tourist sector so that the country earns more from that sector. An economic policy can also be created around a natural resource and how it can be used to create jobs for people and generate wealth for the country as a whole. This was seen in the 1950s when bauxite created a lot of jobs and revenue for Jamaica. In 2018, the World Bank reported that more than 20 countries that were once considered low-income countries improved their status and became middle-income countries by investing in their natural resources, education and infrastructure. Countries that try to build their economy by using their natural resources have to make sure that resources are used sustainably and that wealth is shared fairly in society.

The government has a role in making sure that natural resources are used fairly and safely in Jamaica. They should consider:

- the importance of economic growth, the creation of jobs and incomes for people through the use of natural resources
- how new policies can be used to help economic growth through the use of natural resources
- the importance of the safety of workers, for example in mines and on farms
- the impact of economic development on the natural environment, the need to preserve the resource and protect natural habitats
- the need to provide proper infrastructure in urban areas, for example, providing sanitation, waste disposal, schools, hospitals and businesses as well as transport infrastructure
- making sure that the profits created by using natural resources are shared and reinvested back into local communities.

Discussion

1. What kinds of actions can the government take to make sure that natural resources are used well in Jamaica, to benefit everyone? Why might it be difficult to make sure that the profits of natural resources are used fairly?

2. Think about the various ways in which our natural resources are used. Do you think they are being used in the best ways? What are some alternate ways in which they could be used to earn income for the country and create jobs for people?

Why are some resources used more than others?

Jamaica's mineral resources include metallic ores such as bauxite, copper and nickel; industrial minerals such as limestone, gypsum, silica sand, marble, sand and gravel deposits; some precious and semi-precious stones such as gold, silver, and platinum. Traditionally, bauxite/alumina has been Jamaica's most important export mineral, though it has been subject to major changes in amounts.

- For a long time, Jamaica relied heavily on bauxite due to high demand; Jamaica was the leading producer of bauxite in the early 1950s.
- There is potential for the country to sell other minerals, but in order to do that, they have to make sure adequate environmental standards are in place.
- Mineral exploitation generates a number of environmental issues.
- Although it is known that there is lots more bauxite ore that could be extracted, additional research is being done to estimate the extent of these reserves.
- Other environmental impacts of mining include riverbed and beach erosion due to illegal sand removal, air pollution due to wind-driven dust, loss of beautiful areas of value, and failure to take care of mined out areas to restore them to their previous state.

Future resources that may be more sustainable

As part of the 2030 Vision, Jamaica has committed itself to gaining 50% of its energy from renewable sources by 2030. Jamaica is ideally suited to using renewable energy sources such as wind and solar. Jamaica has a lot of sunlight with strong winds, providing many opportunities for renewable energy alternatives. In order to protect the environment and allow for long term economic growth, alternative resources, not only for energy, need to be sourced. For example:

- solar energy
- hydro (water) energy
- reducing coal and wood burning with alternative energy sources
- composting
- harvesting rainwater for farming and washing and cleaning in homes.

Activity

Working in small groups, identify a natural resource that is underused in your parish. Work together to come up with a proposal of how it could be used to create jobs in your community.

For example, a cave could be opened up for tourist visits, or unused land could be used to grow produce for sale.

You should present your ideas through an art form such as animation, music or poetry.

Remember to include what steps would need to be taken, what jobs could be created and how the earnings would benefit the wider parish.

Invite industry leaders and government representatives to your presentation.

Key vocabulary

economic policy

Questions

See how well you have understood the topics in this unit.

1. _____ are materials that form naturally in or on the Earth.

   a) Chemicals

   b) Renewable energy

   c) Natural resources

2. True or false? Renewable resources are finite. Once used up, they are gone for good.

3. Which of these resources are non-renewable?

   a) Coal

   b) Sun

   c) Water

   d) Wood

4. Provide three examples of the importance of the Sun as a natural resource.

5. _____ refers to the removal of trees or forests.

   a) Desertification

   b) Deforestation

   c) Hydration

   d) Urbanisation

6. Jamaica's recent policy to improve economic development and social and environmental issues is called:

   a) Vision 2020

   b) Vision 2030

   c) GeNNex Elite

7. True or False? Urbanisation is the process where people move from cities into the countryside.

8. Correct this statement: Jamaica's economy relies mainly on renewable energy.

9. How does the use of natural resources help with community development?

10. Write a short definition of the following terms:

Wealth distribution

Policy

Infrastructure

11. Make a list of the problems that mining can lead to.

12. Which two of the following areas have particularly high population density in Jamaica?

a) Portland

b) Kingston

c) St James

d) Manchester

13. Describe what has happened to the population of Jamaica over the past 50 years.

14. Imagine that you work for the government and you want to increase economic development. Write an essay of about 200 words describing how you would use the natural resources to increase development.

Grade 7 Unit 4 Summary

Physical resources and our environment

In this chapter, you have learned about:

- What natural resources are and why they're important
- Classifying natural resources as renewable and non-renewable
- The value of the Sun, land and water as natural resources
- Exploitation of our natural resources.

The overuse of natural resources

In this chapter, you have learned about:

- What greenhouse gases are
- How increased amounts of greenhouse gas emissions contribute to global warming.

The importance of forests and the effects of their misuse

In this chapter, you have learned about:

- The ways forests benefit humans and the physical environment
- What deforestation is
- The immediate and long-term effects of deforestation on humans and the environment
- Finding solutions to the problems created by deforestation.

The natural resources of Jamaica

In this chapter, you have learned about:

- The natural resources in Jamaica and the wider Caribbean
- How natural resources in Jamaica have impacted the development of communities
- The benefits of utilising Jamaica's natural resources
- How the use of natural resources can created problems for communities
- Problems in mining communities.

Economic policies and natural resources

In this chapter, you have learned about:

- What economic policies are
- The link between economic policies and natural resources
- Why some resources are exploited more than others
- Using sustainable or renewable resources in Jamaica.

Checking your progress

To make good progress in understanding utilising our natural resources, check that you understand these ideas.

Explain and use correctly the term *natural resource*.

Describe how forest benefits humans.

Explain how natural resources contribute to community development.

Explain and use correctly the terms *renewable* and *non-renewable energy*.

Name the effects of overuse of natural resources.

Explain the role of the government in the distribution of natural resources.

Explain why the Sun, land and water are important natural resources.

Name the main agricultural products of Jamaica.

Explain how the use of natural resources have contributed to economic growth.

Explain and use correctly the *deforestation*.

Describe what is meant by sustainable development and give examples.

Explain the benefits and problems of using the natural resources in Jamaica.

Unit 5: Utilising Our Resources: Human Resources

Different types of resources

- explain the following concepts: human resources, capital, interdependence
- differentiate among the following: skills, abilities and talents.

Human resource development

- value the importance of human resource in development
- evaluate the provisions that have been made to ensure the training and development of Jamaica's human resources
- the importance of effective training and education in utilising natural resources.

What is a career?

- participate in activities to develop employability skills
- understand what is meant by a career
- understand different types of skills.

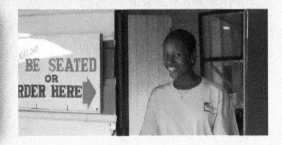

What are work ethics?

- understand how work ethics are important when using human resources.

Jamaica's Economic Structure

- categorise careers as primary, secondary, tertiary and quaternary industries.

How do we classify careers? Career classifications: groups 1–10

- classify human activities into primary, secondary, tertiary and quaternary industries.

How have jobs and careers evolved over time in Jamaica?

- relate historical time periods to changes in industries including new careers that have evolved.

Different types of resources

We are learning to:

- explain the following concepts: human resources, capital, interdependence
- differentiate among the following: skills, abilities and talents.

An economy is made up of businesses that provide **goods** and **services** to meet people's needs. In order to provide goods and services, we need **capital**, which are assets such as the tools and equipment used to produce the goods and services. We also need **land** (or natural resources) and labour.

- A resource is defined as anything natural or physical that can be used to create wealth or improve the standard of living of people. For example, people use land to grow crops or to mine metals and minerals.
- Natural resources come from the natural environment, for example, wood, water and soil. Physical resources are other tangible resources made by people, such as buildings and equipment.
- Human resources are people and their various skills, talents and abilities. People such as teachers, doctors, farmers, office workers, engineers, scientists and shop keepers all have skills that they use to provide goods or services.

Defining human resources (HR):

- workers or employees who offer their labour to an employer
- talents, skills, knowledge and experience that can only be found in people
- training and education are aspects of human resource development.

The ball is a physical resource. The player, his talent and his skill are all human resources.

HUMAN RESOURCES

For each of the following, brainstorm the physical and human resources that it requires:

a) a school   **b)** a restaurant.

What is capital?

Today, economists talk about two kinds of capital – physical capital (including land, which is a physical resource) and human capital. An economy needs human capital and physical capital to run smoothly.

Human capital is developed through education and training.

- Physical capital, including land, is a physical resource that cannot make or provide anything by itself. Physical capital refers to assets that have been made or found that we use to produce goods and services.

- Human capital refers to people, skills, training, experience, education and knowledge. It can only be found in people.

Skills are special abilities people have. They have been learned or developed. Think about the **population** of your country. You will recognise that the young and old people in the country are not able to work, as children and teenagers are still at school while older persons have retired and are no longer working. This means that the human capital used by most countries comes from the working-age population made up of people between the ages of 17 or 18 up to about 65. However, since the younger people (16 and below) are part of the next generation's human resources, it is important for them to be educated and equipped with a range of skills that will help them function effectively.

For a society to work well it needs to have its various parts work well together, relying on each other. For example, the economy depends on the education system to provide the skills needed by the economy to function well. This is known as **interdependence**.

Exercise

1 Choose the correct term to complete each sentence.

resource	human	natural	skill

  a) A _____ is something that we use.

  b) Wood is an example of a _____ resource that we use to make different products.

  c) Someone who has the_____ to play the piano may go on to become a great musician.

  d) The _____ resources of a country lie in its people.

2 List two main differences between human and physical resources.

3 Explain what is meant by interdependence.

4 Look at the picture of the people making up the word 'resources' on the opposite page. What does this picture tell you about human resources?

Key vocabulary

goods

services

capital

land

population

interdependence

Human resources and economic development

We are learning to:

- value the importance of human resource in development.

Economic development is the activity of improving a country's **standard of living** by creating jobs, supporting **innovation** and new ideas, creating **wealth** or making improvements to people's **quality of life**.

When a country has a high standard of education and training, with investment in human resources, there are many benefits to the economy. Skilled, educated people can offer:

- a variety of skills, which in turn offer a range of goods and services
- creative innovations
- expertise that can lead to better planning and use of resources
- new manufacturing and agricultural practices, which can provide for the country's needs more efficiently
- an increase in the wealth generated for the country
- improved creativity, allowing people to solve problems facing the country
- increased levels of production so that more goods and services become available
- more jobs and opportunities, influencing improved standards of living and a decrease in poverty and crime levels.

Creating jobs is a part of improving a country's standard of living.

Discussion

Have a class discussion about the link between education and economic development.

Exercise

1 Write your own definition of economic development.

2 Using your definition, research the examples of economic development activities that you can find in Jamaica.

3 Brainstorm ways that human resources are important to the development of a country.

4 Outline five benefits to a country's economy that skilled people can offer.

5 Write two paragraphs of approximately 250 words on what skilled and educated people can give to a country's economy.

Skills
Which provide a range of goods and services to be sold at home and abroad.

Innovations
A skilled, educated workforce helps to find solutions to challenges in sectors such as healthcare, education, technology, manufacturing and agriculture.

Expertise
A more highly skilled workforce can lead to better planning and use of resources, for example workers are be given tasks that their skills match.

Opportunities
As an economy develops, it requires more skilled people to work in the new sectors – this creates more jobs and opportunities, which in turn influences improved standards of living and helps to decrease poverty and crime levels.

A skilled and educated workforce offers a country's economy

New practices
New practices in key industries such as manufacturing and agriculture, can provide for the country's needs more efficiently, for example manufacturing can be more efficient with new equipment and better production processes.

Production
As levels of production increase, it means more goods and services become available, which in turn helps to contribute to the country's and the workforce's wealth.

Creativity
Problems require solutions, and a skilled workforce, which can solve these problems creatively, helps to contribute to the economy. For example working together as a team, rather than individually makes a business more efficient.

Wealth
The education and training of a country's workforce will determine how well that country's economy will perform – a highly performing economy is both beneficial to the country and the individual.

6 Look at the mind map on this page and look at what a skilled and educated workforce can offer a country's economy. Identify at least one benefit to the economy for each of the following:

   a) building a hospital

   b) establishing a school

   c) providing communication infrastructure.

7 How do you think each of the following could help economic development?

   a) A government offers a free computer training course for 500 school-leavers.

   b) A business offers internships to 20 students.

   c) A bank offers training bursaries for students studying economics and finance, on condition that the students work at the bank for at least one year after qualifying.

Key vocabulary

economic development

standard of living

innovation

wealth

quality of life

The role of importing and exporting labour in Jamaica

We are learning to:

- evaluate the provisions that have been made to ensure the training and development of Jamaica's human resources
- the importance of effective training and education in utilising natural resources.

Every country imports and exports labour, often to fill a gap in an area where the human resources are lacking.

To import means to bring services or goods into a country, while exporting means to send goods or services elsewhere.

Some instances in which Jamaica imported labour include:

- the use of indentured labourers from India and China in the mid-1800s to work on the sugar plantations. After enslavement ended in 1838, the former enslaved Africans refused to continue working on the plantations and so it became necessary for the plantation owners to import labour from elsewhere
- the use of scientists and engineers from overseas to work in the bauxite industry, especially in the early stages of development. This became necessary until local persons could be trained in the operation and maintenance of the machines and different equipment used in the industry
- the use of nurses and doctors from Cuba to combat shortages in the health sector created by local nurses migrating; the use of Cuban teachers to teach Spanish as a second language to students.

Some instances in which Jamaica exported labour include:

- Jamaicans (and other Caribbean nationals) went to Panama to first work on the building of the railway lines in the 1850s and then on the Panama Canal in the 1880s. One of the many factors which influenced this was the conditions that many faced after enslavement came to an end in 1838 (high unemployment, low wages, poverty). An estimated 10 000 Jamaicans went to Panama to work over the period.

- Jamaicans (and other Caribbean nationals) going to the UK after World War II between 1948 and 1970 to help rebuild the country's economy. The UK was suffering from severe labour shortage at the end of the war. The persons who went became known as the "Windrush Generation"; the name of the ship that brought the first group was called the Windrush.

- Jamaicans migrate yearly to the United States and Canada on what is known as the "Farm Work"

Research

Carry out research into the "Windrush Generation". Produce a leaflet explaining why people went to the UK and find out about the kinds of work that they carried out in the UK.

The Panama Canal.

programme and hundreds go to work in the hospitality sectors either in hotels or on cruise lines.

- In more recent times, Jamaican nurses have been heavily recruited by the United Kingdom. Teachers have always been recruited by the United States and UK; Japan and China have now joined the recruitment drive.

Skilled workers in Jamaica ⟩⟩

As Jamaica's economy grows and develops, more and more skilled workers are needed. This has meant that at times, the workforce is short of particular skilled workers.

The Bank of Jamaica: We need more skilled workers

The Bank of Jamaica announced that Jamaica needs to produce more skilled workers to avoid a crisis in the economy. The Governor of the Bank of Jamaica noted that while the bank is encouraged by the employment results, it also presents some issues for further policy debate. Jamaica added 29 200 net new jobs over the year to July 2017. Unemployment rate declined to 11.3%, down 1.6 percentage points from a year earlier.

"This represents the lowest unemployment rate since July 2009 and suggests that employment is growing faster than the labour force," the Governor said. "While these numbers are heartening, they also suggest that Jamaica is beginning to approach its capacity limits in terms of skilled labour. It is therefore critical for the country to increase the pool of skilled workers," he warned.

Activity

Find out two other instances in which Jamaica has either imported or exported labour.

Panama Canal construction, 1913.

Exercise

1. What are 'skilled workers?'

2. What sorts of skills might be necessary to have, working in a bank?

3. Imagine you are in charge of the education system in Jamaica. Write three new policies you would put into place to provide more skilled workers.

4. What will happen without skilled workers in Jamaica?

5. Write an interview schedule, or set of questions you would ask someone about their skills.

Discussion

Discuss why Jamaicans travel overseas to work. Why do Jamaicans seek specialists from outside the Caribbean region to carry out specialised duties? Create a poster explaining the reasons for exporting and importing labour for the exploitation of resources in Jamaica.

The importance of effective training and education in utilising natural resources

Education is the teaching of **knowledge**, ideas, opinions, beliefs and skills.

Investments are made in education based on its importance in economic development. It is recognised that education can:

- improve skills and competencies in the labour force
- produce knowledge and expertise to create new products
- generate ideas and create new markets and opportunities
- pass on cultural values and traditions and help harness them to generate income
- transform the political landscape.

Vision 2030: improving Jamaica's workforce

In the past, Jamaica's workforce had a shortage of highly skilled workers. A workforce is the people who are working. This slowed down economic development. Companies who needed more highly skilled workers had to employ people from other countries. Vision 2030 which was introduced in 2009 outlines strategies to improve the country's workforce by 2030 by improving education.

Vision 2030 logo.

The current aim is to create a globally competitive high quality workforce that will meet the needs of an increasingly knowledge-based economy and society. To this end, the Vision Statement was developed was as follows:

"Well-resourced, internationally recognised, values-based system that develops critical thinking, life-long learners who are productive and successful and can effectively contribute to an improved quality of life at the personal, national and global levels."

This vision is consistent with the national vision statement:

"Jamaica, the place of choice to raise families, live, work and do business."

> **Did you know...?**
>
> The allocation to the Ministry of Education, Youth and Information for financial year 2018/19 was increased by $2.7 billion, moving to $101.6 billion from $98.9 billion in 2017/18.

Effective training and education

It is also recognised that effective training and education are important for the sustainable use of natural resources. A well-trained and educated workforce is needed because:

- resources that are finite and non-renewable require the application of innovative ideas when using them so that they can be preserved and not be depleted

- utilising some natural resources as raw materials to make other products requires expert, and often scientific, knowledge to ensure they are used safely and accurately to achieve the desired end result
- utilising some natural resources creates challenges and issues for both the natural and social environment. Expert as well as creative minds are needed to pre-empt these problems and design solutions to address them and minimise their impact.

Activity

Imagine you are setting up a new bauxite mine in Jamaica. Make a list of the sorts of skills you might need in your workforce to do the following:

a) design the mine

b) build the mine and make sure it is safe

c) protect the environment and manage the waste products

d) interview staff for jobs working in the mine

e) manage the transport of bauxite.

Research

Carry out research into the types of courses you can take as an adult as part of lifelong learning. Why might you need to learn new skills as you move through your career?

Case study

Amelia left school with basic qualifications, and began work in a hotel as a receptionist. After two years, she was promoted to a more senior position in managing the reception, and so she attended adult education college to develop her computer skills. After a year, Amelia was asked to become a junior manager of another hotel, so she returned to adult education to do a management course. One day Amelia hopes to be able to be more involved with running the financial side of the hotel.

Activity

What does Amelia's story tell us about the importance of lifelong learning? What skills might Amelia need in future? How might she gain these skills?

Discussion

In groups, define the term 'education' and discuss the importance of education in developing our human resources. Brainstorm your ideas and write them up in a large mind map. Take the ideas from your discussion. Use them to create a poem, song or poster showing how education benefits the nation.

Lifelong learning can be started in school.

Key vocabulary
....

knowledge

What is human resource development?

We are learning to:

- evaluate the provisions that have been made to facilitate training and development of Jamaica's human resource.

The term **human resource development** (HRD) is used when we talk about **employees** developing their personal and professional skills, knowledge and abilities. It focuses on developing the best labour force possible, so that the company and its employees can achieve their work goals and deliver excellent service to customers or clients.

Training can start earlier. Once a student has graduated from secondary school, they can do further training in institutions such as:

- colleges and technical colleges
- universities
- online colleges or training websites.

People who go on to do further training after school may have a wider choice of careers open to them. They can also earn more money. Once a person is employed, it is still important that they continue to develop their skills and abilities. Some companies and **employers** may offer:

- on-the-job training – training whilst working, to help develop skills within a job
- mentorship (or coaching) – a more experienced employee gives advice and support to someone less experienced
- succession training – where the employee's skills and abilities are developed to prepare them for promotion
- tuition assistance – an employee can go on additional training courses to help build up their knowledge and skills.

> **Did you know...?**
>
> The National Vocational Qualification of Jamaica (NVQ-J) is a certificate of competence that is recognised island-wide as well as in the CARICOM and Commonwealth countries.

A welder doing on-the-job training.

Activity

Visit the website of training centres for adults. Make a list of 10 of the courses that are available. What kinds of jobs might these courses lead to?

Literacy now at 87%

The Jamaican Foundation for Lifelong Learning (JFLL) states that Jamaica's adult literacy rate is now at 87%. This compares to 50% in 1974. There is more to do to improve literacy rates, which are important as this affects the country's productivity and competitiveness.

The foundation is growing and trying to make sure that all adults who need it have access to education. A spokesperson said that having literacy and numeracy skills are very important for adults to gain a good jobs. The foundation is working hard to update its courses so that learners can also develop their computer skills.

Activity

1. What is meant by 'adult literacy rate?'.

2. Give an example of how improved literacy might improve your chances of getting a better job.

3. Why might it be important to have computer skills for work today?

Exercise

1 What is meant by a workforce?

2 Give three reasons why education is seen as an important investment in Jamaica.

3 Define the term 'education'.

4 Why do you think people choose to spend the time and money on further study? Give at least two reasons.

5 Why would employers choose to offer training to their employees?

6 Write a sentence about the role of education in human resources for:

    a) companies   **b)** employees   **c)** the country.

    (Hint: What does education do for the human resources in each of these categories?)

Key vocabulary
....

human resource development

employee

employer

What is earning a living?

We are learning to:

- participate in activities to develop employability skills.

The term 'earning a living' refers to the many ways through which a **wage** or **salary** may be earned.

A wage is a payment to a worker for work done in a particular time period. Payment may be calculated as a fixed amount for each task completed (known as a piece rate), at an hourly or daily rate or based on an easily measured quantity of work done.

A salary is where the employer pays a prearranged amount at regular intervals (such as weekly or monthly), often regardless of hours worked.

Large companies, such as The Bank of Jamaica, pay workers a basic wage, as well as non-salaried benefits called perks. These are benefits such as paid vacations, company vehicles or company medical benefits.

An employer is a person, or organisation, who employs someone to do a particular job. Employers have a responsibility to workers, such as ensuring safe working conditions, and a responsibility to the government to operate lawfully.

Employees are people who work for a company. They are hired to do a job, and are usually paid on a monthly basis. For example, a cashier is paid to sit at a cashpoint and ring up the goods at a shop. Other examples include teachers, nurses, police officers and fire fighters, who are employed by the government to work in schools, hospitals, police stations and fire stations.

Employers have a responsibility to their workers.

What are the ideal qualities of a good employee? 〉〉

There are different qualities needed for different jobs. However there are several basic skills that are necessary for all types of jobs, including:

- honesty – being able to tell the truth is really important, people need to know you as an honest employee
- reliability – being at work on time on a regular basis, doing what you say you will do
- punctuality – being on time and ready to work is very important
- taking responsibility – making sure that if you say you are going to do something you make sure that it gets done properly

- being a good team player – being able to get on with other people and work alongside others is often very important
- being organised and well presented – making sure that you wear appropriate clothing, and making sure that you are ready for work
- listening carefully to instructions – making sure you are clear what it is that you need to do.

Activity

Look at the list of qualities above. Which of these do you think are you best at? Which are the areas you need to work at?

What are the ideal qualities of an employer? »»

In order to encourage workers to want to work hard and be loyal workers, it is important that an employer also demonstrates strengths and skills. To be a good employer you need to have the following qualities:

- Leadership – making changes, taking decisions, helping employees through difficult times, inspiring people to want to work hard
- Management skills – helping manage employees and work situations effectively and efficiently
- Listening skills – understanding how employees feel and think
- Making sure employees feel safe at work – making sure that all health and safety risks are managed
- Organised and efficient – making sure that they set a good example for others and making sure they know what they are doing.

Discussion

What do you think makes someone employable? Imagine you are an employer looking to find the right people for the following jobs:

a) builder

b) office worker

c) nurse.

Exercise

1 In your own words, define the terms employer and employee.

2 Compare the roles of the employer with the employee.

3 What is the difference between a wage and a salary?

4 Name one responsibility an employer has to its workers and to the government.

Key vocabulary

wage

salary

What are work ethics?

We are learning to:

- understand how work ethics are important when using human resources.

Work ethics refer to rules and standards of conduct that are acceptable in the workplace. If rules of conduct are not observed by workers, they can be held accountable by their supervisors and it can be entered in their personal record. This may adversely affect their chances for promotion.

Ethical conduct (the moral principles people live by) is equally applicable to all spheres of life such as at home, school or places of worship.

Acceptable standards of conduct for workers include:

- **honesty** and **integrity**, requiring a worker to be truthful and not to falsify information such as claims of overtime work
- punctuality, being on time to work and other work-related engagements
- respect for the property of the company, such as to refrain from the abuse of vehicles, telephones, copier or fax machines and company materials
- to make sure that tasks are completed in an efficient and timely manner
- work as a team and cooperate with co-workers
- to be properly dressed and to respect the rights of workers or clients
- to be reliable in the course of their work.

Research

Write about 100 words explaining the role that ethics can play in the life of the worker outside the workplace. Then write down a list of the changes you think you ought to make in your life in order to be a diligent person.

Key vocabulary

work ethics
ethical conduct
honesty
integrity

Case study

Top Pop soft drinks

At the Top Pop soft drink factory, workers were reported by supervisors for playing internet games during working hours, and using the company phone for their personal use. Four company workers were seen at a beach with the company vehicle, playing music loudly and making a nuisance of themselves. The workers were summoned to see their managers, where they admitted their actions were not appropriate. They were all demoted for breaking company rules and also made to work extra hours.

Activity

a) Imagine you are an employer looking for a new waiter for your restaurant. Write a list of questions you would want to ask people in the interview. Make sure these questions cover all areas of good work ethic.

b) Imagine you are writing 100 words explaining why you feel you would be a good waiter, including describing your good work ethic.

What characteristics does an ethical worker have?

Always behaves professionally	Professionalism is something you can see the moment an employee walks in the office door. They are professionally dressed in clean, pressed clothes. They arrive a few minutes early to settle in and get their coffee, so that they will be ready to start their shift on time. They are courteous to other employees and don't take random breaks or change lunch schedules without authorisation. They understand their job and are prepared to do it.
Organisation and high productivity	Employees with strong work ethics carry out daily tasks. These are often organised so that they know they are able to devote the required time to any one task. Having a routine and being organised increases productivity. Employees with this trait are able get more done.
Teamwork and cooperation	Part of having a strong work ethic is knowing that you are part of a bigger team and that everyone has a role to play. This understanding allows teamwork and cooperation to ensure that everyone is getting the right information to properly do their jobs. Since those with strong work ethics tend to be more productive and efficient with their time, it means more time to help others to get more done.
Determined to succeed	Those with a strong work ethic have a strong motivation to succeed. A manager will see a determination to succeed in everything the employee does. An employee with a strong work ethic won't wait for someone else to deal with the problem. They will call the right resources, search online for remedies and work the problem until it is resolved.
Consistent and high-quality work	Being an organised timekeeper, with a determination to succeed and a high standard of professionalism, means the work produced by an employee with a strong work ethic is good. Not only is work presented in a neat and professional manner, it often goes above and beyond what was required.

Exercise

1 What examples of work ethics have been broken in the case study?

2 Why do you think it is important to observe proper work ethics while at work?

3 Suggest three ways a company can encourage workers to conduct themselves ethically.

4 What do you think is the meaning of the word integrity?

5 Explain how a worker can show reliability.

6 In groups, brainstorm your understanding of the terms: wages, salary, employer, employee and work ethics.

What is a career?

We are learning to:

- describe ways in which the productivity of the human resource affects the utilisation of natural resources
- understand different types of skills.

A career is the job or profession that someone works in during their working life. The type of career someone pursues is determined by several factors.

- Natural talents, abilities and interests can lead to a particular profession – for example, car mechanic, athlete, dancer, sculptor, doctor or teacher.
- The skill level and previous experience gained from being guided by a skilled senior person lead us to our life occupations – for example, car mechanic.
- Our level of education provides us with the knowledge and skills to perform a job – for example, technical training may lead a person to become a plant supervisor.
- The influence of role models inspires us to select our careers. Olympic gold medallist Usain Bolt may inspire young athletes to become sprinters.
- Your parents will know your natural strengths and advise and guide you in your career choice. They may also influence you according to family tradition.
- Many people consider job satisfaction before choosing a job, because if it is enjoyable people tend to think that they are actually not working.
- The level of wages offered by an employer may be more attractive in a particular career, because some people often rate financial rewards more highly than other factors when choosing a job.
- We may choose a career based on future industries, such as solar and wind power, so that when we qualify as a solar engineer, we can find a job in this industry in the future.

Exercise

In groups, discuss the terms career, employment, unemployment and self-employment and explain the differences between them.

1 In your own words, define the term career.

2 Write down three factors that you would consider before deciding on a career

3 Identify a skill you consider to be your natural ability.

Many people consider job satisfaction before choosing a job.

Activity

In groups conduct research on the role of institutions that offer training for careers:

HEART Trust, NTA, UTECH, UWI, MIND, Caribbean Maritime University, Teachers' Colleges.

Write an article for the class blog using information gathered. Make sure that you comment on the way that the programmes offered help meet the needs of the Jamaican economy. Evaluate how useful each programme is.

Most adults need to work in order to earn a living. After deciding on and taking steps to establish a career most people seek **employment** with a company or with the government. There are some people however who choose be **self-employed**. Self-employed people provide goods or services, and work for themselves. Someone who starts a business, whether it is a shop or a business that provides a service, such as sewing and fixing garments, is self-employed.

Many countries have a problem of **unemployment**. This is the situation where someone is looking for work, or is able to work, but cannot find a job or employment opportunity.

In Jamaica, we have plenty of employment opportunities, but the jobs available do not always match the levels of training and expertise of our human resources. This causes **underemployment**. Underemployment is when people in a labor force are employed at less than full-time or regular jobs or at jobs inadequate with respect to their training or economic needs. You can read some examples of this below. A highly qualified person may be underemployed in a job that does not use their skills or training. If someone feels they are underemployed, they may leave the country to find employment elsewhere. This results in situation known as **brain drain**.

Project

Interview a family member or friend about their career. Make a note of the training they had to complete and what they like best about their job.

Share your findings with the rest of the class.

Level of wages may be more attractive in some industries rather than others.

Case study

Three friends, Shania, Kaliya and Daniel, are all interested in business. After school, they attend university to study business sciences. After they qualify, each graduate goes in a different direction. Shania applies to a bank, where she gets a job as an investment consultant. Kaliya does some research and opens a clothing importation business. Daniel wants to work in a large company, but he can't find a job. He takes a temporary job waiting tables at a local restaurant until he can find a job better suited to his skills.

Research

Carry out a school survey with at least ten students to find out what career they would like to do when they leave school.

Share your findings with the rest of the class.

Questions

1. What do the three friends have in common?
2. Which of the three friends is self-employed?
3. Which of the three friends is underemployed?
4. Two of the friends are paid employees. What is the difference between their situations?
5. What do you think is likely to happen if Daniel does not find more suitable employment?

Key vocabulary

employment
self-employment
unemployment
underemployment
brain drain

What types of industry are there?

We are learning to:

- categorise human activities as primary, secondary, tertiary and quaternary industries.

Today, there are four main sectors of **industry**. They are classified as **primary**, **secondary**, **tertiary** and **quaternary**.

The primary sector

The primary sector involves the extraction of raw materials and natural resources. In Jamaica, people who work in bauxite mining are primary workers. Other examples include agriculture, forestry and fishing.

The secondary sector

The secondary sector turns raw materials into finished goods. For example, factory workers, builders and dressmakers are secondary workers. Manufacturing, refining, processing and construction are part of the secondary sector. Companies in Jamaica that are a part of this sector include:

- oil refining at Petrojam Limited in Kingston
- alumina manufacture at JAMALCO in Clarendon
- food processing by Grace Kennedy Limited
- cement production by Carib Cement.

A forestry worker works in the primary sector.

Oil refining is in the secondary sector.

Research

In groups, research one category of worker, for example, primary. Choose one career within that classification. Research the career and find out why that job is important to the development of the economy of your country. Present your findings in a group report.

1. In your own words, define the terms primary and secondary.

2. Identify which sectors these jobs belong to:

   a) oil refining   **b)** oil drilling

   c) fishing   **d)** sand and limestone quarrying.

The tertiary sector

The tertiary sector involves services rather than physical goods. Examples of people in service industries include waiters, shop assistants and doctors. Persons in this sector are engaged in the provision of direct and indirect services. A direct service sells a service direct to customers for their individual benefit. Direct services include:

- services linked to wellbeing and health – for example, by hospitals and health centres
- education services provided both by the government and private sector from early childhood education to primary, secondary and tertiary university level free of charge
- shoe repair, domestic help, house painting.

An indirect service is one that sells a service to customers but does so through one or more individuals or entities. Indirect services include:

- banking, to pay workers and suppliers, make cash and cheque deposits, automatic teller services
- transport, such as taxis, buses, trucks, ferries, air travel
- food processing services, bottling and packaging
- advertising and promotion of goods and services on the television and radio, and billboards along the nation's highways.

Quaternary industries

Quaternary industries provide knowledge and skills, such as information technology, research and development, innovation industries and the media. Examples of people who work in quaternary industries include those in research and development, science, information and communications technology, and business consultants. A quaternary media industry in Jamaica includes the newspapers – for example, The Gleaner, The Jamaica Observer.

Exercise

1 In your own words, define the terms tertiary and quaternary.

2 Identify which sectors these workers belong to:

   a) teacher   **b)** scientist
   c) bus driver   **d)** newspaper writer.

3 Create a mind map to help explain the terms primary, secondary, tertiary and quaternary. Explain how they are each related to each other.

Healthcare is in the service industry, and so within the tertiary sector.

Research

Working in groups, recall from previous lessons some examples of career types. Your teacher will write responses on the board. Create a table that categorises responses into types of workers, examples of career/job types, the industry to which the job is aligned and the resulting product/service.

Activity

In groups conduct research on careers in the primary, secondary, tertiary and quaternary industries. Create brochures showing the careers to be found in each industry as well as highlighting new careers.

Key vocabulary

primary industry

secondary industry

tertiary industry

quaternary industry

Jamaica's economic structure

We are learning to:

- categorise careers as primary, secondary, tertiary and quaternary industries.

The labour force

The **labour force** is the part of the population that is able and available to work. The characteristics of the labour force are different for every country. In Jamaica, the labour force is made up of people between the ages of 16 and 67. The labour force therefore comprises both persons employed and unemployed.

Unskilled workers are workers who follow primary, secondary, tertiary and quaternary workers and who have no formal training, education or skill. Unskilled workers are usually employed as domestic helpers, cleaners, messengers, sanitation workers or labourers.

The unskilled sector provides services that do not require special skills or heavy physical effort. Usually, a worker in the unskilled sector only has a primary level of education. Examples include sanitation workers at your school, porters at the airport and delivery drivers.

Some of the reasons workers can only find work in the unskilled sector include:

- a lack of basic education, vocational or craft training
- a lack of motivation due to negative effects of a broken home
- an inability to read, write, compute or communicate.

Permanent workers are workers whose job is on a full-time basis. They can often be employed in the same job until they retire – for example, a personnel manager. Some of the advantages of permanent work include:

- the jobs can be highly skilled and of great value to their firms
- benefits include retirement benefits, health insurance, paid holidays and company vehicles
- these jobs provide opportunities for promotion and higher salaries
- the jobs are long-term and employees are paid every month
- there is a higher level of commitment between employer and employee.

Temporary work, or temporary employment, is when an employer offers short-term employment, perhaps to fill a temporary absence or a staff shortage.

Instead of offering a permanent position, the employer may offer a **contract** so that they can pay someone to complete a particular set of tasks.

> **Did you know...?**
>
> Labour force participation rate in Jamaica was 64.50% in the fourth quarter of 2019.

Street vending would be considered as unskilled work.

Once the contract is finished, the worker must find other work. Temporary work is often accepted because it:

- is preferred to no work at all
- may lead to a permanent position
- may open a door to future opportunities
- may provide a young worker with a work history
- maintains production if someone is absent.

One advantage of temporary, part-time work is that workers may work around other projects. Workers can take on more work if they need to earn more money. They can also work from home.

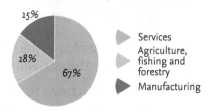

A police officer is an example of someone who works in a permanent role and often is in the job until they retire.

Activity

Using job adverts, explore the different types of jobs that exist. Make a list of the different skills required for each job.

1. In what situation might an employer need some temporary workers?

2. Why do people sometimes take on temporary work? What advantages does this offer?

3. Produce a mind map comparing the advantages and benefits of being **a)** a permanent worker and **b)** a temporary worker.

Exercise

1. Look at the pie chart. Which economic activity employs the greatest number of people?

2. Give three examples of jobs which a person might have in:

   a) services

   b) agriculture, fishing and forestry

   c) manufacturing.

3. In your own words, define the term unskilled worker.

4. Why are some people only able to find unskilled jobs?

5. In your own words, explain the benefits of having a permanent job.

Economic activity in Jamaica, 2017

15%

18%

67%

- Services
- Agriculture, fishing and forestry
- Manufacturing

Key vocabulary

labour force

unskilled worker

permanent worker

temporary work

contract

141

How do we classify careers? Groups 1–4

We are learning to:

- classify human activities into primary, secondary, tertiary and quaternary industries.

The International Standard Classification of Occupations (ISCO) is an international system that places **careers** into different **classifications**.

Occupational classifications are used to group similar job types into categories or groups. This can help people in education and training, career guidance or human resources. In total, there are ten different categories of workers, known as major groups.

The ten different categories of workers are:

1.	Managers
2.	Professionals
3.	Technicians and associate professionals
4.	Clerical support workers
5.	Sales and services workers
6.	Skilled agricultural, forestry and fishery workers
7.	Craft and related trades workers
8.	Plant and machine operators and assemblers
9.	Elementary occupations
10.	Armed forces

Key vocabulary

career
classification
manager
professional
technician
associate professional
clerical support worker

Audley Shaw, Jamaica's minister of industry, is a senior government official and a Group 1 worker.

Group 1: Managers

Managers are senior experienced personnel whose main tasks are to plan, direct, organise and coordinate the activities of their organisation. Typical tasks include:

- giving instructions to workers on how to perform their tasks
- making sure that the workers have the necessary tools and other resources to carry out their work
- making sure that all workers operate as a team and in harmony with each other.

Examples include senior government officials, as well as managers in the fields of sales and marketing, agriculture, manufacturing, healthcare, education and hotels and restaurants.

Group 2: Professionals

Professionals are workers who have advanced qualifications, knowledge and work experience that are applied to their job. Examples include doctors, chemists, scientists, electrical engineers, architects, town planners, midwives, vets, dentists, opticians, teachers, accountants and lawyers.

Exercise

1 How many different types of job classification are there?

2 Why do you think jobs need to be classified?

3 What types of jobs would you do if you were a manager or a professional? Which job would you like to do?

Group 3: Technicians and associate professionals 》》》

Workers in this group are **technicians** and **associate professionals** who work in technical or research-related jobs and who have been educated to university level. Examples include engineering technicians, mining and construction supervisors, air traffic controllers, medical technicians (such as people who create artificial limbs), ambulance workers, dental assistants and government officials, such as immigration and tax officials.

A technician is a Group 3 worker.

Group 4: Clerical support workers 》》

Clerical support workers carry out tasks related to the recording, organising and storing of information. Examples of job types in this group include secretaries, telephone switchboard operators, hotel receptionists, bookkeepers, and office, payroll, bank transport and library clerks.

Workers in this group would be educated to secondary level and would receive on-the-job training while working in their jobs to gain experience.

Research

Using the internet or magazines, research two or three examples of the different jobs for each of the major Groups 1–4. Try to find examples in your country. Create a portfolio which gives the job title and, if possible, add a photograph for each job.

Exercise

4 Which group would the following jobs be classified under?

   a) vet   **b)** assistant vet   **c)** secretary
   d) office clerk   **e)** tax official.

5 Match the activity of the worker to their classification of job.

   a) This worker is the technical expert in the company.

   b) This worker organises, trains and motivates the workers.

   c) This worker is highly skilled, has advanced qualifications in a specialist field and has experience.

Discussion

In groups, discuss the major Groups 1–4. Are there any jobs in these groups that you would like to do?

Career classifications: Groups 5–7

We are learning to:

- classify human activities into primary, secondary, tertiary and quaternary industries.

Group 5: Sales and service workers

This group includes occupations related to the sales and service industries, such as travel, housekeeping, catering, personal care, working and selling in shops or retail and public services. People who work in the sales and service industries are known as tertiary workers. The tertiary sector involves services rather than physical goods. Examples of people in service industries include waiters, shop assistants and porters in hotels.

Examples of job types in this group include:

- cooks, waiters, bartenders
- hairdressers, beauticians
- cleaners and housekeepers in offices and hotels
- street and market sellers, shopkeepers
- **sales workers**, such as door-to-door salespeople, service station attendants
- home healthcare assistants
- public services, such as the police, firefighters, prison guards, security guards.

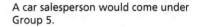

A car salesperson would come under Group 5.

Sales and **services workers** would typically be educated to secondary school level and would receive on-the-job training while working in their jobs to gain experience.

Group 6: Skilled agricultural, forestry and fishery workers

Workers in Group 6 work in the agricultural sector.

Examples of job types in this group include:

- market gardeners and crop growers (growing and harvesting crops)
- animal producers, such as livestock, dairy and poultry
- crop and animal producers
- forestry workers (cultivating, conserving and exploiting forests)
- fishery workers (breeding or catching fish)
- subsistence farmers (producing a variety of animal husbandry products).

Fishery workers are Group 6 workers.

Workers in Group 6 tend to be self-employed and typically are educated to secondary school level and would receive on-the-job training.

Workers in Group 7 work in the building, or construction, industry or in related industries, such as masonry, carpentry, roofing, plumbing, electrical work or welding.

Examples of job types in this group include:

- building workers, such as bricklayers, stonemasons, carpenters
- other building trade workers, such as roofers, plasterers, plumbers, pipe fitters, painters and floor layers
- metal workers, including welders, sheet-metal workers, blacksmiths, toolmakers
- machinery maintenance and repair workers, such as car and aircraft mechanics, agricultural machinery repairers
- handicraft makers, such as musical instrument makers, jewellery makers, glassmakers, potters
- printers and binders
- butchers, bakers, cheesemakers, tobacco workers.

Building workers are Group 7 workers.

Workers in this group are educated to secondary school level and receive on-the-job training.

Did you know...?

The International Standard Classification of Occupations (ISCO) lists armed forces occupations as major Group 10. This includes all jobs held by members of the armed forces.

Activity

Draw a mind map to show what type of job in Group 7 goes with the type of work they do. For example, a bricklayer would build buildings.

Exercise

1 What types of jobs would workers in Groups 5, 6 and 7 do?

2 What type of tasks would someone employed in a Group 6 job be required to do?

3 Using the internet or magazines, research two or three examples of the different types of jobs for Groups 5 and 6. Try to find examples in Jamaica. Add to your portfolio, giving the job title, and add a photograph for each job.

4 In your own words, explain what type of workers belong to the Group 7 classification.

5 Identify whether these job types belong to a Group 7 classification:

    a) baker   **b)** receptionist

    c) jewellery maker   **d)** chef.

Key vocabulary

sales workers

services workers

Career classifications: Groups 8–10

We are learning to:

- classify human activities into primary, secondary, tertiary and quaternary industries.

Group 8: Plant and machine operators and assemblers

Workers in this group operate industrial and agricultural machinery and equipment. It can be a specialised sector to work in and people who work in these jobs need to have experience and understanding of the machinery, as well as an ability to keep up to date with the technology. The types of jobs in this group include:

- mining and quarry machine operators
- metal and chemical machine operators
- textile machine operators, including weaving, knitting, sewing, bleaching, dyeing and shoemaking
- food machine operators, including meat, seafood, dairy, fruit, vegetables and cocoa processing
- assembly line workers
- drivers, including train, motorbike, car, taxi, van, bus, truck and earth-moving machinery
- ship workers and crew.

Workers in this group are also educated to secondary school level and receive on-the-job training.

Plant and machine operators are Group 8 workers.

Group 9: Elementary occupations

Elementary occupations cover jobs which perform simple tasks using basic equipment and some physical effort. They are not regarded as skilled labour. The types of jobs in this group include:

- domestic, hotel and office cleaners
- agricultural, forestry and fishery labourers
- construction, manufacturing and transport labour
- fast-food workers and kitchen helpers
- messengers, odd-job people, rubbish collection.

Key vocabulary

elementary occupations

Jobs in the Jamaica Defence Force (JDF) include the Army, Air Wing and Coast Guard. The role of the armed forces is to defend and protect Jamaica from external forces or threats. The armed forces also help to maintain order in Jamaica as well as carrying out duties seen as necessary by the government. Jobs in this group may include the following activities:

- Maintenance of law and order
- Counter-narcotics operations
- Search and Rescue (SAR)
- Casualty Evacuation
- Humanitarian and disaster relief operations
- Defence diplomacy
- Nation building projects
- Contingency planning
- State ceremonial duties.

Members of the Jamaica Defence Force are part of Group 10: Armed forces.

Activity

Look back over units 5.10–5.12 and the types of jobs in each classification group. Create a graphic organiser which summarises the information for all of these groups. You could include the group type, the type of tasks and job examples.

In groups, make a list of all the teaching, clerical and support staff jobs at your school. Match each one to the job classification system. Create a report of your findings and report back to the class.

Exercise

1   Identify the classification of the following workers:

   a) train driver   **b)** hotel cleaner

   c) cheesemaker   **d)** car mechanic.

2   Make a list of workers in the craft and related trades group that may have been employed to build your school.

3   Using the internet or magazines, research two or three examples of the different types of jobs for each of Groups 7–9. Try to find examples in Jamaica. Add to your portfolio, giving the job title, and add a photograph for each job.

How have jobs and careers evolved over time in Jamaica?

We are learning to:

- relate historical time periods to changes in industries including new careers that have evolved
- analyse the impact of the characteristics of a population in effectively utilising resources.

How were professional and non-agricultural jobs perceived in the past?

In the past professional and non-agricultural roles were seen to include: dentists, lawyers, doctors, police officers and teachers.

Skilled craftsmen in the past were seen to include blacksmiths, bricklayers, wheelwrights, saddlers and shoemakers.

Why have there been changes to the traditional types of jobs?

- Changing technology (computer related jobs, jobs in communication, heavy equipment operation
- Changing lifestyles
- Modification of traditional occupations – new crops in agriculture/hybrid, greenhouse farming, prefabrication in construction industry.

Time period	Nature of jobs and changes in careers
1900 – 1950s	Concentration on agriculture
1950s – 2000	Mining of bauxite and aluminium, tourism and light manufacturing. In the 1980s there was a growth of retail trade, hotel and tourism.
2000 – recent times	There is an increase in young entrepreneurs; people starting their own businesses either as their main source of income or to supplement their income. Many of these are operated online. There is a boom in the service sector, especially in what is known as the Business Processes Outsourcing (BPO) industry. This involves persons working as customer service representatives for overseas entities.

What is the illegal movement of people for forced labour?

The illegal movement of people for forced labour or sexual exploitation is known as **people trafficking**.

Despite the ending of the system which enslaved millions of Africans in the 1800s, modern forms of forced labour have emerged across the globe. The root causes of trafficking

Activity

Collect advertisements online or in newspapers that describe jobs. Compare these with the current courses that are available for training. What are your findings?

vary from one country to another. Trafficking is complex and often caused by social, economic, cultural and other factors:

- The desire of potential victims to migrate is exploited (they believe they are moving for work and a better life)
- Poverty, oppression, lack of human rights, lack of social or economic opportunity, dangers from conflict or instability.

Political instability, militarism, civil unrest, internal armed conflict and natural disasters often cause displacement of families and may result in an increase in trafficking; the destabilisation and displacement of populations increase their vulnerability to exploitation and abuse through trafficking and forced labour.

- Factors 'push' people into migration and hence into the control of traffickers, but other factors that tend to 'pull' potential victims can also be significant.
- The practice of entrusting poor children to more affluent friends or relatives may create vulnerability. Some parents sell their children, not just for the money, but also in the hope that their children will escape a situation of chronic poverty and move to a place where they will have a better life and more opportunities.

Exercise

1 What sort of jobs are there in 'agriculture'?

2 What is an entrepreneur?

3 Explain what people trafficking is, and why it occurs.

How has employment by gender changed over time?

Both men and women play important roles in the ongoing development of Jamaica. Through gender equality in the workforce, the country is able to utilise the skills and talents of all people to help industries run efficiently and therefore contribute to the growth of the economy.

The key benefits of gender equality include:

- Having men and women in employment leads to a bigger workforce, helping the economy to grow.
- When more of the population is employed, it reduces poverty overall so that people can enjoy higher standards of living.
- Gender equality creates a society where both men and women can participate in decision-making.

Activity

In groups, collect information from STATIN to find out how employment has changed in Jamaica from 1960 to the present day. Make notes on what you find and share with the rest of the class.

Discussion

How do traditional ideas about being male and female influence the kinds of jobs people choose? Discuss, and include examples of what might be considered typically 'male' and 'female' jobs.

Are traditional ideas about men and women changing over time?

What can be done to encourage females into 'male' jobs and vice versa?

Exercise

4 In your own words, explain why gender equality is important in the workforce.

5 Imagine you are working for a construction company and you want to increase the number of females in employment. Write an email to your boss to explain why this is a good idea.

Key vocabulary

people trafficking

Questions

See how well you have understood the topics in this unit.

1. Explain what is meant by:

   a) human resources

   b) interdependence

   c) underemployment

2. Complete the following table:

Type of activities	Explain the type of activities this involves	Examples of careers
Primary		
Secondary		
Tertiary		
Quaternary		

3. Describe population distribution in Jamaica and explain how it affects the utilisation of resources.

4. Explain what is meant by importing and exporting.

5. Give examples of two imports and two exports of Jamaica.

6. What is human trafficking?

7. Correct the following statement:

   > Push factors are what attracts a person to work somewhere and pull factors are what make someone feel they must leave a place

8. State one reason education is important for human resource development and for natural resources to be utilised well.

9. Give examples of jobs in each of the following categories:

   a) Managers

   b) Professionals

   c) Technicians and associate professionals

   d) Clerical support workers

10. What is meant by 'brain drain'?

11. Identify two problems with temporary work.

12. Name three careers that have been created in recent years in the service industry. Explain why they now exist.

13. What career options does a person have when leaving school?

14. What is self-employment? Give an example.

15. Write a 100 word summary on 'work ethics' giving examples.

16. Write a short essay on why Jamaicans may go abroad to work, and why people with specialised skills may be employed from abroad to work in Jamaica.

Grade 7 Unit 5 Summary

Different types of resources

In this chapter, you have learned about:

- What different types of resources there are
- What economists mean when they talk about capital
- The difference between physical capital and human capital.

Human resources and the development of the economy

In this chapter, you have learned about:

- What is meant by economic development
- The importance of human resources to an economy and the economic development of a country
- How a skilled and educated labour force helps a country to utilise its natural resources and improve the economy
- Instances of the importation and exportation of labour to benefit Jamaica's economy.
- The usefulness of the facilities that are in place to train and develop Jamaica's human resources
- The strategies outlined in Vision 2030 to improve the capacity of Jamaica's workforce by 2030.

Human resource development

In this chapter, you have learned about:

- What is meant by human resource development and the types of training opportunities that employers offer their employees
- What it means to earn a living and the difference between a wage and a salary
- The ideal qualities of an employer
- The importance of work ethics and ethical conduct in the workplace
- The meaning of the terms career, self-employment, unemployment and underemployment
- What types of industry there are.

The economic structure of Jamaica

In this chapter, you have learned about:

- The labour force
- Classifying human activities as primary, secondary, tertiary and quaternary industries
- The International Standard Classification of Occupations which places careers into different groups
- How modern opportunities have changed the general view of professional and non-agricultural jobs over time
- The factors that lead to people trafficking.

Checking your progress

To make good progress in understanding utilising human resources, check that you understand these ideas.

Explain and use correctly the term *human resources*.

Describe how a person becomes a skilled worker.

Explain the differences between skills, abilities and talents.

Explain and use correctly the terms *workforce* and *population*.

Name the ideal characteristics of good ethics at work.

Explain the role of the education system in ensuring that skilled workers are provided for the economy.

Explain and use correctly the term *underemployment*.

Name the key imports and exports of Jamaica.

Explain how careers have changed in Jamaica.

Explain and use correctly the terms *primary*, *secondary*, *tertiary* and *quarternary*.

Describe the different types of careers that a person can have.

Explain the functions of agencies provide training and skills throughout life.

Unit 6: Social Groups and Institutions

Objectives: You will be able to:

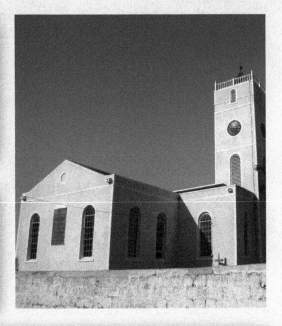

Groups in society

- define the term group
- identify and examine the different groups to which people belong
- explain the functions and characteristics of groups.

Institutions and types of social institutions

- identify and differentiate between social, economic and political institutions
- assess agents of socialisation.

Understanding social norms

- understand what is meant by social norms, folkways, mores and taboos.

Different types of groups

- identify different types of groups and their characteristics
- explain the differences between primary and secondary groups
- explain the differences between formal and informal groups.

Benefits of groups

- explore the benefits of being a member of a group
- explain roles and responsibilities in groups and group cohesion
- examine ways groups can overcome issues that arise.

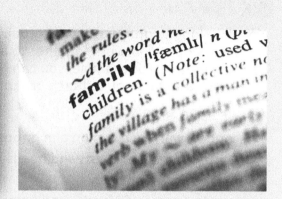

Leadership

- define the terms leader, leadership, power and authority
- state the qualities of a good leader and examine the role of a leader in a group.

Groups in society

We are learning to:

- define the term group
- identify and examine the different groups to which people belong.

Groups ❯❯

We all belong to **groups**. A **social group** is made up of two or more people who work together to achieve a common purpose or goal. For example, you can be a part of a family, a club or class at school, a church group or a sports club.

Groups allow us to:

- work towards a common aim or goal/objective
- share common interests and needs
- create a sense of **unity**
- create a sense of identity and **belonging**
- do activities together or **interact** together often
- have common rules of behaviour, sanctions or rewards.

Groups that do not have these characteristics are not classed as social groups, because they are temporary or do not fulfil all or any of the above characteristics; for example, a crowd at a sporting event.

One of the first groups you are part of is the family group, as you are born into that group. Later you will become part of a wider community group, and then as you go through life you will become part of a number of groups.

Family and community groups are the first types of group that you will be part of.

Discussion

In groups, brainstorm the definition of 'group' and think of as many different types of group as you can.

Key vocabulary

groups

social group

unity

belonging

interact

primary groups

secondary groups

formal groups

informal groups

Examples of groups ❯❯❯

People can belong to many different groups. Groups can be classified in different categories. For example:

- **primary groups** – small groups which people interact with often; for example, your family
- **secondary groups** – usually larger groups which meet less often; for example, your class at school
- **formal groups** – groups which have a structure, membership requirements, and rules and regulations; for example, a church group
- **informal groups** – more casual groups than a formal group, which see people come together with a common interest; for example, a sports club.

1 Write your own definition of 'social group'.

2 Give two examples of a social group.

3 What do groups allow us to do?

4 Is a crowd of people at a sporting event classed as a group? Give a reason for your answer.

5 Name the first social group that you became a member of.

Each group type has goals or objectives that are unique to that group. Some objectives are clearly defined and can be carried out over a long period of time, while other goals can be specific to a particular group's needs.

Here are some examples:

Group type	Example	Goal/objective of the group
Social (family and friends)	Family, close friends, school friends, neighbourhood friends, your class at school	To provide physical and emotional needs Families also have customs and traditions which bind them together
School	In class or in school clubs	To learn new skills in a subject over a school year To learn social skills with peers
Religious	Church, mosque, temple	To share a common faith
Sports	Tennis club, soccer club, hockey club, swimming club, football team, cricket team, netball team	To improve skills To socialise with peers
Charity and community	Lions, Rotary, youth outreach clubs	To help members of the community
Cultural	Drama group, debating club, Toastmasters, choir, orchestra or band	To put on a stage show

Exercise

6 Name four different categories of groups.

7 Look at the table. Choose two group types – for example, sports and cultural – and choose one example of a group in that 'type' you are a member of. Describe the goal(s) of the group.

The functions of groups

We are learning to:

- explain the functions of groups.

Functions of groups

A **function** refers to how something works or operates, the job something does. Groups have many different functions. The mind map summarises the functions of a group.

Opportunities for leadership
Learning to organise and manage people; for example, giving people jobs to do

Self-esteem
Feeling good about oneself; for example, helping other people

Behaviour
Learning how to behave in social situations.

Sense of purpose/achievement of specific goals
As a group working towards common aims; for example, raising money for a community project

Functions of Groups

Sense of belonging and identity
The feeling of belonging and being associated with a group or group of people

Opportunities to learn new skills and talents
Learning how to do new things

Companionship and friendship
Enjoying the company and friendship of other people

Safety and security
Anxieties and feelings of insecurity are reduced and feelings of comfort and safety increased

Read what these students say they get from belonging to groups.

My debating club has improved my communication and leadership skills.

In my church youth group, we all cooperate to help our community. I've also made some great friends.

With my choir I get to display my singing talent. I love singing!

My friendship circle is so important to me. I can confide in my friends and trust them.

My photography club is helping me reach my goal of becoming a photographer and journalist.

Exercise

1 For one group that you are member of, create a mind map which shows its functions.

2 Complete this quiz by matching each group function to the statement that fits best.

   i) A sense of belonging

   ii) A sense of identity

   iii) Companionship

   iv) A sense of purpose/ achievement of goals

   v) Developing leadership ability

   vi) Opportunities to develop and learn new skills and to show talents

   vii) Safety and security

   a) We have made some amazing changes in our community.

   b) I feel safe and happy among my friends.

   c) We are all different, but we are learning how to do something new.

   d) I am learning how to organise and lead a group.

   e) I enjoy spending time together with the people in my group.

   f) I feel at home here – everyone understands me and I fit in.

   g) This is who I am!

3 Look at the speech bubbles. Write a short sentence for each one, explaining why you think that group is helping the student.

4 Identify and explain in 250 words the functions of a group.

Project

Think about a group you belong to. Use a concept map to emphasise the functions of that group. Use the example on page 158 to help you.

Discussion

Discuss the ways groups can effectively carry out their functions.

Key vocabulary
....

function

The characteristics of groups

We are learning to:

- describe the characteristics of groups.

Characteristics of groups ⟩⟩

We categorise groups in different ways, according to several characteristics. The mind map summarises the characteristics of a group.

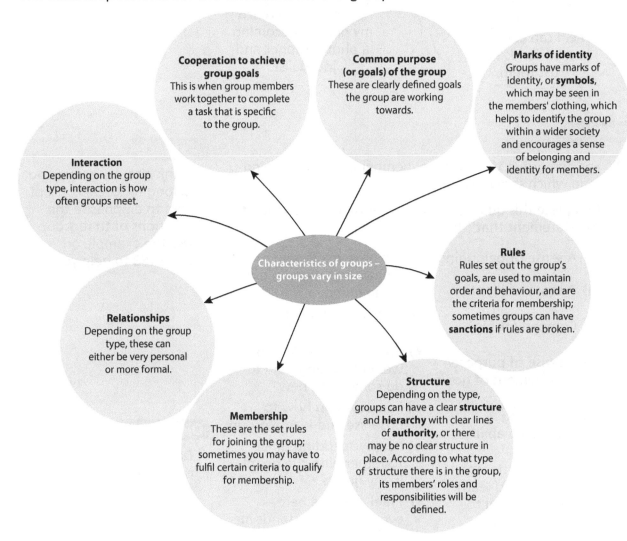

Cooperation to achieve group goals
This is when group members work together to complete a task that is specific to the group.

Common purpose (or goals) of the group
These are clearly defined goals the group are working towards.

Marks of identity
Groups have marks of identity, or **symbols**, which may be seen in the members' clothing, which helps to identify the group within a wider society and encourages a sense of belonging and identity for members.

Interaction
Depending on the group type, interaction is how often groups meet.

Characteristics of groups – groups vary in size

Rules
Rules set out the group's goals, are used to maintain order and behaviour, and are the criteria for membership; sometimes groups can have **sanctions** if rules are broken.

Relationships
Depending on the group type, these can either be very personal or more formal.

Membership
These are the set rules for joining the group; sometimes you may have to fulfil certain criteria to qualify for membership.

Structure
Depending on the type, groups can have a clear **structure** and **hierarchy** with clear lines of **authority**, or there may be no clear structure in place. According to what type of structure there is in the group, its members' roles and responsibilities will be defined.

Exercise

1 Explain in your own words the main characteristics of a group.

2 Think about any of the groups that you belong to. Do your groups show any of these characteristics? If so, which ones?

Marks of identity ⟫⟫

Marks of identity are used by groups to give their group an identity or sense of belonging. Examples include:

- a school uses a letterhead, a uniform and a badge to identify its members from other groups
- a sports team uses a symbol or badge on their kit
- a Scout or Girl Guide group uses a logo as part of the group's identity
- a youth club may have a logo to identify themselves
- a church group may use a symbol from their faith
- a political party may use a symbol associated with their politics
- a trade union uses a logo with a message that reflects the objectives of the group.

Project

In groups, discuss a group you would like to form. It could be a sports club, a reading club – anything you like. In 400 words, write down four characteristics that your group would like the group to have.

Size of groups ⟫⟫⟫

Groups come in different sizes. They can vary from just two to many hundreds. The size of a group can also help to determine how well the group stays together.

- A **dyad** is a group of two. It is the smallest group. If one person doesn't cooperate, the group falls apart.
- A **triad** is a group of three. If there is conflict between two members, the third member may help the others reach a solution. If the members cannot agree, and one leaves, the group may continue to exist as a dyad.
- Larger groups have more than three members. In very large groups, the members may not even know each other. For example, some large companies have hundreds or thousands of members. The citizens of a large country such as China make up a group of more than a billion members.

Cub Scouts, Brownies and Girl Guides all wear uniform to identify their group.

Exercise

3 Decide if each of a) to d) are a dyad, a triad or a larger group.

a) a Grade 7 class   **c)** a church youth group

b) two girls in class   **d)** three children from the same neighbourhood.

4 Give an example of a dyad, a triad and a larger group that you belong to.

5 In groups, brainstorm ideas about characteristics of groups and see if you can think of at least two examples of each one. Put your ideas into a graphic organiser, like the one opposite, to help formulate your ideas.

Key vocabulary

symbol

sanctions

structure

hierarchy

authority

dyad

triad

Institutions and types of social institutions

We are learning to:

- identify and differentiate between social, economic and political institutions.

Institutions

A large group that helps to organise society is called an institution; these are found in all societies. It consists of a group of people who have come together for a common purpose. These institutions are a part of the social order of society and they govern behaviour and expectations of individuals.

All institutions are established structures, governed by norms. **Norms** outline the ways that people should act. Individuals are **socialised** into institutional norms and regulations. Socialisation is the process of internalising norms and values of a society. **Values** refer to ideas or beliefs that are seen as important in society. These norms, rules and regulations become binding on the members of society.

Institutions are a means of making sure that basic and vital needs are met for the continued existence of society.

> **Did you know...?**
>
> Values are reflected in laws and human rights, such as the right to life, the right to safety, the right to privacy.

What are the different types of social institutions?

There are five basic institutions that help to meet the needs of a society. These are the family, **education**, **religion**, the economy and the **political system**. There are many other institutions that work along with these five units to help organise and satisfy the needs of a complex modern society. They tend to fall into three broad groups:

- Social – these types of institutions are those which meets the needs of society and the individual, for example the family, religion, education and healthcare. The school is an important social institution, as one of its roles is to educate citizens about how society works, a person's role in society and the different functions of society.

- Political – political institutions are organisations that create and enforce laws and legislation at both local and central government. Each country has a different political system, for example Jamaica has a parliamentary system, and this has an impact on how political institutions in that country are run.

- Economic – economic institutions are organisations within a country which help run and keep the economy going. For example, the government makes economic policies and implements them, for example to help grow businesses and implement taxation, but there are also other institutions such as banks which we use on a daily basis.

Social

Social institutions are those that help to organise life outside work; they impact our social wellbeing and development. For example:

- The family
- The school system (education)
- Religion and sports

Economic

Economic institutions help govern and organise our work lives as well as ensuring that the distribution of wealth and income takes place. These institutions include:

- Taxation system
- Work and pensions system
- Finance companies such as banks
- System of social benefits from the government

Types of social institutions

Political

Political institutions help to regulate laws and policies that maintain society in good working order. For example:

- The legislature (law-making body)
- Justice system/system of courts
- The police
- Prisons

Banks are economic institutions.

Courts are political institutions.

Exercise

1. Explain what is meant by an institution.

2. What is a norm? Give an example of norms in Jamaica. How do these norms differ from what exists in other countries?

3. Give examples of different values in the Jamaican society.

4. Explain the differences between social, economic and political institutions.

5. Work in groups to discuss whether the different social institutions have all the characteristics of a social institution.

Did you know...?

Values are reflected in laws and human rights, such as the right to life, the right to safety, the right to privacy.

Key vocabulary

norm

socialised

value

education

religion

political system

Agents of socialisation

We are learning to:

• assess the agents of socialisation.

As we saw earlier, socialisation refers to the process of internalising norms and values that occurs throughout life. We may also describe socialisation as the process through which the cultural traditions within a society are passed on and learned by individuals.

Parents teach children table manners, which is an example of primary socialisation.

There are two types of socialisation

• Primary – **primary socialisation** occurs in early life, before a person begins school. Primary socialisation is carried out by family members, friends, religious ideas and practices and possibly also by the media, such as the television programmes a child watches.

• Secondary – **secondary socialisation** refers to the internalisation of norms and values that takes place from the age a person begins school throughout their entire life. Agencies involved with secondary socialisation include friends, or peers, schools, religious ideas and practices, laws, police, the media.

Schools begin secondary socialisation.

Socialisation through family and friends or peers is considered informal as there is no set structure in terms of how norms and values are passed. In fact most of what is learnt happens through observing and imitating, even though some direct teaching may take place. Socialisation, especially through the school system or education system is considered formal as there is a set curriculum and set there are rules, codes of behaviour and sanctions in place. Some socialisation through the school system takes place through what many call the hidden curriculum where children are directly taught certain things but they learn them based on how persons behave and the structures that are put in place.

Agencies of socialisation

Agency	How do they socialise?	Examples
The family	Parents, grandparents, siblings teaching children appropriate norms and behaviour	Teaching manners, how to resolve conflict, preparing children for school, allowing adults to talk about problems
Education	Teaching children about how to behave outside the home, how to transition from home into the workplace	Teaching students' rules How to manage conflict How to dress and act appropriately outside the home Preparing students with correct skills, norms and values

Agency	How do they socialise?	Examples
The media	Shaping individual behaviour, perceptions, norms and values	Encouraging gendered behaviour (how to behave as male or female) Encouraging people to want to be consumers, to buy goods and services Shaping social attitudes
The law	Providing guidance on what is right and wrong – values through punishment	Policies and laws that shape our behaviour, for example, not speeding, not fighting or being violent Consequences such as fines and imprisonment reinforce ideas about boundaries
Religion	Provides moral guidance about what is right and wrong, beliefs and values	Religious texts, sermons, religious festivals reinforce particular ideas such as being charitable.

Formal social control refers to any agency of socialisation where there are written rules or laws which can be broken.

Informal social control refers to any agency of socialisation where there are no written rules or laws which can be broken. Rather there may be effects of deviating social norms such as being ignored by friends or told off by parents if your behaviour is considered wrong.

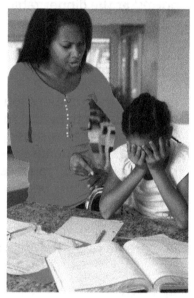

Parents correcting children is a form of socialisation.

Exercise

1 Using your own words, define socialisation.

2 What is the difference between primary and secondary socialisation?

3 Are the following examples of formal or informal social control?

    a) Being grounded by your parents

    b) Getting a fine for parking in the wrong place

    c) Going to prison

    d) Your friends ignoring you.

4 Think about the formal and informal types of socialisation that occur in your school. Make a list of examples of each.

5 Write a short essay on how socialisation has changed over time. How were people socialised differently in Jamaica in the past?

Key vocabulary

primary socialisation

secondary socialisation

Understanding social norms

We are learning to:

- understand what is meant by social norms, folkways, mores and taboos.

Every society has a set of social norms, or what is agreed to be 'normal' behaviour. These norms ensure that:

- people behave in ways that are acceptable and approved
- society functions smoothly
- we can predict and understand the way that people will behave
- when people stray or deviate from the norms, we can respond in appropriate ways.

Discussion

In small groups create a list of what are considered 'norms' at the dinner table. What behaviour is expected? What happens when someone breaks those norms?

Expected dinner table behaviour is a social norm.

Case study

In Japan, the number "four" is avoided because it sounds very similar to the word for death. As in Western culture where the No. 13 is considered an unlucky number, so is the No. 4 in Japanese culture, and is used as little as possible. In Japan, you must always avoid giving anyone something in fours because it can be seen as a very ominous gift.

Elevator labels will often be missing a fourth floor — and in extreme cases, they will not have floors.

Activity

Think about the following situations where norms are expressed:

Situation	Norms (examples)	Values (what is seen as important)
Meal times		
In a formal meeting		
Greeting a friend		
Giving a gift		
Birthdays		

Folkways and mores

Folkways and **mores** refer to the traditional behaviour or way of life of a particular community or group of people. These are sometimes known as customs. Some examples common in Jamaican society include standing in line, holding the door for someone, nodding at or greeting fellow passengers at a bus stop (perhaps varies from city to the countryside), waiting for fellow diners' food to arrive before you start eating.

Here are some examples of social mores:

- It is not considered acceptable or mainstream to abuse drugs, particularly Class A drugs, such as heroin and cocaine.
- It is not considered acceptable to drive at 90 mph in a residential area.
- It is expected that one would hold the door for a person behind him or her when entering a building.
- It is expected that one will be on time for work the majority of the time.
- It is not acceptable to wear casual clothes in most fine dining establishments.
- Talking to oneself in public is not considered normal behaviour.
- Stealing is considered unacceptable under any circumstance.
- Adults are expected to work in order to support themselves.

Taboos

A **taboo** is a social or religious custom prohibiting or restricting a particular practice or forbidding association with a particular person, place, or thing. Taboos, like customs, folkways or mores vary from place to place.

To eat some animals, for example, is considered taboo, such as frogs, snails, cats and dogs. In other parts of the world, these might be considered a delicacy.

Exercise

1. Why are roles important?

2. What are folkways and mores? Give examples of each.

3. Give an example of a taboo subject in Jamaica.

Being courteous to other travellers on public transport is a folkway.

Activity

Can you think about some of the folkways in your life? Think about what happens during your average school day. Write a list of all the folkways you practice. Have any of these changed over time?

Discuss

What are considered to be taboo subjects in Jamaica? Have these changed over time? Do taboos vary between different groups in the society?

Did you know...?

In Malaysia it is a taboo for pregnant women to eat pineapples.

Key vocabulary

folkway

more

taboo

Different types of groups

We are learning to:

- identify different types of groups and their characteristics.

Primary groups ⟩⟩

The **characteristics** of a primary group include:

- They are small in size.
- The relationships are very personal and intimate.
- Contact often takes place, and is face-to-face.
- Because they are a small size, each member often interacts with all the others.
- They create a sense of belonging and loyalty.
- The bond between members is based on emotions.
- Members are accepted because of who they are and what they are like.

Primary relationships are often those first experienced in life and cannot be replaced. Examples are family and close friends, who provide each other with love, care and support.

Secondary groups ⟩⟩⟩

The characteristics of a secondary group include:

- They are a larger size than a primary group.
- The relationships are less personal.
- Contact is less frequent, impersonal and more formal.
- Members only interact with some of the other members, but not all.
- Members may only be accepted if they contribute something to the group, like completing a task.

People join these groups based on shared interests and activities. Examples are sports groups and political organisations.

Exercise

1. Define primary and secondary groups..

2. Explain the difference between primary and secondary groups. Give an example of each.

3. Secondary groups are your family and friends. True or false?

A sports club is an example of a secondary group.

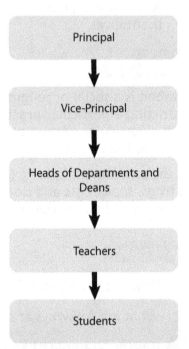

Principal

⬇

Vice-Principal

⬇

Heads of Departments and Deans

⬇

Teachers

⬇

Students

Example of hierarchy in formal groups.

Formal and informal groups >>>

Groups can be classified as formal or informal depending on their organisation, structure and characteristics. A formal group is often formed to fulfil a task or activity, while an informal group is made up of people with shared interests and likes.

A formal group has:

- written rules – what the members must follow, and what happens if they do not follow the rules
- a clear division of work and power – who does what, and who takes responsibility and makes decisions
- a hierarchy or structure, which explains different levels of authority
- membership requirements – what to do to join and a procedure for replacing members
- fixed meeting times – when and where it meets
- organised activities – what the group does.

Examples are churches, schools, companies and service organisations.

An informal group has the following features:

- It is small to medium-sized.
- It has goals but these are not usually written down.
- Activities can change quickly.
- Members usually know each other or have a personal connection to one another.
- There is no strict structure; leadership may come from age, status, experience or who has been in the group the longest.

Examples are our families and friendship circles.

Discussion

As a class, discuss why it is important for formal groups to have rules. What would happen if there were no rules in your school?

Research

Identify one example of one type of group. Collect and present information on the characteristics of the group chosen.

Exercise

4 List groups that you belong to. Mark each group with 'P' for primary or 'S' for secondary. Are there more primary or secondary groups?

5 Write your own definitions of a formal and informal group and give one example of each.

6 What are the main differences between formal and informal groups?

7 Why do you think informal groups are usually small to medium-sized? (Think about what is needed for a larger group.)

Key vocabulary
....

characteristics

Differences between groups

We are learning to:

- explain the differences between primary and secondary groups
- explain the differences between formal and informal groups.

Primary and secondary groups 》》

We have seen that primary groups are small and close, while secondary groups are larger and are not as close or intimate. Each type of group has other differences and these are summarised in the table below.

	Primary	Secondary
Size of group	Small in size and confined to a small area	Large – can contain thousands of members
Rules	No set rules	Can have more formal rules
Goal	Main aim is to fulfil all the needs of its members; provides emotional benefits such as love, care, support and security	Aim is to satisfy the specific needs of its members; helps its members to complete tasks and goals
Activities	Emotional depth; activities are often spontaneous	Superficial relationships
Degree of interaction	Intimate, face-to-face, informal	Less intimate, not face-to-face, informal
Membership requirements	Share close, personal, intimate and long-lasting relationships	Temporary and voluntary
Structure/ hierarchy	Position in the group is according to birth, age or sex	Position in the group is by role
Examples	Family, the neighbourhood, close friends	Political parties, voluntary organisations, trade union, sport, cultural groups

Exercise

1 What are the main differences between primary and secondary groups?

2 Give an example of a primary and a secondary group.

3 Think of a group that you belong to. Is it a primary or secondary group? Why do you think this is?

4 Explain in your own words the goals of both a primary and a secondary group.

We have seen on page 169 that a formal group is often formed to fulfil a task or activity, while an informal group can be formed within the formal group and is made up of people with shared interests and likes.

	Formal	Informal
Size of group	Determined by the aims of the group, but are usually large	Tend to be small
Rules	Written rules with sanctions	There are no written rules
Goal	Clearly defined and lasting; can last for several years	Can change as activities change in the group; can have a short time span
Activities	Has organised activities, fixed meeting times	Activities occur spontaneously
Interaction	Interaction may be formal and limited	Is unstructured and open
Membership requirements	Must satisfy certain guidelines	No fixed criteria; members can join and leave very quickly
Structure/ hierarchy	Clearly defined hierarchal structure, with status, roles and clear lines of authority	No clear structure, with an unofficial leader
Leadership emergence	Leaders are **appointed** or **elected**	Leaders may come from age, status, experience or who has been in the group the longest
Examples	Sports club, school, political party, trade union, scouts	Friendship groups in church, school, playing in the street

Exercise

5 What are the main differences between formal and informal groups?

6 Write approximately 250 words that explain the differences between two named groups in formal and informal or secondary and primary groups.

7 Which type of group shows the following characteristics:

a) the meetings can be at fixed times

b) it has no clear structure

c) these types of groups can last for several years

d) have written rules.

Key vocabulary
....

appoint

elected

Benefits of groups

We are learning to:
- explore the benefits of being a member of a group
- explain roles and responsibilities in groups and group cohesion.

Benefits of group membership ⟩⟩

Each group is different. Members participate in groups for a wide variety of reasons. Let's look at benefits that groups offer their members and what happens when members no longer experience these benefits. Belonging to a group can bring a number of benefits to someone:

- gaining a sense of their own **independence**
- a sense of belonging is a strong part of being part of the group
- groups allow their members opportunities to display their talents or to learn new skills
- taking **responsibility** for their role within the group
- cooperating with other members of the group and working together as a team
- making well-informed decisions
- learning to resolve problems and differences
- helping create a sense of identity and understanding who you are and what you believe in
- accepting authority and being loyal to the group
- giving opportunities for leadership
- dealing with different personalities and being tolerant of others' views and ideas.

Exercise

1 Read the statements below. Match each statement to one of the factors above.

  a) 'At my youth group, I feel like I am part of something.'

  b) 'My church group keeps me strong in my faith. That's part of who I am.'

  c) 'At my art club, I get to display my special talent for drawing.'

  d) 'My choir group has a lot of rehearsals. But we're all committed to attending every rehearsal. No one wants to let the others down.'

Activity

You are the PRO (Public Relations Officer) of a community basketball group. Write an article for the school newspaper to highlight the benefits of being a member of the group.

It is important for a group to work well together to achieve their goals.

Project

Write a 5-minute presentation about a group that you belong to outside of school. Perform your presentation to the class.

Roles and responsibilities ▶▶▶

Each member of a family has certain roles and responsibilities. When these roles and responsibilities are not fulfilled the family cannot carry out its functions.

This applies to any other groups, no matter their size, whether they are formal or informal, primary or secondary.

Each person in a group has their own role and responsibility, and if everyone does not do their part it cannot function properly. For example, if you play in a sports team, and you don't turn up at the match, the team cannot play.

When any group members do not carry out their specific role or responsibility, it will become difficult for that group to achieve its goals.

Members will also start to lose their sense of belonging to the group and the group may break up.

Group cohesion is the group's ability to stick or stay together and last.

There are a number of factors which make good group cohesion:

- good communication and cooperation
- the same goals and interests
- commitment from the members
- a sense of belonging to the group
- a good strong identity for the group
- effective leadership
- plenty of opportunities to use new skills
- working together as a team.

School is an example of a formal group.

Discussion

As a class, discuss the benefits of belonging to a group.

Exercise

2 Think of a group you belong to. List three benefits of being in that group.

3 Write a letter inviting other students to join a basketball group. Outline the benefits of joining the group.

4 In your own words, define the terms role and responsibility.

5 Name three factors that contribute to group cohesion.

Key vocabulary

independence

group cohesion

Overcoming group issues

We are learning to:

- examine ways groups can overcome issues that arise.

Issues within groups

Sometimes issues can happen within a group. There can be many reasons for this.

- People are individuals and sometimes they just disagree with each other or are not happy with other members' behaviour.
- Dissatisfaction with the leader – are the leaders capable of guiding the group? Are there opportunities for developing new leadership skills? Sometimes a leader can be too **controlling** and will not empower members to do the tasks that they should be doing.
- Lack of cooperation – do members cooperate well? If members do not cooperate, the group's aims will not be met.
- Members may be in **competition** with each other. For example, they both may want the same position of leader in the group.
- Peer pressure. This is a feeling that one must do the same things as other people within a social group in order to be liked or respected by them. For example, a person started drinking alcohol in high school because of peer pressure.

We have seen how, if everyone fulfils their roles and responsibilities, the group will stay together. Those same factors which make a group cohesive can also create problems in a group:

- bad communication and lack of cooperation
- different goals and interests
- lack of commitment from members
- no sense of belonging
- lack of identity
- ineffective leadership
- lack of opportunities to use new skills
- not working together as a team, but as individuals.

People have to work together to achieve results.

Discussion

Think about how peer pressure might affect your behaviour. Think of examples of peer pressure that are in your interests (and good for you) and examples of where peer pressure works against your interests. Produce a noticeboard in groups with images of what peer pressure can be like and how to avoid it.

Activity

A local group is having problems with lack of cooperation between its members to achieve its goals. In groups, discuss strategies to deal with this.

Key vocabulary

controlling
competition
compromise

Exercise

1 Give three reasons why you think that issues can sometimes arise within groups.

2 Why do members of a group need to cooperate and work well together?

3 Choose three factors which should make a group cohesive but can pull a group apart. Suggest how these could be overcome.

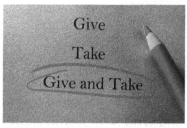

Give

Take

Give and Take

Compromising is often a balance of giving and taking.

Ways to overcome issues

When issues begin within groups, it needs to be dealt with quickly, so that they do not begin to affect the overall running of the group and put the aims of the group at risk. Resolving issues can involve:

- **compromise** – this is finding a way between two conflicting members, opinions or ideas. Each side has to make a concession, meaning that they find common ground that they can agree on to *solve the problem* and reach their common goal
- talking to the leader of the group about the problems and ask them to resolve it. If the problem in the group is the leader themselves, then this needs to be discussed as a group with the leader
- cooperating more closely together and working together as a team to achieve the group's goals.

Case study

We couldn't keep our charity group together

What kind of group did you start? A charity club.

What was it called? The Mandeville Helpers.

Where was it based? At our school in Mandeville, Jamaica.

How many people were interested? Lots of students seemed interested, but only 12 came to the first meeting. Then it got smaller each time.

What were the problems? We couldn't agree how to start. Some people wanted to work with children and others wanted to work with elderly people. There were sub-groups that didn't agree with the rest of the group. The leader of the group made decisions the rest of the group did not agree with.

Questions

1. What factors caused the charity group to fail?

2. What should they have done differently?

3. What would you have done to make the charity successful?

4. Think of a problem you have experienced in a group you belong to. Create a comic strip of the issue and how it was resolved.

Leadership

We are learning to:

- define the terms leader, leadership, power and authority
- state the qualities of a good leader.

What is a leader?

A **leader** is someone who leads or guides a particular group, and who is in overall charge of that group. A leader is someone whom the rest of the group follows.

Leadership is shown when the leader (or leaders) influence the group to achieve a common objective. Leadership has a direct impact on the way in which a group functions. It is important to have effective leadership that encourages cohesion within groups. When we talk about leadership qualities, we mean those personal qualities that make someone good at leading others.

Leadership qualities

Good leaders must have good leadership qualities. A good leader should be able to:

- *communicate well* with the members
- be able to *deal* with people
- *set goals* for the group and *put members'* needs first
- *allocate resources* to achieve the group's goals
- *motivate and persuade* other members to achieve the group's goals
- be *honest, reliable* and fair
- be *responsible*
- *command respect* of the members and *be respectful* towards them
- be *open and apply good ideas* from members
- be *influential* on how people think and act.

Exercise

1. Explain in your own words the terms leader and leadership.
2. Write a list of the qualities that you believe people need in order to become leaders.
3. Decide on the three most important qualities in a leader. Use the word cloud to help you.

Discussion

In groups, discuss the difference between power and authority.

honest trustworthy persuasive reliable disciplined having integrity selfless fair hardworking responsible respectful kind calm good communicator tolerant

Activity

Describe qualities a good leader should have. Write about 150 words.

Key vocabulary

leader

leadership

honest

reliable

responsible

respectful

A good leader needs to have **power** in their group to make the group function. Power is the ability of one person or group to exercise influence and control over others.

Authority is the right to exercise power over others. There are three types of authority that we accept in free society:

- **Charismatic authority** – A charismatic leader has a strong personality and a special ability to inspire others. Groups follow this kind of leader because they want to, not only because a law or tradition tells them to.

- **Traditional authority** – Traditional leaders get their power from customs or traditions. Often, they are connected to the religious tradition of a country or group. Kings and queens are examples of traditional leaders.

- **Rational-legal authority** – In many groups, organisations and countries, people elect leaders into power by **voting**. They are voted into power, and when they resign, or when they no longer receive any votes, their authority ends.

Case study

Great leaders from around the world

Nelson Mandela is famous for helping to unite South Africa to end apartheid. He was a great advocate for peace and forgiveness, even though jailed for 27 years while doing this. Despite this, Mandela was able to gain the respect and trust of all his followers, and other world leaders, which helped South Africa to heal the wounds of apartheid.

Dr Eric Williams was one of the great leaders of Trinidad and Tobago. He made a huge contribution to the nation, which eventually led to independence. He believed that all humans are equal and spent his life working towards this goal. To help do this, Williams reformed education and economic development.

Questions

1. What type of leader do you think Nelson Mandela was?

2. What qualities as a leader did Dr Eric Williams have?

3. Write your own definitions of the terms power and authority.

4. Explain in your own words the three types of authority in society.

Project

Find out more information about one of the leaders on this page. Consider the following:

- When were they born?
- Where did they come from?
- What was their most famous achievement?
- What qualities do you think they had?
- Why do you think they were successful leaders?

Nelson Mandela was imprisoned for 27 years in his fight to end apartheid in South Africa.

Key vocabulary

power

charismatic authority

traditional authority

rational-legal authority

voting

The role of a leader

We are learning to:

- examine the role of leaders in groups
- defend the qualities of a good leader.

Role of leaders in a group

We have already looked at the qualities that a leader of a group should have, that they should be able to use their power and authority effectively, as well as the types of leader and the differences between leadership types. But what is the role of a leader?

A leader has many roles to fulfil in a group. These help them to:

- achieve their goals or aims and allow members to be happy and comfortable
- represent the group they lead, both within the community and with other local groups, and to be a role model
- stay **focused**, give direction and provide guidance on achieving their goals
- **mediate** on issues which arise in the group
- keep a sense of order and structure within a group.

Each of these roles can be applied in our everyday groups – such as our youth group – but they can also apply to leaders who work in the community, at council level, government level or world leaders.

lead achieve goals represent community focused give direction give guidance mediate give support issues keep order structure aims happy

Exercise

1 Draw a mind map to illustrate what you understand by the role of a leader in a group. Use the word cloud to help you.

2 Add to the mind map the qualities a leader should have for each of these roles.

3 True or false? A leader's role is to:

a) let a group get on with things in their own way

b) mediate between members who disagree

c) help the group achieve their goals

d) help the group choose a different goal each week.

Activity

Students work in groups to role-play a dramatic piece which highlights one role of a leader.

Project

Roleplay a situation in which two students imagine that they are campaigning to be a leader of a formal group. Get them to reflect on the qualities they possess to be leader or wish to develop to become a leader.

Case study

Defending leaders

Being a leader is a difficult job. We have already seen that group cohesion is important for keeping a group together, but sometimes a group, and in particular the leader, can face unexpected problems or challenges.

Often it is not the leader who has caused the problem or difficulties, but they get criticised by the other group members anyway. Sometimes it is easier to blame the group leader, because they are in the position of leadership and authority, rather than to accept that the problems may have been caused by the group members.

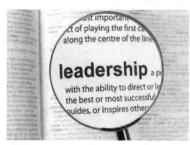

Leadership is the ability to give direction.

Matthew has been running a youth club group in Portmore for three years. The club has a committee which has six members, including Matthew.

All this time, Matthew has been managing the finance, finding venues and resources, and running the sessions. Some of the committee members are not doing their roles in the way they should be, but because Matthew enjoys the sessions with the children he has not said anything. All the children respect Matthew as their leader, and like him because he listens to them and lets them act out their ideas. The children's parents are happy with Matthew as the leader.

Two of the committee members want Matthew to be replaced as leader because they do not think he is running the club correctly. The children and parents have heard about this and are sad that Matthew may have to go. They are campaigning to let him continue as leader.

Research

Using books or the internet, research one famous leader and outline their achievements and role as a leader. Make a short presentation to the class.

Discussion

In groups, discuss what you think are the most important qualities in a leader.

Questions

1. What role does Matthew have at the youth club?

2. Do you think the group shows good group cohesion? Why/why not?

3. Do you think Matthew is doing a good job, or should he be replaced as the leader of the group? Why?

4. If you were Matthew, what would you do?

5. Why do you think it is difficult being a leader?

6. Your youth group is about to choose a new leader. Outline the three qualities you want this leader to have.

Key vocabulary

focus

mediate

179

Questions

See how well you have understood the topics in this unit.

1. Match the key vocabulary word with its definition.

   i) groups

   ii) informal group

   iii) formal group

   iv) leader

   v) leadership

   a) a group that has written rules, a clear division of work and power, and procedures for replacing members

   b) a group is made up of two or more people who do things together to achieve their common goals

   c) when a leader (or leaders) influences a group to achieve a common objective

   d) a group that does not have written rules or objectives or a strict hierarchical structure

   e) an individual who influences the behaviour or actions of another person, or who directs and guides a group towards decisions

2. Complete this table with the group type: school, social (family and friends), sports, cultural, religious, charity and community.

Example	Group type
Family, close friends, school friends, neighbourhood friends, your class at school	
In class or in school clubs	
Church, mosque, temple	
Tennis club, soccer club, hockey club, swimming club, football team, cricket team, netball team	
Lions, Rotary, youth outreach clubs	
Drama group, debating club, Toastmasters, choir, orchestra or band	

3. Name four functions of a group.

4. Complete this sentence about the characteristic of a group: 'Groups have _____ which may be seen in the members' clothing, which helps to identify the group within a wider society.'

5. True or false?

    a) A characteristic of a primary group is its large size.

    b) A characteristic of a secondary group is that it meets less often.

    c) A characteristic of a formal group is that it has written rules to follow.

    d) An example of an informal group is your family.

6. Name four benefits of belonging to a group.

7. Give three examples of a problem that you can get in a group.

8. Explain why compromising is one way to solve group problems.

9. Which of these qualities should a leader of a group have?

    a) communicate well

    b) not able to deal with people

    c) be unreliable

    d) set goals for the group

    e) show respect

10. Match these terms with their definition.

    i) charismatic authority

    ii) traditional authority

   iii) rational-legal authority

    a) a form of leadership in which people come to a position of power through traditions or customs, because it has always been that way

    b) a form of leadership in which people come to positions of power through a fair system of rules and laws

    c) power that comes from one's exceptional personality or character, or powers of persuasion

11. Name three roles that a leader has in a group.

12. This word cloud shows some of the qualities a good leader should have. Take three of these words and write a sentence for each one describing the quality a leader should show.

honest trustworthy persuasive reliable disciplined selfless having integrity fair hardworking responsible respectful kind calm good communicator tolerant

13. Explain what is meant by:

    a) institution   **b)** folkways   **c)** taboo

14. Complete the following table:

Type of activity	Political, economic or social institution	Why?
Establishing tax rules		
Arresting people		
Arranging family life		
Investment companies		

Grade 7 Unit 6 Summary

Groups in society

In this chapter, you have learned about:

- Groups and the different categories of social groups that people belong to
- What groups allow the members of society to do
- The functions of groups for the individual and the wider society
- The characteristics of groups.

Institutions, including social institutions

In this chapter, you have learned about:

- Institutions as large groups that help to keep society organised and orderly
- The five basic institutions that meet the needs of society
- The two types of socialisation
- The agencies of primary and secondary socialisation that transmit the norms and cultural traditions of a society.

Social norms

In this chapter, you have learned about:

- What is meant by social norms
- What is meant by folkways and mores
- What a taboo is.

Different groups and the benefits of belonging to them

In this chapter, you have learned about:

- The features of primary and secondary groups, and formal and informal groups
- The differences between primary and secondary groups, and formal and informal groups
- How members of society benefit from group membership
- The roles and responsibilities of group members
- Issues that can occur within groups
- Solutions to group issues when they occur.

Leadership

In this chapter, you have learned about:

- Leadership and leadership qualities in a group
- The differences between charismatic, traditional and rational-legal authority
- The role of the group leader and the qualities of a good leader.

Checking your progress

To make good progress in understanding social groups and institutions, check to make sure you understand these ideas.

Explain the term *group*.

Identify the different groups to which people belong.

Name the different categories of groups.

Explain the functions of groups.

Describe the characteristics of groups.

Explain the differences between groups.

Name the benefits of belonging to a group.

Examine how groups can overcome issues within groups.

Identify factors which help keep groups together.

Identify what is meant by an institution.

Identify examples of taboos, folkways and mores.

Examine the role of peer pressure in affecting people's behaviour.

Unit 7: Social Groups: The Family

Objectives: You will be able to: ≫

Where do I belong?

- define and use correctly the terms family and kinship
- identify and describe the different types of families in our society
- compare the different family types.

Unions and relationships

- identify possible advantages and disadvantages of various different family types
- define and use correctly the terms union, common law, visiting relationship, marriage
- identify and describe the different types of unions in our society.

Family history

- define and use correctly the terms family tree, origins, ancestry, customs, traditions
- develop an awareness of our family histories
- construct a family tree.

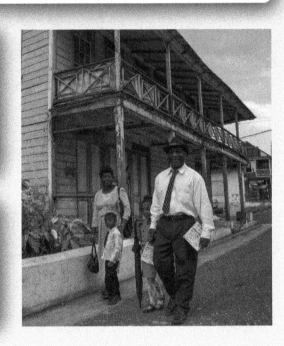

Functions of the family

- explain the relationships that exist within families
- describe the functions of the family
- describe the five functions of the family.

My roles and responsibilities

- define and use correctly the terms role and responsibility
- describe the roles of an individual
- describe the roles, relationships and responsibilities of family members
- examine the consequences of not fulfilling responsibilities.

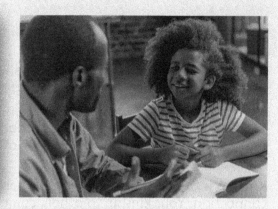

What are some of the challenges faced in Jamaica?

- analyse challenges faced within the family.

Where do I belong?

We are learning to:

- define and use correctly the terms family and kinship
- identify and describe the different types of families in our society
- compare the different family types.

Different types of families

A **family** is a group of individuals, usually living together and related by blood, marriage or some type of union, such as adoption.

The adults in a family usually take responsibility for caring for the children. There are different types of families, but there is no wrong or right type of family.

Kinship is the most basic form of human relationship or connection. Your kinship to others comes from either:

- **blood ties**, which trace your descent from common ancestors
- unions such as marriage, adoption or other connections.

The four main family types in the Jamaican family are **nuclear, extended, sibling** and **single parent** families. There are also **reconstituted families**.

> **Discussion**
>
> Have a class discussion about the term 'family'. What makes a family? Let each student identify their main family members, and suggest which type of family they belong to.

Nuclear family
A mother, father and their children living together in one household.

Extended family
A larger family, with additional family members such as grandparents or married siblings.

Reconstituted family
These are families where one or more parents have children from previous relationships.

Sibling household
A household in which the parents are absent, so the older brothers and sisters take care of younger siblings.

Single parent
One parent living with his or her children.

Exercise

1 Define the terms 'nuclear family' and 'extended family'.

2 Describe the advantages and disadvantages of each family type.

Case study

Three different families

A. Michael and Joanne were classmates. During their studies, they began dating. After two years of **courtship**, followed by a six-month engagement, they got married. They have two children, David and Rebecca. They work to support their family, and also dedicate a lot of time and attention to their children's education and growth.

An example of an extended family, here showing three generations of the same family.

B. Goodman and Rianna met each other on holiday in Jamaica. After a whirlwind three-month romance, they got married. Soon, Rianna was pregnant with their son, Daniel. When Daniel was two, however, Goodman and Rianna realised the relationship was not working. They got divorced. Rianna lives with Daniel in Kingston.

C. Kayla (16), Anisha (11) and Benjamin (9) are three children who live alone since their parents died and they became orphans. Kayla takes care of the younger two. They do not have income, so they rely on help from neighbours and from social workers.

Questions

1. Which case study describes:

   a) a nuclear family?

   b) a single parent family?

   c) a child-headed household?

2. Describe the challenges you think may be faced by Family B and Family C.

3. Define the words:

   a) courtship

   b) engagement

   c) divorce.

4. How can courtship and engagement contribute to a happy family life? Write a paragraph for your answer. Describe your own family type.

Project

Your teacher will show you a slide show or presentation of different family types.

Collect data on the different family types in your class. Complete a tally table with the numbers of each family type and then represent your data on a bar graph.

Key vocabulary

family

kinship

blood ties

nuclear family

extended family

sibling household

single parent family

reconstituted family

courtship

Unions and relationships

We are learning to:

- identify possible advantages and disadvantages of various different family types
- define and use correctly the terms union, common law, visiting relationship, marriage
- identify and describe the different types of unions in our society.

Advantages and disadvantages of different family types »

The four main different types of families have advantages and disadvantages for the members of the family.

Activity

As a class, work with your teacher to discuss the advantages and disadvantages listed below, and list them in tables under family type - nuclear, extended, sibling and single parent. Remember, some advantages and disadvantages may apply to more than one type of family. Be respectful of each other's opinions and listen when classmates are sharing their own experiences.

Advantages

- Siblings do not get split up if their parents are not available, for example, siblings being placed in different foster homes
- No fighting between parents
- Parents support each other
- Strong support network
- Strong bonds of love and affection between siblings
- Children take more responsibility to help parent(s)
- Two role models to teach appropriate behaviour
- Children learn to cooperate with others
- Strong development of responsibility
- Strong communication between parent and child
- More financially secure; stable and caring environment
- Strong sense of belonging
- Smaller family to support
- Caring home environment helps good self-esteem
- Family shares what they have and protect each other

Disadvantages

- There can be disagreements and conflicts
- Children may be too young to look after siblings
- One parent takes all the responsibilities: very tiring
- Can be isolated from other relatives
- May have a traditional hierarchy where older men have the most power
- Children may leave school to look after siblings
- Child may spend more time alone or with peers
- Parents may lack support of extended family
- No source of income, adult guidance or help
- Discipline and supervision fall to one parent which can be difficult when juggling work commitments
- Children may have less experience of a range of opinions and views
- Children may be vulnerable to abuse
- Only one income
- Less opportunity for problem-solving

Most families form when two people form a **union**. There are three different types of unions:

- **Marriage** – a legally or formally recognised union.
- **Common-law union** – a couple live together as husband and wife without getting married. In Jamaica, persons in common-law relations are considered to be 'spouses' having lived continuously together for five years. Legal recognition of such unions may occur if one or both persons apply to the court for a declaration of their union.
- **Visiting relationship** – a long-term partnership where the partners do not live together, but one visits the other from time to time; they may have children.

A wedding party on the beach, Jamaica.

Case study

A. Brandon and Emma met while they were studying. At first they were just classmates, but then they developed stronger feelings for one another. They dated for two years and then they decided to move in together. That was six years ago. They never got married, but they have a baby girl together and they live together as a family.

B. Jenelle still lives with her parents. She has been in a relationship with her boyfriend, Leroy, since she was 18 and he was 24. Now she is 22 and has two children. Her parents help her take care of the children as Leroy still lives with his family.

Questions

1. Describe the types of union in the examples above.
2. Do you think Brandon and Emma should get married? Suggest advantages or disadvantages to support your answer.
3. Why would Jenelle choose to continue living with her parents? Suggest two possible reasons.

Discussion

The nuclear family is usually considered the ideal family type. Do you agree? Which family type would you prefer to be in?

Exercise

1 In your own words, define the terms 'marriage', 'common-law marriage' and 'visiting relationship'.

2 What type of unions do you have in your family?

3 Which type of union would you like or dislike? Write sentences using the following frames:

    a) I would like to be in a ____ because _____.

    b) I would not like to be in a ____ because _____.

Key vocabulary

union

marriage

common-law union

visiting relationship

Family history

We are learning to:

- define and use correctly the terms family tree, origins, ancestry, customs, traditions
- develop an awareness of our family histories
- construct a family tree.

Family customs and traditions »

Your **origins** are where you come from. In a family with records that go back several generations, it is possible to trace your **ancestry**. This is the line of relatives starting with your parents and **grandparents** and going back in time to each generation's parents and grandparents. Within your family you are linked to your origins through your family's **customs** and **traditions**.

Customs and traditions are thoughts, actions or behaviours that a group of people do and have done for a long time, which help to identify them as part of that group. Read the examples of family traditions opposite.

Exercise

1 What do all the family customs have in common?

2 Does your family have any of these family customs? Which ones? If not, why not?

3 Describe a tradition that you do not have, but would like to have in your family. Explain why.

Once a week, we have a family meal together.

Our family tradition is an annual holiday with all our cousins.

One of our family traditions is walking to church each Sunday. It gives us all a chance to spend some time together without any distractions.

We always take a moment for thankfulness before meals.

Family histories and family trees »»

Each person has some awareness of their family history from their personal experience of their own family. In addition to this, we each hear stories about older family members and ancestors from the previous generations.

A more formal way of finding out about family histories is by interviewing elders. Family records, such as photographs and old birth and death certificates, can tell us more about our families.

A family tree »»»

An awareness of family history helps a person to understand who they are and where they come from. A **family tree** is a **genealogical** diagram that shows a person's ancestors and how that person is related to each of their ancestors and siblings.

Project

Construct your own family tree showing at least three generations. Present your family tree as a project on a large piece of card.

In other words, your family tree shows how you are related to your parents, grandparents, siblings, aunts, uncles and cousins.

A family line (also called lineage) is a line of descent that you can trace to a common ancestor. A matriarchal family tree shows the lineage on the mother's side of the family. A patriarchal family tree shows the lineage on the father's side. A family tree showing both sides of the family is bilineal. Family trees also reveal parts of your family's history: which family members got married, and when, and dates on which children were born.

Look at this family tree and answer the questions that follow.

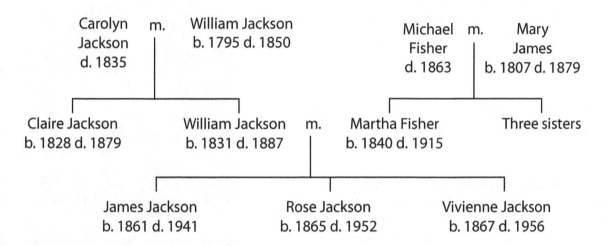

Exercise

4 What do the letters b., d. and m. stand for on the family tree?

5 Why do some people only have one date under their name?

6 How many children did Martha have?

7 Name Rose Jackson's grandfathers.

8 Name Vivienne's aunt on her father's side.

Research

Create a questionnaire for the elder members of your family. Research some stories in your family's history. Give a three-minute oral presentation with some of the most interesting details you found out.

Key vocabulary

origin

ancestry

grandparents

custom

tradition

family tree

genealogical

Functions of the family

We are learning to:
- explain the relationships that exist within families
- describe the functions of the family.

Family relationships ⟫

A family relationship describes the way two people are connected to each other within a family. It may describe the blood tie or the union that connects the people. The family tree below shows the **relationships** that can exist within families.

Grandparents: the parents of your parents are your grandparents. Your mother's parents are your maternal grandparents. Your father's parents are your paternal grandparents.

↓

Parents: mothers and fathers are responsible for taking care of their children.

↓

Children/siblings: from birth to 18 years, a person is considered a child. **Siblings** are children born to the same parents. Your brothers and sisters are your siblings. Half-brothers and half-sisters are siblings who share one parent rather than both.

↓

Aunts, uncles and cousins: your parents' brothers and sisters, and their spouses, are your aunts and uncles. Their children are your cousins.

↓

Nephews and nieces: when your brothers and sisters have children of their own you become an aunt or uncle. Your siblings' daughters are your nieces. Your siblings' sons are your nephews.

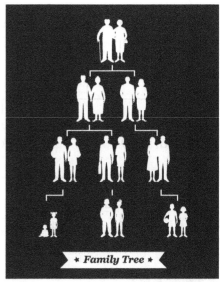

★ Family Tree ★

Family trees are often represented as above.

Exercise

1 Identify each family relationship:

   a) Your mother's parents are your _____.

   b) Your parents' other children are your _____ and _____.

   c) When your siblings have children, they are your _____ and _____.

   d) Cousins are the _____ of my parents' _____.

Discussion

Discuss the functions of the family in groups. Collect photographs to show each of these functions and make a collage to show to the rest of the class.

There are five broad functions of the family:

BIOLOGICAL: having children is the **biological function** of families. Most families begin with a marriage or partnership that results in one or more children.

ECONOMIC: every individual has basic needs for food, shelter, security and clothing. The **economic function** of the family requires that some members of the family work or have some way of bringing in income for the family's needs.

FUNCTIONS OF THE FAMILY

EMOTIONAL: human beings need love, attention and support as much as they need basic things like food, water and shelter. Part of the family's function is to provide for the emotional needs of its members.

SOCIALISATION: in the family, children learn how to interact and communicate with others and how to form relationships. This is known as socialisation.

CULTURAL/ EDUCATIONAL: within a family, a child acquires knowledge, skills, values and attitudes that form part of his or her education. Beliefs and traditions, morals and values all form part of the cultural function of families.

Exercise

2 Into which of the five functions does each of the following fit?

   a) comforting a younger sibling when they are upset
   b) a parent showing a child how to prepare for Christmas celebrations
   c) a couple planning to have a child
   d) grandparents explaining to a child when to say please and thank you
   e) an aunt paying for her niece's school fees.

3 In your opinion, which is the most important and least important of the family functions? Write a one-page essay, or present a one-minute oral presentation, explaining your opinion.

Key vocabulary
....

relationship

siblings

biological function

cultural/educational function

The five functions of the family

We are learning to:

- describe the five functions of the family.

Biological »

Not all unions result in children. However, in society as a whole, human beings need to reproduce in order to continue human society. Therefore, the most basic function of the family is to produce children.

Emotional »»

Families provide love, affection, support and attention. Children whose parents have loving relationships tend to have higher self-esteem, greater confidence and can usually cope well with stress and conflict. This can benefit the wider Jamaican society by making sure that children are brought up to be calm, kind and patient. As such, this will help them to become good members of social communities in the future.

However, even in families with high levels of conflict and negative emotion (such as anger), family members still rely on each other for support and for a sense of family identity.

Families provide children with love and affection.

Socialisation »»»

Socialisation is where children gain the knowledge, language, **social skills** and values to fit into social groups, such as their family and community. This is done by giving children:

- a sense of who they are and where they belong
- guidance about how to behave and interact with others
- a sense of their roles and responsibilities
- guidance on how to form and sustain relationships.

Language is a big part of socialisation. Children learn to speak a language and they also learn what kinds of language are appropriate in different settings. Being able to communicate effectively with others isn't just important for families, but also within Jamaican society as a whole.

Exercise

1 Suggest a family structure that does not have a biological function.

2 Look at the picture above. Which family functions can you see suggested in the picture?

Discussion

Your teacher will show you pictures representing the different functions of the family. Discuss what each picture represents.

Economic

Everyone has basic needs and families are structures that provide for these needs. In order to provide these, a household needs the following to survive:

- Income: money to pay for goods and services. The person who earns the greatest proportion of money for the family is the **breadwinner**.
- Domestic work: this includes cooking, cleaning and laundry. This may be shared out among the family.
- Childcare: in many families both parents work, so another relative may look after the children or the family may pay for childcare services.
- Care of the elderly or disabled: elderly or disabled members of the family may need care. This may be provided by a relative or by a paid service provider.

Children gain social skills by mixing with other children.

Cultural and educational

The educational function is to teach children information and skills they will need throughout their lives. Children are highly **impressionable** and develop much of their understanding and knowledge about the world from their family home.

Part of socialisation and education involves teaching family members about their culture. This may include:

- religious beliefs and traditions
- language, accent and style of speaking
- beliefs, morals and values
- customs and heritage.

Most families participate in culture that reflects the groups they belong to within their community. For example, if you are born into a Jamaican family, you will grow up familiar with the Jamaican accent and way of speaking, popular Jamaican dishes and the celebrations of your community.

Exercise

3   How many members of your family work? Who is the main breadwinner?

4   Who does the domestic work in your home? Is this work shared equally between family members? If not, who is responsible for it and why is it not the responsibilities of others?

5   Who looks after the children or elderly in your family?

Activity

Describe three important functions of the family in approximately 300 words. Remember to explain how these functions help to positively impact the wider Jamaican society.

Key vocabulary

social skills

breadwinner

impressionable

My roles and responsibilities

We are learning to:

- define and use correctly the terms role and responsibility
- describe the roles of an individual
- describe the responsibilities of each role
- describe the roles, relationships and responsibilities of family members
- examine the consequences of not fulfilling responsibilities.

Benefits of family cohesion

Family cohesion describes the close bond between family members, providing care, love and support to one another, including extended family members and close friends.

A cohesive family is able to communicate effectively and openly. This means that they can usually resolve conflicts easily through calm discussion. Cohesive families have access to good emotional support, which can lead to greater happiness and less stress for the members.

Having a cohesive family unit also helps to ensure that traditions are passed on, and that strong morals and excellent standards of behaviour carry on through the generations.

In a cohesive family model, parents or caregivers work well together, ensuring that children have a stable homelife. This allows the younger members of the family to focus on their education and get support when they need it. Cohesion can be ensured when family members carry out their roles and responsibilities.

Roles and responsibilities

Each member of a family plays their own **role**. A role is a pattern of behaviour that comes from your position in the family. For example, a parent's role is to take care of the children and make decisions for the household. Along with this role may come several **responsibilities** – the things we are expected to do as part of our role – such as providing food, paying rent, buying clothes and so on.

As an individual, your role may change depending on where you are and who you are with. For example, at home you may be a son, an older brother to a sibling, a younger brother to another sibling, and a grandchild to your grandparents.

Discussion

Discuss which individual (or individuals) in your family takes on responsibility for each of the following: earning money, running the household, caring for the family.

Exercise

1 Identify two different roles you play in your family and explain two responsibilities for each role. Write these in your portfolio.

2 In your own words define 'roles' and 'responsibilities'.

Identity

A person's roles and responsibilities affects identity. Your identity refers to the way you are seen and how you see yourself. Your identity can be about your roles, gender, position in the family, religion, where you live, and much more.

Traditional roles and responsibilities

In traditional societies, men were breadwinners and the head of the house, responsible for making decisions. Women took care of the children and housework. Girls helped their mother with the housework and childcare. Boys helped with work such as gardening.

Today, women and men may both work and spend equal amounts of time earning money for the family. This gives both men and women the right to make decisions such as how money is spent. Today there is greater awareness of women's and girls' rights to **equality**. However, some families still expect members to follow traditional roles.

Consequences of not fulfilling roles and responsibilities

If one person fails to fulfil their responsibility in a family, this can cause the whole family to suffer. It may mean that someone else has to take responsibility for a role that is not rightfully theirs. This can lead to jealousy, resentment or depression. Distribution of family roles can sometimes be unfair - one person can be responsible for much more than another.

Case study

"We were a family of five – my mother, my oldest brother, my grandmother and me. My dad died a few years ago, so my oldest brother started working to help my mother support us. With my mother and brother working, my grandmother looked after me most of the time. But she is very old. I worry about something happening to her. Then I would be on my own at home during the day." James

Questions

1. Identify the responsibilities that each person in James' family takes on.
2. List the consequences if no one in the family can:
   a) earn money to support the family
   b) stay at home to look after the children
   c) take care of housework.

Grandparents
- provide support for parents
- help with looking after the children
- provide financial assistance if they are able
- help the child's social and emotional growth
- pass on customs, traditions and family history.

Parents
- meet basic economic needs
- provide emotional support, love and affection
- socialise children
- educate children
- pass on traditions and customs.

Children
- show respect for their parents
- help with chores
- care for siblings and elderly family members
- attend school and take responsibility for their studies
- do not waste family money or possessions.

Causes and effects of changing roles of family members ⟫⟫

There are a number of reasons for the changing roles of family members in Jamaica.

Women's changing roles in Jamaican society

According to an anti-discrimination committee, in the past, despite women's great academic achievements, they occupied few positions in Jamaica of real power and influence. This is still true to some extent today, but more women are making their marks in Jamaican history. For example, Portia Simpson Miller was the first woman to be head of the government. Equality in Jamaica may be a slow process but it is progressing.

Jamaican Prime Minister Portia Simpson Miller with US President Barack Obama in Kingston, 2015.

Some traditional customs are still practised in Jamaican homes, but more and more families include women who work and men who assist with taking care of the children and domestic chores. There are also a lot of women and men in Jamaica who are raising their children alone. While some traditional roles remain, there are changes taking place in the family.

Discussion

In groups discuss the importance of female role models in Jamaican society. Discuss examples of women in powerful positions and the impact of gender equality on society.

Exercise

3 Explain what male and female roles used to be like in Jamaica.

4 Give three reasons why family roles are changing.

5 Are there any problems with raising children as a single parent?

Activity

In groups, choose a scenario where roles have changed in a family. Create a dramatic presentation to show the impact on different family members and perform it to the rest of the class.

Activity

Role-play the different roles and responsibilities of individual family members. Use the flow chart on page 197 to help.

Key vocabulary

role

equality

There are a number of causes and effects of the changing roles in the family:

Cause	Effects on family life
Women are increasingly staying in education longer	Women see other women role models succeeding in education and they are able to go on to university or higher level training. This means they may choose not to get married or start a family, or choose to start a family later in life.
Women are increasingly in paid work and focusing on their careers	With more women working, childcare is now often shared with men, or families now depend on nurseries and after-school care services.
	Some women may choose not to have children or to have fewer children so that they can have a career as well.
Attitudes are changing, towards greater gender equality in society	There are now laws and policies making sure that women and men are treated more equally. These may encourage women to go into paid work and to expect greater equality at home, for example, sharing household chores.
Divorce is increasing	Women can afford to divorce and to support themselves and their children, making divorce more likely.
People are choosing to get married later, or not at all	There are fewer traditional nuclear families, and more people living together instead of being married. There may also be fewer children born, and as a result, smaller families.

Research

Do you think that the nuclear family is in decline? Write a questionnaire to hand out at school to find out how many people live in different family structures. What are your conclusions?

Activity

1. Carry out research into the number of women who work in Jamaica.

2. What is the average pay of women compared with the average pay of men?

3. How many single parent families are there in Jamaica? How many of these are headed by women?

4. What are some gender differences in the workplace and family life?

Did you know...?

In 2020, women in Jamaica are 23% less likely to have equal economic participation and opportunities than men. There is a gender pay gap of approximately 38%. This means that, on average, women's income was estimated to be around 38% lower than that of men.

What are some of the challenges faced in Jamaica?

We are learning to:

- analyse challenges faced within the family.

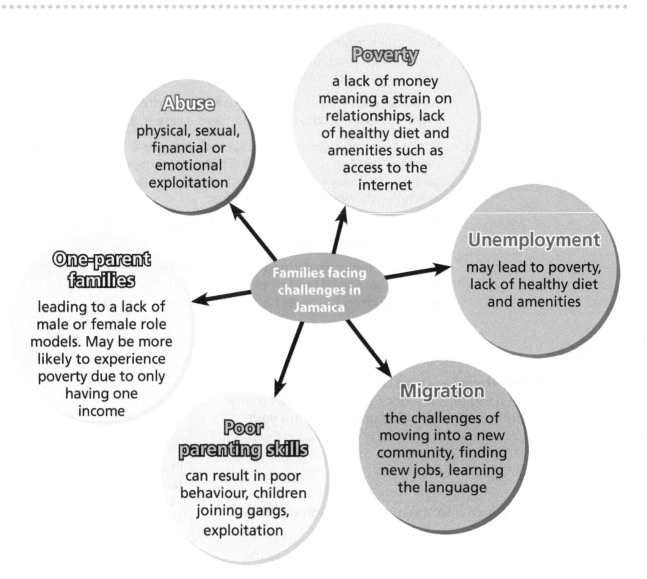

Poverty
a lack of money meaning a strain on relationships, lack of healthy diet and amenities such as access to the internet

Abuse
physical, sexual, financial or emotional exploitation

One-parent families
leading to a lack of male or female role models. May be more likely to experience poverty due to only having one income

Families facing challenges in Jamaica

Unemployment
may lead to poverty, lack of healthy diet and amenities

Migration
the challenges of moving into a new community, finding new jobs, learning the language

Poor parenting skills
can result in poor behaviour, children joining gangs, exploitation

Which agencies and programmes support the family?

In Jamaica there are specialist services and programmes designed to support families that are having problems. For example:

1. families experiencing **poverty**
2. families that include members who have **disabilities**

Discussion

Discuss how these problems may be overcome in the family.

3. families that have members who have health issues

4. families where members are considered to be vulnerable or at risk, for example, of abuse

5. problems with drugs and alcohol within the family

6. problems with violence, crime or other illegal behaviour.

There are several agencies in the government set up to help support families, for example:

1. **National Family Planning Board** – responsible for planning and implementing programmes for family planning; focuses on sexual and reproductive health. Some of its services include the distribution of contraceptives, testing for sexually transmitted infections (STIs), counselling and training for parents and young adults.

2. **Child Development Agency** – responsible for care and protection of children, works with children beyond parenting control, institutional placement and supervision, foster care placement and supervision, adoption, home and family services.

3. **Programme for Advancement through Health and Education (PATH)** – provides assistance for low income families and vulnerable persons such as the elderly and those with disabilities. The programme offers assistance with food and schooling for children on a monthly basis.

4. **National Health Fund** – helps with paying for prescription drugs for people with long term health issues.

The Role of UNICEF in supporting families in Jamaica

"At UNICEF Jamaica, we are a small team dedicated to one big goal: to help fulfil the rights of every child. We work towards this by partnering with the government, non-governmental organisations and change-makers in civil society to influence and improve laws, policies, programmes and services for children.

We are in a unique position to collaborate with everyone from the most impassioned advocates and service providers who work up close with children and their families, to the country's elected leaders who work at the policy and legislative level on their behalf. And most importantly, with children and adolescents – engaging them on the issues that affect their lives.

Focusing our attention on the most vulnerable children, we have four priority areas in our current country programme (2017–2021): safety and justice, health promotion, lifelong learning and social protection.

Activity

Carry out research into the work of the Child Development Agency. What are their aims? What do they do? Present your findings in a PowerPoint to present to the rest of your class.

Unicef is the world's leading organisation working for children in danger.

Everything we do is guided by the Convention on the Rights of the Child, which Jamaica ratified in 1991. Our work is also informed by and contributes to the Vision 2030."

UNICEF estimate that one in four children live in poverty in Jamaica.

Case study

UNICEF

According to UNICEF, one in four of Jamaica's children lives in poverty and, as a result, is more exposed to health issues, more vulnerable to **exploitation**, has reduced access to adequate water and sanitation facilities, and is more likely to be exposed to violent discipline. Girls in the poorest population quintile are also more likely to become teenage parents. An estimated 35 000 children under age 14 have a disability and are at risk of being excluded or discriminated against. Jamaica has state-run social protection programmes, including the PATH conditional cash transfer programme. However, a significant number of deserving children still fall outside of this targeting mechanism.

Exercise

1. How are UNICEF and the Jamaican government working together to protect children at risk?

2. Which types of children are at risk?

3. Carry out research into the PATH programme. How is it aiming to support children?

Agencies that support families ›››

The Child Protection and Family Services Agency (CPFSA) is responsible for protecting children and helping to promote child friendly policies and programmes to help support families. The agency employs over 600 staff, working across many different parishes. It plays several roles including:

- providing residential childcare services. This includes eight government children's homes and places of safety as well as monitoring and another 40+ private homes
- The Children and Family Support Unit which focuses on working with other agencies in helping to keep children out of State care, through counselling and other interventions to families and abused victims
- providing adoption services, making sure that children are placed safely with suitable parents
- running the children's summit which is an annual event.

Research

Carry out research into the work of UNICEF in Jamaica. Find out what current projects exist and describe how they are addressing the following four priority areas:

- safety and justice
- health promotion
- lifelong learning
- social protection.

Write a leaflet describing the project and present it back to your class.

Activity

Imagine you are a government worker and you are given the job of designing a new policy to protect and support families in Jamaica. Decide what your policy will do, set out its aims and create a policy document highlighting these aims. Present this to your class.

Child Protection and Family Services Agency

Protecting Children, Empowering Families, Securing the Future

Case study

Maxfield Park Children's Home

The Maxfield Park Children's Home was established in September 1918 and is located on 6½ acres of land which was donated by Major Maxfield to the Government for social purposes. The facility is the largest and oldest children's Home in Jamaica and it is a place of safety for many children who have been abandoned or made homeless.

There are presently 86 children in care, ranging in age from babies to 18 years old.

The Home seeks to train and prepare the children in activities that help to broaden their horizon and bring out their full potential. These activities include:

- The Rotoract Spelling Bee Competition
- The Reading Competition
- The Debating Competition
- The Dorm Competition
- The Homework Programme
- Basketball Team

There are currently two schools on the property. The special school serves children with learning challenges and also provides education for newly admitted students until they are integrated into regular school. The basic school serves children aged 3 to 6 living in the Home. Over the years, a number of the children have obtained passes in GSAT, CXCs & City & Guild examinations. Recently, two students were accepted at the G.C. Foster College and the U.W.I (Mona campus) to pursue tertiary education.

Due to the overall economic climate, the children's home is experiencing financial difficulties as there has been a significant decrease in donations, hence the need for assistance to maintain the current infrastructure. Funds are urgently needed to undertake major renovations to infrastructure and repairs to plumbing and electrical work. They are also in urgent need of a bus to transport those challenged children who attend school off property, as current buses are old and malfunctioning.

Source: Children Of Jamaica Outreach website.

It is the responsibility of the whole country to protect at-risk children.

Exercise

4 Describe the work of the CPFSA.

5 Why do care homes exist?

6 Explain the current challenges faced by care homes in Jamaica.

Key vocabulary

poverty

disabilities

exploitation

Questions

See how well you have understood the topics in this unit.

1. List one similarity and one difference for each pair:

   a) nuclear family and extended family

   b) single parent family and sibling household

   c) sibling household and extended family.

2. Match each example below to one of the following functions of family: biological, emotional, social, economic, cultural or educational.

   a) giving a child love and attention

   b) teaching a child to swim

   c) earning money to support a family

   d) taking a child to church.

3. List all the different roles you play. You can choose from the mind map below or add any other roles you can think of.

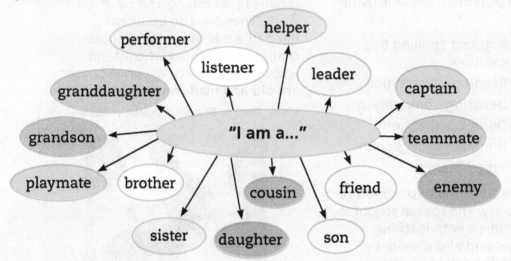

4. Which of the following circumstances does not describe a single parent family?

   a) The parents get divorced and the children live with one parent.

   b) The father has died, so the children live with their mother.

   c) The parents are having difficulties, so the children go to live with their aunt, uncle and cousins.

5. Describe the following types of family structures:

   a) nuclear

   b) reconstituted

   c) extended family.

6. Describe three roles you play in your life (these may be roles at home, at school or in your community). List two responsibilities of each role.

7. Draw part of your family tree, showing at least three generations.

8. What is meant by the following terms?
   a) procreation
   b) breadwinner
   c) identity

9. Explain three reasons why roles have changed within the family.

10. Identify two consequences of the changing role of women on family life.

11. How does the government provide families with support?

12. Why might families need support from the government or other agencies?

13. What do UNICEF do to support families in Jamaica?

Grade 7 Unit 7 Summary

Belonging, unions and relationships

In this chapter, you have learned about:

- What is meant by family and the types of families
- The advantages and disadvantages of the different types of family
- Three different types of unions in Jamaica.

Families

In this chapter, you have learned about:

- Family customs and traditions
- Family histories and using family trees to trace ancestry
- How to interpret the information on a family tree
- The different types of family relationships shown on a family tree
- The biological functions of family
- The emotional functions of family
- The social functions of family
- The economic functions of family
- The cultural and educational functions of family.

Roles and responsibilities

In this chapter, you have learned about:

- The roles and responsibilities of members within the family unit
- The consequences of not fulfilling the roles and responsibilities expected within the family unit
- The factors that cause the changing roles of men and women in the family
- The effects of the changing roles of members on family life.

Challenges and the family

In this chapter, you have learned about:

- The social and economic challenges faced by families in Jamaica
- The categories of agencies and programmes that support the family in Jamaica.
- How UNICEF supports Jamaican families
- The roles of Child Protection and Family Services Agency play in supporting families in Jamaica.

Checking your progress

To make good progress in understanding more about social groups: the family, check to make sure you understand these ideas.

Explain what is a family.

Explain what is kinship.

Name the four main of family types in the Caribbean.

Identify the potential advantages and disadvantages of the various different family types.

Explain why there are different types of unions.

Describe the characteristics of the five functions of the family.

Explain the roles and responsibilities of three family members and why it is important they fulfil their roles.

Describe the consequences of not fulfilling these roles and responsibilities.

Describe the changes in the role of women in the family.

Describe what is meant by an agency that supports the family.

Outline the problems faced by some families.

Explain how government and non-governmental agencies help support families.

End-of-term questions

See how well you have understood ideas in Unit 4.

1. Explain the difference between renewable and non-renewable resources.

2. Make a list of the benefits of the Sun, land and water as a natural resource.

3. Write about 200 words on the use and overuse of natural resources and the negative effects on the environment.

4. Match these definitions to the correct terms:

    a) sustainable

    b) deforestation

    c) exploitation

    i) The removal of trees or forests

    ii) The overuse of a resource

    iii) Means an action that can be kept going for ever, something that can continue to be done without it having damaging consequences that might limit that activity in the future.

5. Briefly describe the benefits of forests for humans and the physical environment.

6. What are the solutions to deforestation? Give an example.

7. Explain the potential problems of the use of natural resources on communities in Jamaica. Write about 200 words.

8. Explain the role the government can play to make sure that natural resources are used fairly and safely in Jamaica.

See how well you have understood ideas in Unit 5.

9. Explain what is meant by human resources.

10. Explain the differences between physical and human resources.

11. Provide two examples of physical resources.

12. Give two examples of factors that affect human resources.

13. Explain what is meant by an unskilled, semi-skilled and highly skilled worker.

14. What can skilled, educated people offer an economy?

15. Match these terms with their definitions.

   a) on-the-job training

   b) mentorship

   c) succession training

   d) tuition assistance

   i) An employee can go on additional training courses to help build up their knowledge and skills.

   ii) Where the employee's skills and abilities are developed to prepare them for promotion

   iii) Training whilst working, to help develop skills within a job

   iv) A more experienced employee gives advice and support to someone less experienced.

16. Outline four acceptable standards of conduct that workers should follow.

Questions 17–20 ⟩⟩⟩

See how well you have understood ideas in Unit 6.

17. Explain what is meant by a social group.

18. Why are social groups important? Write a short paragraph to explain.

19. Write a short essay of six paragraphs in which you mention at least three types of institutions in Jamaica. You should explain why there is a need for these institutions and what each institution does.

20. Explain the difference between primary and secondary socialisation.

Questions 21–24 ⟩⟩⟩

See how well you have understood ideas in Unit 7.

21. What are the main family structures found in Jamaica?

22. Write a paragraph explaining what a family tree is, and why it is useful.

23. Write a short essay explaining the reasons why roles may be changing in the family in Jamaica, and the consequences of these changes on family life.

24. Give an example of an agency that supports family life, explaining what it does.

Unit 8: Movements of the Earth

Objectives: You will be able to:

The effects of movement of the Earth
- describe the effects of rotation and revolution on the Earth.

World geography: locating places
- describe the characteristics and purpose of lines of longitude and latitude
- locate places and give locations using longitude and latitude.

History of longitude and latitude
- appreciate the work of inventors of latitude and longitude.

Locating the Caribbean
- locate the Caribbean on a world map.

Time Zones

- identify the location of the Caribbean and Jamaica using lines of latitude and longitude.

How differences in time, climate and seasons affect human activities around the world

- describe the seasonal types experienced in the five climatic zones.

How the climate affects how we live

- examine the ways climate influences ways of life.

The effects of movements of the Earth

We are learning to:

- describe the effects of rotation and revolution on the Earth.

The effects of rotation and revolution of the Earth 〉〉

In order to understand the effects of the movement of the Earth, it is important to understand its position in the **solar system**.

The solar system 〉〉

The solar system is the Sun and the many objects that **orbit** it. To orbit means to take a curved path around an object. These objects include eight planets and at least five dwarf planets and countless asteroids, meteoroids and comets. The surrounding objects are kept in orbit by the pull of the Sun's **gravity** which has an influence for many millions of kilometres. Gravity is the force that attracts an object or body towards the centre of a planet, star or other body.

Rotation is the spinning of Earth on its axis once every 24 hours. Earth's axis is an imaginary line running through its centre tilted at 23½ degrees. The Earth spins from west to east.

Revolution is the movement of Earth around the Sun once every 365.25 days. Since our calendar years have only 365 days, we add an extra leap day every four years to account for the difference. The time taken for Earth to orbit the Sun is influenced by its distance from the Sun. Planets closer to the Sun have a shorter orbit.

> **Did you know...?**
>
> Earth has two main movements, it **rotates** and it **revolves**.

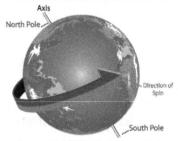

Earth's axis is an imaginary line running through its centre, tilted at 23½ degrees.

Activity

Build a model of the solar system, labelling the planets, the Sun, dwarf planets, asteroids, meteorites and comets. Explain the model to the rest of your class.

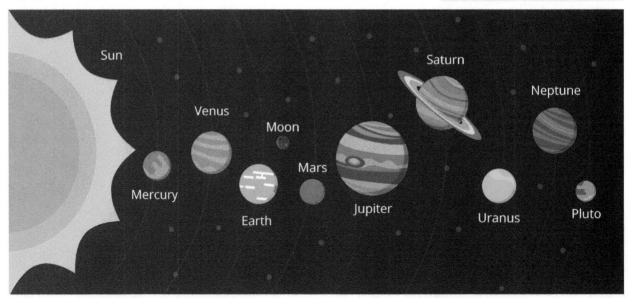

Day and night ▶▶▶

The Earth turns round on its **axis** every 23 hours and 56 minutes and it is this rotation that is responsible for the daily cycles of day and night. At any one moment in time, one half of the Earth is in sunlight, while the other half, facing away from the Sun, is in darkness. As the Earth rotates day slowly changes to night and night slowly changes to day. Rotation also creates the apparent movement of the Sun from east to west across the sky.

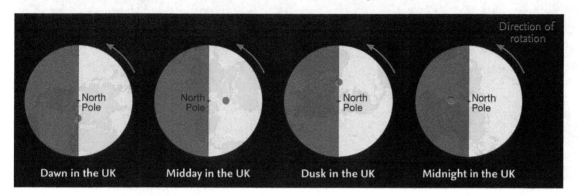

Direction of rotation

| Dawn in the UK | Midday in the UK | Dusk in the UK | Midnight in the UK |

The seasons and length of day ▶▶

The tilting of Earth on its axis causes different parts of the globe to be tilted either towards the Sun or away from it at different times of the year. This causes variations in the amount of sunlight received and results in the four seasons, Spring, Summer, Autumn and Winter, as the Earth revolves around the Sun. For example, in June each year, the Northern Hemisphere is tilted towards the Sun causing it to receive more direct sunlight and experience warmer temperatures and longer days. This marks summer in the Northern Hemisphere, The Southern Hemisphere at this time will experience winter as it is tilted away from the Sun and receiving less direct sunlight. It therefore experiences cooler temperatures and shorter days.

The summer Solstice (first day of summer) marks the longest day of the year. Some places on Earth receive 24 hours of sunlight on this day. The winter Solstice (first day of winter) marks the shortest day of the year. Some places experience 24 hours of darkness on this day.

The distinct changes in the four seasons are only experienced by places found between the Tropic of Cancer and the Arctic Circle and between the Tropic of Capricorn and the Antarctic Circle. Places in the Tropics such as Jamaica and other Caribbean countries do not experience these distinct changes.

Did you know...?

In the spring and autumn, each hemisphere receives similar amounts of light. On two specific dates each year, called the equinoxes, both hemispheres get illuminated equally.

Key vocabulary

solar system

orbit

gravity

rotate

revolve

axis

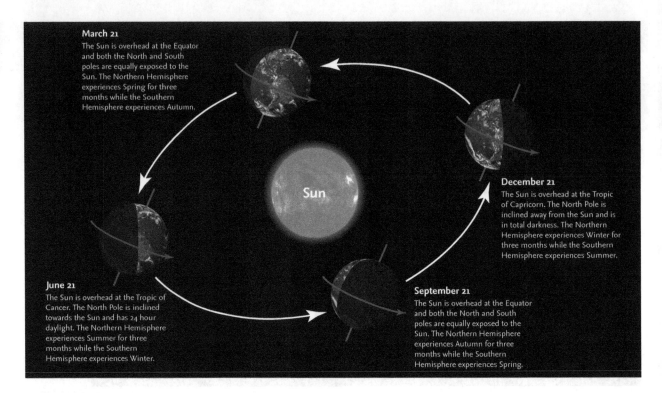

March 21
The Sun is overhead at the Equator and both the North and South poles are equally exposed to the Sun. The Northern Hemisphere experiences Spring for three months while the Southern Hemisphere experiences Autumn.

Sun

December 21
The Sun is overhead at the Tropic of Capricorn. The North Pole is inclined away from the Sun and is in total darkness. The Northern Hemisphere experiences Winter for three months while the Southern Hemisphere experiences Summer.

June 21
The Sun is overhead at the Tropic of Cancer. The North Pole is inclined towards the Sun and has 24 hour daylight. The Northern Hemisphere experiences Summer for three months while the Southern Hemisphere experiences Winter.

September 21
The Sun is overhead at the Equator and both the North and South poles are equally exposed to the Sun. The Northern Hemisphere experiences Autumn for three months while the Southern Hemisphere experiences Spring.

Exercise

1 What is gravity?

2 Explain why seasons exist.

3 If it is night in Jamaica, name one place on Earth where it is daytime.

How is life on Earth supported through movement of the Earth?

Earth is the only planet known to maintain life. Like Venus and Mars, Earth has mountains, valleys, and volcanoes. But unlike other planets, almost 70% of Earth's surface is covered in oceans of liquid water that average 2.5 miles deep. The unique atmosphere here nourishes life on Earth as well as the way that it moves:

- The Earth moves within a relatively stable solar system.
- The Earth is at an ideal distance from the Sun so that we can use its energy.
- We have an ozone layer to block the harmful rays from the Sun.
- Our moon has a stabilising effect on the Earth that makes sure that it keeps its tilted angle, ensuring that the climate and seasons stay the same.
- The moon influences the flow of the sea. Lunar tides were important in helping early life migrate (move)

Discussion

In small groups discuss how the movement of the Earth and its effects influence how people live and the activities they engage in. You may look how changes in seasons influence how we dress, reactional activities, activities such as farming and many others.

from the oceans to tidal flats and, eventually, onto the land. Although the Sun also influences ocean tides, it does so with relatively little effect.

What does the Moon do? ▶▶▶

Everyone knows that the Moon is partly responsible for causing the tides of our oceans and seas on Earth, with the Sun also having an effect. However, as the Moon orbits the Earth it also causes a tide of rock to rise and fall in the same way as it does with the water. The effect is not as dramatic as with the oceans but nevertheless, it is a measurable effect, with the solid surface of the Earth moving by several centimetres with each tide.

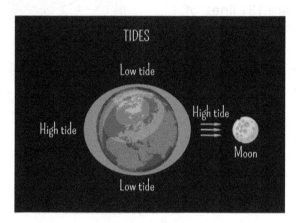

What is Earth like as a planet? ▶▶

Here are some interesting facts about why planet Earth is so unique:

- Our home planet Earth is a rocky, terrestrial planet. It has a solid and active surface with mountains, valleys, canyons, plains and so much more.

- Earth is special because it is an ocean planet. Water covers 70% of the Earth's surface.

- Our atmosphere is made mostly of nitrogen and has plenty of oxygen for us to breathe. The atmosphere also protects us from incoming meteoroids most of which break up in our atmosphere before they can strike the surface as meteorites.

- Earth is warm so living things like us can be there. It's the only planet in our solar system we know of that supports life.

- Earth is the third planet from the Sun in our solar system. That means Venus and Mars are Earth's neighbouring planets.

Source: Visit the NASA website 'Space Place' and search for 'All About Earth'.

It is thought that the Moon was created when a rock the size of Mars slammed into Earth, shortly after the solar system began forming about 4.5 billion years ago.

Activity

Design and create a 3D model showing how rotation of the Earth leads to night and day.

What you will need:

1. Balloon (representing the Earth)

2. Small flashlight

Instructions:

1. Inflate a balloon to represent the Earth.

2. As you rotate the Earth model, observe how different parts of the Earth receive sunlight at different times. One half facing the light source experiences daytime, while the other half in shadow experiences night-time.

World geography: locating places

We are learning to:

- describe the characteristics and purpose of lines of longitude and latitude
- locate places and give locations using longitude and latitude.

Characteristics of lines of latitude

Lines of latitude are imaginary lines that run horizontally from east to west. Latitude is measured in degrees (°) north or south of the Equator. The North Pole is at 90° north and the South Pole is at 90° south. There are 181 lines of latitude. The main lines of latitude you will notice on maps are:

- the Equator is at 0° – this line divides the Earth into northern and southern **hemispheres**
- the Tropic of Cancer (23.5 °N)
- the Tropic of Capricorn (23.5 °S)
- the Arctic Circle (66.5 °N)
- the Antarctic Circle (66.5 °S)
- the North Pole (90 °N)
- the South Pole (90 °S).

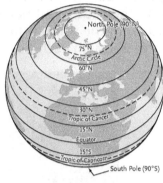

Lines of latitude.

Characteristics of lines of longitude

Lines of longitude are imaginary lines that run vertically from north to south. They are measured in degrees.

The most important line of longitude is the **prime meridian** (0°). This is also known as the Greenwich Meridian, because it runs through the Greenwich Observatory in Britain. Exactly halfway round the Earth from the Greenwich Meridian is the International Date Line, at 180°. The Eastern and Western hemispheres are situated to the east and west of the prime meridian.

Cayo Coco's latitude is halfway between 22°N and 23°N. Its longitude is halfway between 78°W and 79°W. We can write its position as 22°30'N, 78°30'W.

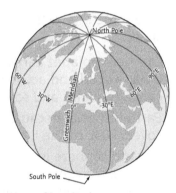

Lines of longitude.

Discussion

In pairs discuss the purpose of lines of latitude and longitude, and identify two characteristics of both longitude and latitude.

Purpose of longitude and latitude ⟫⟫

Remember, lines of longitude and latitude do not exist in real life. They are tools that help people locate places on maps and describe positions.

Look up Jamaica in an atlas. Next to the name of Jamaica, you will see the page number, followed by a grid reference and then the coordinates (18°10'N 77°30'W). The coordinates for Jamaica tell you that it is situated 18 degrees and 10 minutes north of the Equator and 77 degrees 30 minutes west of the Greenwich Meridian.

The table shows you the longitude and latitude of cities in Jamaica, as well as some of the major cities of the world.

City	Coordinates
Kingston, Jamaica	17°59'49" N 76°47'37" W
Montego Bay, Jamaica	18°28'16" N 77°55'8" W
New York, USA	40°42'51" N 74°00'21" W
Paris, France	48°51'12" N 2°20'55" E
Cape Town, South Africa	33°55'33" S 18°25'23" E
Sydney, Australia	33°52'04" S 151°12'26" E
Beijing, China	39°54'26" N 116°23'50" E

The International Date Line ⟩

In 1884, delegates attended the International Meridian Conference in the USA to work out an international prime meridian. They agreed on the Greenwich Meridian.

Fortunately, this meant that the 180° meridian (exactly opposite the 0° meridian) mostly passed over water. This line is known as the International Date Line (IDL).

When it is Monday to the left of the IDL, it is Sunday to the right of the IDL. People who cross the line from east to west skip forward by one day. People who cross the line from west to east repeat the day.

Exercise

1 Name the line of latitude that is:
   a) furthest to the north and south of the Equator
   b) at 23°S and at 23°N.

2 Lines of longitude are given in degrees east or west of the Greenwich Meridian. Is the International Date Line 180°W or 180°E of the Greenwich Meridian? Explain your answer.

3 Complete the following sentences:
   a) St Lucia is situated _____ of the Equator and _____ of the Greenwich Meridian.
   b) Belize is situated _____ of the Equator and _____ of the Greenwich Meridian.

4 Look at the cities in the table above. Which city/cities:
   a) are in the southern hemisphere?
   b) is furthest north?
   c) is furthest east?
   d) is closest to the Equator?

Activity

On a globe of the world, find the Equator, the Tropic of Cancer and the Tropic of Capricorn. Also identify the Greenwich Meridian and the International Date Line. For each line, identify two countries that have that line passing through them.

Key vocabulary

line of latitude

hemisphere

line of longitude

prime meridian

History of longitude and latitude

We are learning to:

- appreciate the work of inventors of latitude and longitude.

Latitude ≫

For thousands of years, people have used the skies to help with navigation.

The Phoenicians were part of an ancient civilisation in the Middle East. They were known for exploring the world by boat. As long ago as 600 BC, the Phoenicians used the Sun and stars to work out their latitude. The Polynesians also used the movement of the stars to work out their latitude.

The ancient Greeks started using grid lines to show latitude and longitude. This was a suggestion by Greek astronomer Hipparchus around 300 BC. Hipparchus also found a way to locate places on Earth by observing the positions of the Sun, moon and stars.

Around 225 BC, Eratosthenes, a Greek mathematician and astronomer, measured the circumference of the Earth (the distance around the Earth) by calculating the distance between Alexandria in Northern Egypt and Syene in Southern Egypt. Once he worked this out, he was able to work out the circumference of the Earth.

This discovery helped the Greeks to draw maps as they then were able to find their latitude easily using trigonometry and the positions of the Sun, moon and stars.

Ancient scholars also made many mistakes in their ideas and writings about geography. The Roman scholar Ptolemy believed that the circumference of the Earth was shorter than it actually is.

As a result, Christopher Columbus made the mistake of believing he could reach Asia by sailing west from Europe.

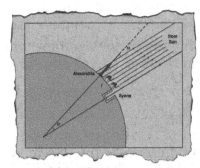

Eratosthenes' knowledge of the Sun's position and distance between points enabled him to calculate the Earth's circumference.

Research

Work in groups. Each group chooses and using the internet researches one of the following navigation instruments:

- back staff
- kamal
- astrolabe
- octant
- sextant
- quadrant
- bearing compass
- magnetic compass
- ring dial.

As a class, make a timeline with pictures of the different navigational instruments at the correct places, showing when they were invented or used.

Exercise

1 Name three ancient civilisations that learned to navigate using the Sun, moon and stars.

2 Name two ancient Greeks whose discoveries helped navigators to find their latitude position.

Up until the 18th century, there was no internationally accepted system for calculating longitude. This was a problem for sailors because as soon as they set sail from their own country they were 'at sea', an expression that came to mean lost.

Scientists had problems working out how far they had travelled from east to west. It was easier to calculate latitude because they could work out the length of the day, the height of the Sun or the distance of the stars above the horizon.

Early mariners used a 'dead reckoning'. They threw a log overboard and timed how long it took for the log to pass the boat. They would use this to work out how fast they were travelling, and from that calculation work out how far they had travelled. However, this was very inaccurate because the boat's speed could easily increase or decrease.

John Harrison, 1693–1776, inventor of the device to find the longitude of a ship at sea.

In 1707, five British naval ships got lost in heavy fog. Because there was no system of longitude, they miscalculated where they were and 2 000 sailors died as a result of the mistake. In response to this, in 1714, the English parliament offered a prize of £20 000 to anyone who could solve the longitude problem.

One solution was to measure the time at sea and to measure the time on a clock at another place and compare the difference between the two clocks.

However, this was not simple. Clocks at this time operated using metal **pendulums**. A pendulum swings around wildly during storms at sea and metal expands and contracts with changes in temperature, which affected how they worked.

A clockmaker called John Harrison eventually won the prize, after many years of work.

Today, **Global Positioning Systems (GPS)** have made it possible to identify coordinates from anywhere on Earth.

Activity

In groups, create a jingle of two stanzas using the names of the people who created longitude and latitude.
(Tip: Eratosthenes and John Harrison)

Exercise

3 Why was it easier to work out latitude than longitude?

4 Create a jingle about the history of latitude and longitude.

5 Create a timeline about the history of longitude and latitude. Add any photos you can find from the internet.

Key vocabulary

pendulum

Global Positioning System (GPS)

Locating the Caribbean

We are learning to:

• locate the Caribbean on a world map.

Locating the Caribbean

To find the Caribbean on a world map:

• First find the continents of North America and South America.

• Look at the narrow strip of land that joins the two continents.

• To the east you will see the Gulf of Mexico and the Caribbean Sea.

• The Caribbean region is located in and around the Caribbean Sea.

• It is found between 10 and 25 degrees North and between 60 and 90 degrees West.

Activity

Your teacher will hand out blank maps of the Caribbean. Insert the Tropic of Cancer, the Caribbean territories and their capitals, and the surrounding bodies of water.

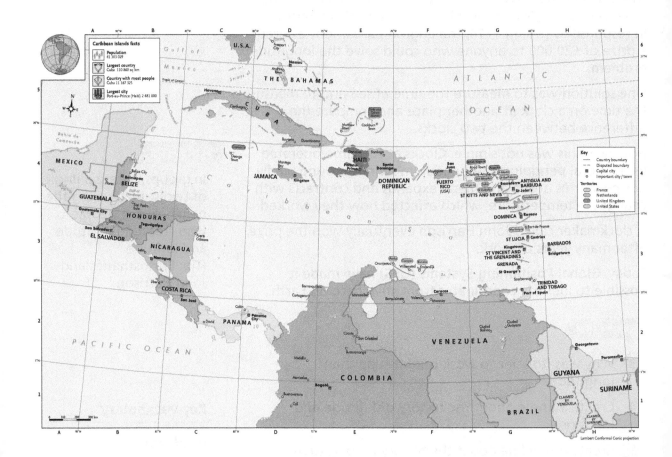

Jamaica is an island country of the West Indies, the third largest **island** in the Caribbean Sea, after Cuba and Hispaniola. It is located at 18 degrees North and 77 degrees West. Jamaica is about 146 miles (235 km) long and varies from 22 to 51 miles (35 to 82 km) wide. It is situated 100 miles (160 km) west of Haiti, 90 miles (150 km) south of Cuba, and 390 miles (630 km) northeast of the nearest point on the mainland, Cape Gracias a Dios, on the Caribbean coast of Central America.

Jamaica

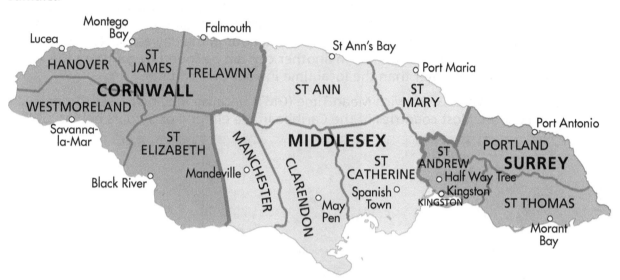

Exercise

1 Copy and complete.

   a) The Caribbean region is located in the _____ Sea.

   b) To the east of the Caribbean is the _____.

   c) Many Caribbean territories have the ___ Sea on their southern coast and the ___ Ocean on their northern coast.

2 Find out the longitude and latitude of Jamaica's position.

3 Name three countries that are closest to Jamaica.

Discussion

The countries of the Caribbean are considered part of North America although they are closer to South America. Why? Do you agree that this should be the case?

Key vocabulary
....

island

Time zones

We are learning to:

- identify the location of the Caribbean and Jamaica using lines of latitude and longitude.

What are time zones? 〉〉

Time varies around the world due to the Earth's rotation. This causes different parts of the world to be in light or darkness at any one time.

To account for this, the world is divided into 24 standard **time zones** based on 15° intervals of longitude (1 hour of time). All places in a time zone have the same time of day. The shapes of some zones have been adjusted so that all of the country or region lies in the same zone. There is one hour difference between each zone – one hour in the day earlier to the west, one hour later to the east. The local time in another city can be found by counting the number of hours earlier or later than the local time in your own country.

The time at 0° is known as Greenwich Mean Time (GMT) because the line passes through Greenwich in London. Most countries of the Caribbean are either 4 or 5 hours behind GMT.

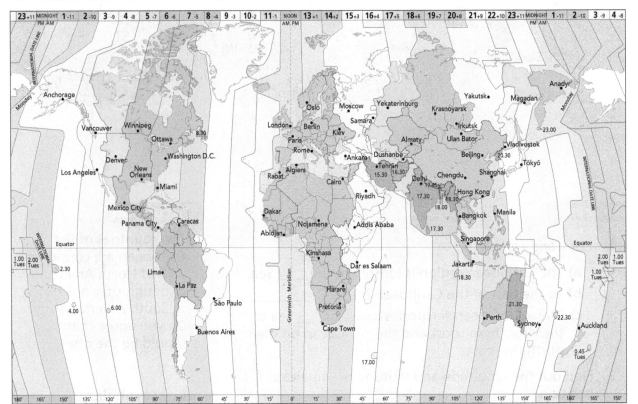

Exercise

1 Explain what is meant by a 'time zone'.

2 How much time is there between each zone?

3 Write 100 words explaining why it is important to know how to calculate time.

Why do we need time zones?

Time zones give specific areas on the Earth a time of day that is earlier or later than the neighbouring time zones. This is because when it is daytime on one side of the Earth, it is night-time on the other side. There are 24 time zones dividing the Earth into different times, each with its own name, like the Eastern Standard Time Zone.

When did time zones begin?

Greenwich Mean Time (GMT) began in 1675, when the Royal Observatory in Greenwich, London, was built to help ships find their longitude at sea. GMT was a standard reference for time keeping when each city kept a different local time. When railways began carrying many people quickly among cities keeping different times, they adopted time zones to simplify operations. By about 1900, almost all time on Earth was in the form of standard time zones.

GMT is now called UTC (Coordinated Universal Time). UTC is the time standard of the world. All other parts of the world are offset (plus or minus) according to their longitude. Most of the zones are offset by a full hour, but there are some offset by half an hour or 45 minutes.

Some parts of the world follow Daylight Saving Time (DST), and during this period of time in summer they add one hour to their normal solar hour.

The time zones are numbered in relation to the UTC, so in Los Angeles the time zone will be UTC−8, in London UTC+0, in Rome UTC+1, and in New Delhi UTC+5:30.

Activity

Draw a map with the time zones of the Caribbean.

Do some research about the time the Sun rises and sets in Jamaica compared with a country in Europe.

The Royal Observatory in Greenwich, London.

Exercise

4   When did Greenwich Mean Time begin?

5   Explain what is meant by UTC.

6   Write a paragraph explaining why we need time zones.

7   You are travelling to Spain for a holiday. You are due to land at 11:00am local time. What time will it be in Jamaica?

8   The cricket World Cup is being held in Cape Town, South Africa, starting at 6:00pm local time. Calculate when you should start watching in Jamaica.

Key vocabulary

time zone

Time, climate, seasons and human activities

We are learning to:

- describe the seasonal types experienced in the five climatic zones.

What are seasons? ➤

Seasons are how a year is divided and they generally have specific weather patterns associated with each season. For example, Jamaica has a rainy and dry season. Europe and North America have cold winters, warm summers, as well as spring and autumn.

Research

Using books or the internet, research how seasons in other parts of the world impact tourism in Jamaica. In groups, create a presentation to share what you find out with the rest of the class.

Key vocabulary

seasons

climate zones

latitudes

What are climate zones? ➤➤

Climate zones are horizontal belts found at different **latitudes** and have varying average weather conditions. Each climate zone has different weather conditions and seasons. There are three broad climatic zones which are separated by the main lines of latitude. These are the tropical zone, temperate zone and polar zone. Within each zone, the climate is further influenced by different factors, creating specialised climates for specific places.

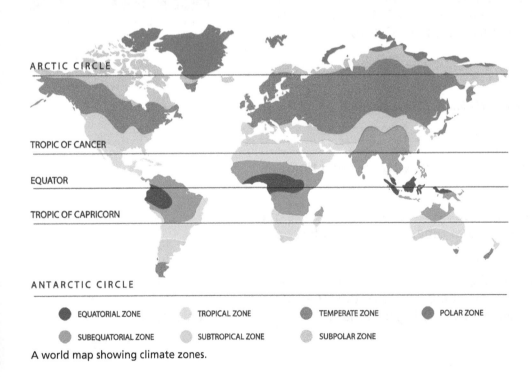

ARCTIC CIRCLE

TROPIC OF CANCER

EQUATOR

TROPIC OF CAPRICORN

ANTARCTIC CIRCLE

- EQUATORIAL ZONE
- TROPICAL ZONE
- TEMPERATE ZONE
- POLAR ZONE
- SUBEQUATORIAL ZONE
- SUBTROPICAL ZONE
- SUBPOLAR ZONE

A world map showing climate zones.

EQUATORIAL (TROPICAL) CLIMATES

Location:
10° north and south of the Equator; referred to as tropical climates as they are found between the Tropic of Cancer and the Tropic of Capricorn.

Countries:
Brazil, Venezuela, Guyana

Temperatures:
average about 27°C

Rainfall:
around 1 500 mm per year

Seasons:
only one season throughout the year

HOT DESERT CLIMATES

Location:
20° and 35° north and south of the Equator

Countries:
Egypt, Saudi Arabia, United Arab Emirates

Temperatures:
can be as high as 50°C but will fall at night; temperatures are hottest between April and October

Rainfall:
very little rainfall in hot desert regions; in order to be classed as a desert, there must be less than 250 mm of rain every year

Seasons:
two seasons – summer and winter

MEDITERRANEAN CLIMATES

Location:
30° and 45° north and south of the Equator

Countries:
Italy, Spain, southern Australia

Temperatures:
hot in summer months (up to 40°C); winter temperatures average 10–15°C

Rainfall:
there is rainfall in most months of the year other than June, July and August

Seasons:
two main seasons – summer and winter

TEMPERATE CLIMATES

Location:
40° and 60° north and south of the Equator

Countries:
UK and western states in the USA

Temperatures:
summer months average 20°C; winter months can be cold, often falling below 0°C

Rainfall:
rainfall all year round, including the summer months, although autumn and winter have the most rainfall

Seasons:
four seasons – spring, summer, autumn, winter

TUNDRA (COLD DESERT) CLIMATES

Location:
60° and 75° north and south of the Equator

Countries:
Greenland, northern Canada, northern Russia

Temperatures:
summer months reach 10°C; coldest during the winter, when temperatures can go down to –50°C

Rainfall:
very low in cold desert regions – less than 250 mm of rainfall; precipitation is most likely to fall as snow rather than rain in these regions

Seasons:
two seasons – summer and winter

How the climate affects how we live

We are learning to:

* examine the ways climate influences ways of life.

How do the weather and climate affect us day to day?

What the weather is like affects us in our everyday lives. It influences our decisions about what we wear and what we do each day. Weather and climate affect people, industries and the environment all over the world.

Clothes worn

If you live in a very warm country, you will want to wear loose clothes made from cotton or linen, as these are cooling in warm temperatures. You will most likely wear shorts and T-shirts in warm countries, to try to stay as cool as possible.

In contrast, if you live in cold countries you will want to wrap up really warm and wear as many layers as possible. In some of the coldest countries in the world, such as northern Russia, people wear **animal hides** (skin) to keep warm. The hides of animals such as caribou and hares can be worn to protect people from the very cold air, because if you wore short sleeves in these countries you could very easily get **frostbite**. There is a phrase used in Iceland that says, 'There is no such thing as bad weather, just bad clothing.'

The sunny climate in the Caribbean means that the cricket season takes place between November and May.

Health problems

Climate affects what diseases are found, and spread, in different countries. Most diseases are very heavily influenced by the weather, and many diseases need specific weather conditions. For example, malaria is a very dangerous disease spread by mosquitoes. Mosquitoes are found all over the world and they are not all harmful. However, tropical areas, where temperatures are warm and the air is **humid** (moist), make excellent breeding conditions for mosquitoes and for this reason malaria is a problem in these areas.

Some other medical conditions that may be associated with warm conditions include heat stroke and heat exhaustion. In cold climates, hyperthermia is common and some conditions such as bronchitis and pneumonia are sometimes made worse by cold conditions.

Sporting activities ▶▶

The climate affects the different sporting activities that are possible in a country.

For example, countries that have snow in the winter months can be very popular ski and snowboarding destinations. Countries such as New Zealand, France and the USA (for example, in Colorado) are all very popular ski areas. Many people visit these countries from all over the world.

Sports such as cricket are heavily influenced by the climate. In the Caribbean, where the cricket season takes place between November and May, whereas in the UK – which has far less reliable sunshine – the season can only be played in the warmer months, between April and September.

Crops planted ▶▶▶

Farming is a very important industry around the world. It is not necessarily a big industry in many countries now, but it is still a very important industry and one that is highly dependent on the climate. Not all crops need the same weather conditions.

While it is true that most crops need sunshine and rain to grow, too much sunshine or too much rainfall will not produce many crops.

Countries that are very hot, such as Ethiopia, struggle to grow crops because the temperatures are so high and there is very little rainfall.

Some regions, such as certain states in the USA (for example, Alaska), cannot grow crops easily because there are very low temperatures and very little rainfall.

Some of the best regions to farm are in temperate areas, where there are no extreme weather conditions.

Farming is an important industry and highly dependent on climate.

Exercise

1. How do the weather and climate affect our decisions about what to wear?
2. What health problems are caused by the weather?
3. Give examples of sports that need specific weather conditions.
4. How is farming affected by the weather?

Key vocabulary

animal hide

frostbite

humid

Questions

See how well you have understood the topics in this unit.

1. A/An _____ means to take a curved pathway around an object.

    a) orbit
    b) alien
    c) planet
    d) axis

2. The Earth's axis is _____, causing us to have seasons.

    a) straight
    b) tilted
    c) horizontal
    d) vertical

3. A/An _____ is the two points in the year where both hemispheres get the same amount of light.

    a) season
    b) axis
    c) equinox
    d) solstice

4. GMT stands for:

    a) Greenwich Median Time
    b) General Median Time
    c) Greenwich Mean Time.

5. True or False? Lines of latitude are imaginary lines which run in a north to south direction around the globe.

6. Correct this statement: most countries of the Caribbean are either 4 or 5 hours ahead of GMT.

7. Explain what is meant by the Equator.

8. Write a short definition of the following terms:

    Solar system
    Gravity

9. Make a list of how seasons affect human activities around the world.

10. Which two of these affect the tides:

    a) The Sun

    b) The stars

    c) The Moon

    d) The sky.

11. Explain how longitude and latitude are used to locate a particular place.

12. Explain what is meant by climate zones?

13. Name the five climate zones.

14. Explain the differences between the climate in a tundra zone compared with a desert zone.

15. What makes the Earth a suitable place for life? Write a short essay.

Grade 7 Unit 8 Summary

The movement of the Earth

In this chapter, you have learned about:

- The composition of the solar system
- Differentiating between rotation and revolution
- How the rotation of the Earth causes day and night
- How the Earth's revolution around the Sun causes the seasons of the year and the length of the day
- How the rotation and revolution of the Earth supports life on Earth
- The effect of the Moon on the tides of the Earth's seas and oceans
- What makes the Earth a unique planet.

Longitude, latitude and time zones

In this chapter, you have learned about:

- The characteristics of the lines of latitude and lines of longitude
- Using lines of longitude and latitude to locate places on the map and describe global positions
- What the International Date Line does
- How ancient voyagers, mathematicians and astronomers devised lines of latitude and longitude to determine location of vessels and calculate travel time and distance
- How to locate the Caribbean on a map
- How to locate Jamaica on the world map
- What is meant by time zones
- The importance of time zones
- The history of time zones and how they improved time keeping for travellers.

The impact of seasons and climate on human activities

In this chapter, you have learned about:

- The different seasons of the year
- The differences between the three main climate zones and the specialised climates of specific places
- How weather and climate affect the clothes people wear, their health problems, their sporting activities and agriculture.

Checking your progress

To make good progress in understanding the movements of the Earth, check that you understand these ideas.

Explain and use correctly the term *rotation*.

Describe how the Earth moves.

Explain the effects of the movement of the Earth.

Explain and use correctly the terms *longitude* and *latitude*.

Name the ways that longitude and latitude are used.

Explain the solar system.

Explain and use correctly the term *time zones*.

Name the key parts of the solar system.

Explain how the seasons affect people.

Explain and use correctly the term *seasons*.

Describe the ways life is supported on Earth.

Explain the role of the Sun and moon in maintaining the seasons.

Unit 9: Interdependence Among Communities and Countries

Objectives: You will be able to:

Relationships between communities

- define relevant terms and concepts: regional integration, bilateral agreement, cooperation, dependence, economy, interdependence, region.

Community development and cooperation

- name organisations in Jamaica that promote community development
- design a programme to address a community problem.

Regional cooperation: The West Indian Federation, CARIFTA, CARICOM and CSME

- define relevant terms and concepts: multilateral agreement, multinational corporation
- describe the Caribbean integration process from the 1950s to the present
- outline the objectives and membership of institutions/bodies which form part of the integration process.

Cooperation in the Caribbean: sport, education, medicine, culture and disaster preparedness

- identify non-political areas of cooperation within the Caribbean region: sports
- assess the role of regional agencies in facilitating the integration process.

Benefits of regional integration and cooperation

- analyse ways in which the individual, businesses and countries benefit from regional integration.

Individual role in regional integration

- discuss ways the individual, and countries can deepen regional integration
- role of individual citizens in the integration process.

Relationships between communities

We are learning to:

- define relevant terms and concepts: regional integration, bilateral agreement, cooperation, dependence, economy, interdependence, region.

Regional integration is when countries in a **region** cooperate and work together towards common goals. This has been a priority since the 1950s, when the first attempts were made by Caribbean states to work cooperatively towards common goals. This came about because states wanted to be less dependent on former colonial powers.

Carnival is an event where people from different cultural backgrounds can come together.

Integration >>

To **integrate** means to bring together ideas and people so that they work together or become part of the same group. The aim of integration is to give members equal status in a group and to share the advantages and strengths that the group brings. There are several types of integration:

- **Social integration** happens when people of different cultural backgrounds learn tolerance and respect for each other.
- **Racial integration** is when people of different races are treated equally so they can live and work together.
- **Economic integration** is achieved when two or more states in a geographic area set common economic goals and reduce the barriers to trade between them. This complements a country's own economy, which is made up of businesses that provide goods and services to meet people's needs.

Discussion

Work in groups and discuss how interdependence can help the states in the Caribbean to develop.

Cooperation >>

Cooperation means working together and helping each other to achieve common goals. For example, we need to cooperate with our neighbours and other members of our community. If there is a problem in a community and everyone cooperates fully, the problem can be solved.

Exercise

1 In your own words, define regional integration.

2 How many different types of integration are there? Write your own definition of each.

3 Why do you think social integration is important in Caribbean countries?

Project

Do your own research in groups. Take one of the terms explained on these pages, and find out more about the term. Then look in newspapers and find examples of events that illustrate what it means. For example, a community event could illustrate integration in an area.

Dependence >>>

To depend on something is to rely on or be controlled by it. **Dependence** on other people has many disadvantages, because it means you are not free to do as you wish.

During colonial times, Caribbean colonies were dependent on their colonial masters (for example, the United Kingdom) and were forced to live by the social and economic laws and rules of their colonisers.

Colonies had little or no control over their own laws or the economic and social development of their own countries.

In the 1960s, when many Caribbean states gained independence, foreigners still owned much of the good farming land and also many of the businesses. The profits from these economic activities were not used to develop the Caribbean countries.

From the 1950s onwards, Caribbean states tried to lessen their dependence on their former colonial rulers in order to strengthen their economies.

Countries began to establish **bilateral agreements** – agreements where two countries help each other – and treaties to help develop the region as a whole.

US President Barack Obama (centre, third from the left) takes part in meeting with Caribbean Community (CARICOM) leaders at the University of the West Indies (Kingston) on 9th April 2015.

Interdependence >>

Countries that help each other or rely on each other are **interdependent**. The leaders of states in the Caribbean saw **interdependence** as the way forward and as a means of strengthening the development of states in the region.

This interdependence started in the 1950s with the West Indian Federation and continues today through organisations like CARICOM and the Association of Caribbean States (ACS).

Exercise

4 In your own words, define the terms dependence and interdependence.

5 Did the Caribbean colonies have control of their own laws when they were a Crown colony?

6 In what way were the Caribbean colonies once dependent on the United Kingdom?

Key vocabulary

regional integration

region

integrate

social integration

racial integration

economic integration

cooperation

dependence

bilateral agreement

interdependent/ interdependence

Community development and cooperation

We are learning to:

- name organisations in Jamaica that promote community development
- design a programme to address a community problem.

There are various organisations that help promote community development and cooperation. It is important that you understand the role that they play and how they work. Community development refers to making sure that a group changes in a positive way so that social problems can be identified and resolved. Community cooperation refers to where different groups in the community continue to work together positively.

Case study

The Linstead Community Development Committee (CDC) is a **community organisation**, based in the parish of St Catherine. It was founded in 1999 and its main purpose is to invest in the growth and development of the community.

In 2017, it embarked on its 12th staging of its annual summer school. Chairman of the CDC Devon Smith said that "What is exciting about this year is, the volunteers are students from the area who were once summer school attendees and are excelling in their classes," said Smith. "One important feature of the curriculum this year is the move to emphasise cultural activities, nature walks, art and craft and community tours."

The CDC also has a programme, 'Operation Clean Sweep', which is an initiative sponsored by USAID to promote environmental awareness. "We came out on top having attained first place in the programme that emphasises the recycling of plastic bottles. We saw the need to continue because of its value to the environment," said Smith.

Source: adapted from Jamaica Gleaner.

Working together will help to solve problems in the community.

The Peace Management Initiative (PMI) was set up in 2002. Based in Kingston it uses alternative **dispute resolution methodologies** to treat community based violence. With its partners the PMI aims to achieve what was once thought to be impossible: zero murders for the entire year.

The PMI works in communities where murder has affected life, but also work to prevent this happening.

The PMI intervenes in communities and works to interrupt violence and build peace, by bringing together a coalition of youths, residents, NGOs, government, police, schools, churches and even gangs.

T3M, is a recording studio in Mountain View and is one of several organisations collaborating with the PMI. T3M is run by youths who see music as both a career and a vehicle for change within the community. "Music, for us, gets us out of violence because it is a different way for us to express our emotion." says Donai Singleton of T3M. "We're basically role models for the younger ones."

Source: adapted from UNICEF blogs.

Questions

1. Explain the importance of both the CDC and PMI in their local communities.

2. Explain why people and organisations working together help to improve lives in communities.

Research

Find out more about the following key organisations. Their web sites are a good place to start.

The Social Development Commission (SDC)

The SDC is the principal community organisation agency working with Jamaica's 775 communities.

The Parish Development Committees (PDC)

The PDC are stakeholders drawn from local businesses, civil society, elected officials, state agencies and other groupings, which coordinates and monitors the development processes at the local level.

Jamaica Social Investment Fund (JSIF)

The JSIF was established in 1996 as a component of the Government of Jamaica's (GoJ's) national poverty alleviation strategy.

Activity

In small groups, identify a social problem in your area.

a) Design a programme of activities which will address this problem.

b) Write out your plan, explaining each activity and describing the different groups in the community that will be involved.

c) Produce a poster outlining the community development programme.

Exercise

1 What is meant by community development?

2 What is meant by 'outreach'? Give some examples.

3 Why does cooperation generally mean better outcomes for a community?

Key vocabulary

community organisation

dispute resolution methodologies

Regional cooperation: The West Indian Federation

We are learning to:

- define relevant terms and concepts: multilateral agreement, multinational corporation
- describe the Caribbean integration process from the 1950s to the present: West Indian Federation
- outline the objectives and membership of institutions/bodies which form part of the integration process: West Indian Federation.

West Indian Federation

The first significant attempt at integration by Caribbean states took place in 1958, when 10 Caribbean countries, who were all still British colonies at the time, formed the **West Indian Federation** as an attempt at a political union.

The West Indian Federation was the first example in the region of an organisation that was based on **multilateral agreement**. A multilateral agreement usually refers to agreements between more than one country or **multinational corporation** (a large organisation that has business interests in more than one country). The West Indian Federation is an example of a multilateral agreement.

The flag of the West Indies.

Objectives and membership of the West Indian Federation

At the time of its formation in 1958, the membership of the West Indian Federation was:

- Antigua and Barbuda
- Barbados
- Dominica
- Jamaica
- Grenada
- St Kitts-Nevis-Anguilla
- Montserrat
- St Lucia
- St Vincent and the Grenadines
- Trinidad and Tobago.

The main aim of the Federation was to reduce dependence on (and ultimately to achieve independence from) Britain.

Exercise

1 When was the West Indian Federation set up?

2 Name the members of the West Indian Federation.

3 What were the main advantages of creating a Federation?

Did you know...?

The following states were members of the Federation:

- Antigua and Barbuda
- Barbados
- Dominica
- Grenada
- Jamaica
- Montserrat
- St Kitts-Nevis-Anguilla
- St Vincent and the Grenadines
- St Lucia
- Trinidad and Tobago.

The Federation is disbanded >>>

The West Indian Federation was **disbanded** in 1962 when Jamaica and Trinidad and Tobago decided to leave. There were a number of reasons for this:

- Trinidad and Tobago and Jamaica were the biggest countries in the Federation and they were expected to bear most of its costs. This was considered to be unfair.

- The smaller countries feared that the more powerful countries would dominate the Federation.

- There was disagreement as to where the capital of the Federation should be.

- Jamaica objected to the colonial status of the Federation and felt that it was holding back independence from Britain.

- The most respected leaders of the time preferred to stay on as leaders in their own country, rather than lead the Federation,

- In September 1961, Jamaica held a **referendum** in which the people of Jamaica elected to pull out of the Federation.

Activity

Look up the word disbanded. What does it mean?

Exercise

4 Outline the reasons why the West Indian Federation disbanded.

5 Your teacher will play you the calypso 'Federation,' by Mighty Sparrow. Listen carefully to the lyrics and then discuss these questions.

   a) Why, in the opinion of Mighty Sparrow, did Jamaica want to pull out of the Federation?

   b) What reasons did Mighty Sparrow give for the collapse of the Federation?

   c) What is Mighty Sparrow's opinion of the Federation? Was it a good thing or not?

   d) Do you think Trinidad and Tobago was to blame in any way?

6 Compile a timeline of the key dates of the history of the West Indian Federation.

Key vocabulary

West Indian Federation

multilateral agreement

multinational corporation

disbanded

referendum

Regional cooperation: CARIFTA

We are learning to:

- define relevant terms and concepts: free trade
- describe the Caribbean integration process from the 1950s to the present: CARIFTA
- outline the objectives and membership of institutions/bodies which form part of the integration process: CARIFTA.

CARIFTA 》》

The next attempt at integration occurred when the **Caribbean Free Trade Association (CARIFTA)** was formed in 1965 with the signing of the Dickenson Bay Agreement. This was a much more successful attempt, which later led to the formation of CARICOM – an organisation that is still very active today.

CARICOM member flags.

Membership of CARIFTA 》》

The idea of a **free trade** region was first discussed at meetings between the leaders of Trinidad and Tobago, Guyana (then called British Guiana), Antigua and Barbuda and Barbados – the original members of CARIFTA.

The Prime Minister of Trinidad and Tobago organised this meeting in 1963 after announcing that the country intended to pull out of the West Indian Federation. As a result of these discussions a formal agreement was drawn up, and the Caribbean Free Trade Association (CARIFTA) was formed in 1965 with the signing of the Dickenson Bay Agreement.

On 1st July 1968, Dominica, Grenada, St Kitts and Nevis, Anguilla, St Lucia and St Vincent and the Grenadines joined CARIFTA. A few years later in 1971, Belize (then called British Honduras) joined as well. By this time, several of the states had achieved independence.

> **Did you know...?**
>
> The members of CARIFTA were:
>
> - Antigua and Barbuda
> - Barbados
> - Belize
> - Dominica
> - Grenada
> - Guyana
> - Jamaica
> - Montserrat
> - St Kitts and Nevis
> - Anguilla
> - St Lucia
> - St Vincent and the Grenadines
> - Trinidad and Tobago.

1 What do the initials CARIFTA stand for?

2 Which countries first discussed the idea of a new trade association?

3 Name the countries that became members of CARIFTA.

4 What role did Trinidad and Tobago have in the formation of CARIFTA?

Objectives of CARIFTA

The main objective of CARIFTA was to unite the economies and improve relationships between each of the member states.

The best way of doing this was to increase trade between members of the organisation. It was thought that this would also encourage development in the region.

The agreement encouraged member states to:

- buy and sell more goods between themselves
- diversify and expand the variety of goods and services available in the region
- make sure there was fair competition, especially for smaller businesses
- make sure that the benefits of free trade were shared fairly among member states.

Bananas being packed in Dominica for sale in the UK, as part of a special agreement between Caribbean islands and the UK.

Discussion

Discuss why it is a good idea if countries unite for trade reasons. Are there any potential problems?

Key vocabulary

CARIFTA

free trade

5 What were the main objectives of CARIFTA?

6 Explain in your own words what free trade means.

7 What are the advantages of free trade?

8 Why do you think it was so important for newly independent states in the Caribbean to form strong ties?

9 Which countries played leading roles in the development of CARIFTA? Why?

10 Compare the West Indian Federation and CARIFTA. What were the similarities and differences between them?

11 Compile a timeline of the key dates of the history of CARIFTA.

Regional cooperation: CARICOM and CSME

We are learning to:

- define relevant terms and concepts: globalisation
- describe the Caribbean integration process from the 1950s to the present: CARICOM, CSME
- outline the objectives and membership of institutions/bodies which form part of the integration process: CARICOM, CSME.

CARICOM and CSME

The success of CARIFTA encouraged member states to think of ways to increase cooperation in the Caribbean.

The CARIFTA agreements did not allow for:

- the free movement of workers or of capital between the member states
- it did not allow for the coordination of agricultural, industrial and foreign policies.

A meeting of CARICOM leaders.

Therefore it was decided to improve the association and call it a new name: the Caribbean Community or **CARICOM**. This came into being in 1973 and replaced CARIFTA, although the CARIFTA Games and sporting events continued.

Membership of CARICOM

CARICOM is an organisation of Caribbean states that promotes cooperation and integration between member states, especially in areas like trade and transportation. It also coordinates foreign policy. This has resulted in many benefits for the citizens of Caribbean states. People can move around freely to study and to look for work, and goods and services can be traded easily between these countries.

CARICOM was formed with the signing of an agreement at Chaguaramas in Trinidad and Tobago, between Trinidad and Tobago, Barbados, Jamaica and Guyana. The organisation grew quickly and now includes 15 member states:

- Antigua and Barbuda
- the Bahamas
- Barbados
- Belize
- Dominica
- Grenada
- Guyana
- Haiti
- Jamaica
- Montserrat
- St Lucia
- St Kitts and Nevis
- St Vincent and the Grenadines
- Suriname
- Trinidad and Tobago.

> **Did you know...?**
>
> The CCs on the CARICOM flag are like the links on a chain. A linked chain represents unity. The fact that the links are not complete represents a break with the colonial past. What do you think the colours of the flag represent?

In 1989, the CARICOM heads of government agreed to increase economic integration. As well as this, CARICOM wanted to find ways to respond to globalisation. This led to the creation of the CARICOM Single Market and Economy (**CSME**).

Globalisation is a process of making the world more connected, with goods, services and people moving and communicating easily and quickly all around the world.

The main economic objectives of the CSME are:

- improved standards of living and work
- full employment of labour and other factors of production
- coordinated economic development
- expansion of trade and economic relations with other states
- greater economic power in dealing with other states
- members working more closely together on economic policies
- the CSME also allows for the free movement of money and skilled labour between member states, the right to set up a business in another member state, free movement of goods and a common trade policy.

The CARICOM flag.

Exercise

1 What are the main objectives of CARICOM?

2 Why was the CSME agreement signed?

3 If they want to set up a new business, what advantages do businesspeople from CARICOM member states have?

4 Compile a timeline of the key dates in both CARICOM and the CSME's history.

Activity

Work in pairs and look online and in newspapers for interesting reports about CARICOM activities. Select a report, then describe what you have discovered to the class.

Key vocabulary

CARICOM

CSME

Cooperation in the Caribbean: Sport

We are learning to:

- identify non-political areas of cooperation within the Caribbean region: sports
- assess the role of regional agencies in facilitating the integration process.

Economic affairs were not the only concern of Caribbean leaders. In order to promote unity amongst people in the Caribbean, integrated sporting events were also set up. These have proved to be most successful.

CARIFTA Games ⟩⟩

The CARIFTA Games were held for the first time in 1972. They consist of athletic field and track events, including sprints, middle-distance running races, hurdles, jumping events, throwing events and relay races between teams.

The Games are held annually. There are two categories: one for athletes under 17 years old, and the other for athletes under 20. Athletes are only allowed to compete if they are from countries that are members or associate members of CARICOM.

Sport can bring communities together.

Purpose of the CARIFTA Games ⟩⟩⟩

The CARIFTA Games were founded to improve relations between people of the English-speaking countries of the Caribbean. Since then, athletes from French- and Dutch-speaking countries have also been encouraged to take part.

Location of the Games ⟩⟩⟩⟩

The CARIFTA Games have been held in many different countries, including Trinidad and Tobago, Jamaica, Barbados, the Bahamas, Martinique, Guadeloupe, Bermuda, Grenada, Turks and Caicos, St Kitts and Nevis and St Lucia. New sports facilities have been built in many places in order to host the games.

Did you know...?

Cricket West Indies (CWI) is one of the oldest examples of regional cooperation. It was founded in the early 1920s, when it was called the West Indies Cricket Board.

Exercise

1. When were the CARIFTA Games first held?

2. Which sporting events feature in the CARIFTA Games?

3. What was the purpose of founding the CARIFTA Games?

4. In which countries have the games been held?

Research

Work in pairs. Visit the Cricket West Indies website (cricketwestindies.org) and research the mission, values and vision of this organisation. What do they aim to achieve?

Successful athletes

The CARIFTA Games have been a starting point for many athletes who have gone on to become world record holders, and world and Olympic champions. These include:

- Usain Bolt (sprinter from Jamaica)
- Darrel Brown (sprinter from Trinidad and Tobago)
- Veronica Campbell-Brown (track and field athlete from Jamaica)
- Kim Collins (track and field athlete from St Kitts and Nevis)
- Pauline Davis-Thompson (sprinter from the Bahamas)
- Alleyne Francique (track athlete from Grenada)
- Obadele Thompson (sprinter from Barbados).

The West Indies cricket team is made up of players from CARICOM countries.

West Indies cricket team

The West Indian cricket team, commonly known as the Windies, is one of the most successful cricket teams in the world.

The team is made up of players from CARICOM countries. It competes successfully in international tournaments and is an example of the benefits of regional cooperation between CARICOM countries. Cricket West Indies encourages regional development as part of the International Cricket Council's development programme.

Some of the best cricketers in the world come from the West Indies. Over the years, players like Sir Garfield Sobers, Gordon Greenidge, Brian Lara, Clive Lloyd, Malcolm Marshall, Sir Andy Roberts, Sir Frank Worrell, Sir Clyde Walcott, Sir Everton Weekes, Sir Curtly Ambrose, Michael Holding, Courtney Walsh, Joel Garner and Sir Viv Richards have made the Windies a force to be reckoned with.

Many players have been rewarded for their great contributions to the game of cricket.

The Windies have won the ICC Cricket World Cup, the ICC World Twenty20 and the ICC Champions Trophy. The Under 19 teams have also been successful.

Discussion

Your teacher will help you to arrange a class debate. You will discuss whether or not West Indies cricket benefits the Caribbean. Some of the class should argue that it does have benefits for the region, while others should suggest that is does not. Prepare your case and think of good reasons to back up your arguments.

Exercise

5 Which countries form the West Indies cricket team?

6 Work in pairs. Find out about the medals (gold, silver and bronze) that have been won by athletes from your country in the CARIFTA Games. Find pictures of the athletes and report back to the class.

Cooperation in the Caribbean: Education and medicine

We are learning to:

- identify non-political areas of cooperation within the Caribbean region: education, medicine
- assess the role of regional agencies in facilitating the integration process.

Education (University of the West Indies) ❭❭

This University of the West Indies (UWI) developed from the University College of the West Indies, which had been established in 1948 as an independent external college of the University of London. UWI became completely independent in 1962, at a time when many countries in the Caribbean achieved independence. This helped in efforts to make the region more **autonomous** and less dependent on former colonial rulers. UWI aids in regional development by providing tertiary education and research facilities.

Students and their lecturer at the university campus in Kingston, Jamaica.

UWI is internationally recognised for its excellence. Graduates of the university have helped to provide leadership in Caribbean states and to promote economic and cultural growth. Graduates of the university include many current and former prime ministers as well as Nobel laureates and Rhodes Scholars.

The university has three main campuses:

- Mona – in Jamaica
- St Augustine – in Trinidad and Tobago
- Cave Hill – in Barbados.

There are several smaller campuses in other states, as well. The Open Campus of the university provides for online learning.

The university offers diplomas and degrees in engineering, humanities, education, law, medicine, science, agriculture and social sciences.

> **Did you know...?**
>
> Sir Derek Walcott, the Caribbean poet and playwright who won the Nobel Prize for Literature in 1992, was a graduate of the University College of the West Indies. He studied in Jamaica.

Exercise

1. How long has UWI been a fully independent Caribbean university?

2. What courses can you study at this university?

3. Analyse the role that UWI plays in the development of the Caribbean.

Entry requirements for students to degree courses require CSEC (Caribbean Secondary Education Certificate) and CAPE (Caribbean Advanced Proficiency Exam) passes in relevant subjects, for example if you wish to pursue a B. Ed. in history, you would need five CSEC subject passes and two double Units CAPE subjects.

Research

Using the website for the University of The West Indies at Mona, research the entry requirements for one degree or diploma in the following faculties:

- Faculty Of Humanities & Education
- Faculty Of Medical Sciences
- Faculty Of Law
- Faculty Of Engineering
- Faculty Of Science & Technology
- Faculty Of Social Sciences
- Institute for Gender & Development Studies.

What other qualifications are acceptable?

Medicine

Promoting good health is essential to the development of the Caribbean. There is widespread cooperation between healthcare providers across the Caribbean.

One example is the Caribbean Environmental Health Institute (CEHI). This was set up in 1989 by CARICOM to respond to the environmental health concerns of its members.

The CEHI provides advice to members in all areas of environmental management, including:

- water supplies, liquid waste and excrement disposal
- solid waste management – for example, from shelters and health facilities
- water resources management – for example, collecting and distributing treated rainwater
- coastal management, including beach pollution
- air pollution, occupational health
- disaster prevention and preparedness, such as planning for floods
- natural resources conservation
- environmental institution development
- social and economic aspects of environmental management.

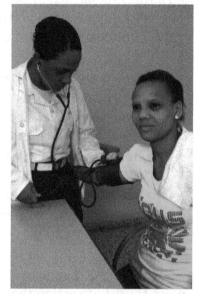

Promoting good health is essential to the development of the Caribbean.

Exercise

4   How and why is medical expertise shared across the Caribbean?

5   Why do you think it is important to share such expertise?

6   In your own words, explain the services that CEHI provides and why it is important to the wellbeing of the people of the Caribbean.

Key vocabulary

autonomous

Cooperation in the Caribbean: Culture and disaster preparedness

We are learning to:

- identify non-political areas of cooperation within the Caribbean region: culture, disaster preparedness
- assess the role of regional agencies in facilitating the integration process.

Other forms of cooperation between Caribbean states include **cultural festivals** like **CARIFESTA** (Caribbean Festival of Arts) and a combined disaster management agency called CDEMA.

Culture (CARIFESTA)

Since this first festival in 1972 in Guyana, CARIFESTA has been strengthening the **cultural bonds** between the people of the Caribbean. The aims of CARIFESTA are as follows:

- to depict the life of the people of the region – their heroes, morale, myths, traditions, beliefs, creativeness and ways of expression
- to show the similarities and the differences between the people of the Caribbean and Latin America
- to create a climate in which art can flourish so that artists are encouraged to return to their homeland
- to awaken a regional identity in literature
- to stimulate and unite the cultural movement throughout the region.

The festival has achieved its aims and created numerous benefits for the people of the Caribbean. It has become a major tourist attraction that unifies Caribbean nations and expresses their diversity at the same time.

The festival has helped to create a unique **identity** for people from the Caribbean. The festival has also promoted cultural activities as a form of entertainment as well as creating opportunities for many artists to forge good careers.

Research

Work in pairs and find newspaper articles about CARIFESTA. Find out how the celebrations help to bring people of the region together. Report back to the class with a summary of what you have discovered.

Exercise

1 What would you expect to see and do at CARIFESTA? Make a list of 10 items or activities.

2 What is a regional identity and how does CARIFESTA promote this?

3 How do you think the people of the Caribbean region have benefited the most from CARIFESTA?

Discussion

a) In a class discussion, express your opinions about the benefits of CDEMA to Caribbean unity. Has CDEMA really been effective?

b) Work as a class and express your opinions about the benefits of CARIFESTA and its contribution to regional unity.

CDEMA (the Caribbean Disaster Emergency Management Agency) was set up to coordinate responses to **natural disasters** such as hurricanes, volcanoes, earthquakes and tsunamis in CARICOM member states and associate member states. The responsibilities of CDEMA include:

- managing and coordinating disaster relief
- getting reliable information on disasters
- reducing or eliminating the impact of disasters
- setting up and maintaining adequate disaster response.

Case study

Read this press release issued by CARICOM after the 2010 earthquake in Haiti and answer the questions.

'More than 300 persons from 11 Caribbean Community (CARICOM) Member States and Associate Members have so far been involved in the response to the devastating earthquake which struck Haiti on 12th January. The Region's initial response was spearheaded by Jamaica, the subregional focal point with responsibility for the northern geographic zone of CDEMA which includes Haiti.

Personnel from Antigua and Barbuda, Barbados, Belize, the Bahamas, Dominica, Guyana, Grenada, St Lucia, St Vincent and the Grenadines and the British Virgin Islands provided support after the initial search and rescue, medical, security and engineering teams had been supplied by Jamaica within 48 hours of the earthquake.

CARICOM's continuing interventions in Haiti include: emergency response coordination; medical assistance; logistics, inclusive of the distribution of relief supplies and engineers assessments; security; CARICOM civilian evacuation and resource mobilisation.'

Questions

1. How did CARICOM respond to the 2010 earthquake in Haiti?
2. Which members of CARICOM were involved in the response?
3. Which country led the response team? Why do you think they led it?

Activity

Write a report about the benefits of belonging to regional integration organisations. Outline the advantages and any disadvantages.

Did you know...?

Members of CDEMA include:

- Anguilla
- Antigua and Barbuda
- the Bahamas
- Barbados
- Belize
- British Virgin Islands
- Dominica
- Grenada
- Guyana
- Haiti
- Jamaica
- Montserrat
- St Kitts and Nevis
- St Lucia
- St Vincent and the Grenadines
- Suriname
- Trinidad and Tobago
- Turks and Caicos.

Key vocabulary

cultural festival

CARIFESTA

cultural bonds

identity

CDEMA

natural disaster

Benefits of regional integration and cooperation

We are learning to:

- analyse ways in which the individual, businesses and countries benefit from regional integration.

The benefits and achievements of regional integration and cooperation

Integration in the Caribbean has brought many benefits to the region.

Free movement of goods, labour and capital

Regional integration has improved the ability to move goods, **labour** and **capital** freely across the region, increasing opportunities to grow regional economies and to improve levels of employment.

Unemployment is a big problem within the Caribbean region, but access to greater resources can lead to better job opportunities, a larger population can offer more skills and a larger regional economy is more attractive for investment.

Regional integration has given businesses and industries in the Caribbean access to a larger market.

Expansion of trade

Regional integration has given businesses and industries in the Caribbean access to a larger market. Trade expansion means a diversification of products available to larger markets, which leads to greater economic growth. Regional integration assists trade expansion because:

- the entire region becomes a market of goods and services starting from within the region
- the region can trade more effectively on the world market.

Various **trade agreements** between member countries of organisations such as CARIFTA, the removal of trade barriers and a larger market to trade in have resulted in more goods being traded between Caribbean countries. There is also a greater awareness in the world about goods and services provided by the Caribbean.

Discussion

Have a class discussion about the ways young people and adults can help promote Caribbean integration and the development of a Caribbean identity.

Exercise

1. In your own words, explain the benefits of regional integration for trade. Write 100 words.

2. How can unemployment be reduced by greater regional integration?

Improvement in the quality of life

Regional integration, along with steady economic growth and prosperity, means that there is more money available for social programmes (better housing, healthcare, **sanitation**). It also creates jobs, which means people have more money. There is better access to education, as well – for example, the University of the West Indies.

Increased cooperation among member states

Regional integration has increased cooperation among the member states. Participation in organisations such as CARIFTA (trade), CARICOM/CSME (economy), OECS (unity), ACS (heritage and sustainable tourism), CARIFESTA (culture) and CDEMA (disaster preparedness) contributes to increased cooperation between member states.

Closer cooperation between member states also helps to reduce the cost of government (CARICOM, for example, provides many services that individual countries could only provide for themselves at a much higher cost), reduces duplication of effort and increases bargaining power with markets outside the region. Member states that work closely together create a stronger community sense and a closer-knit region that already has a long shared history.

Better response to global environment

Regional integration offers greater opportunities for the region to compete on a global scale and to take part in globalisation.

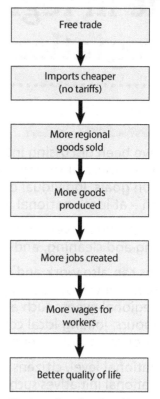

The benefits of regional integration.

Project

Students work in groups to create a jingle or advertisement that informs individuals and businesses about ways they can support regional integration.

Exercise

3   In your own words, explain how regional integration can improve the quality of life in the region.

4   Name the organisations that help to improve regional integration and explain what they do.

5   Name three ways that quality of life can be improved through regional integration.

Key vocabulary

labour

trade agreement

sanitation

Individual role in regional integration

We are learning to:

- discuss ways the individual, and countries can deepen regional integration
- role of individual citizens in the integration process.

Role of the individual

We have been discussing integration at a regional level, which involves countries working together to achieve common **goals**. Individual citizens also have a role to play, though – at local, national and regional level.

At an individual level, citizens share family duties, such as washing and cleaning, and looking after family members.

Citizens can also work and cooperate together at a community level, by taking part in community events (and regional events such as CARIFESTA), helping their neighbours, joining local community groups, such as youth groups or sport clubs, neighbourhood watch groups.

At a national level, citizens can help the local authorities with national initiatives such as looking after the environment.

The role of the citizens at a regional level can include:

- being informed – citizens should be aware of issues (social, political, economic, cultural) at local, national and regional level
- purchasing regional products – buying local goods and products helps local producers rather than producers in other parts of the world
- showing solidarity and mutual support towards regional fellow citizens – the Caribbean is a multicultural region and on each island there are people from different cultural backgrounds; it is important to respect people who come from different backgrounds.

One of the roles of being a citizen, is to show solidarity and support towards fellow citizens.

Discussion

In groups discuss this question: 'Do individuals benefit from regional integration or not?'

Exercise

1 At which levels can individuals help their community and country achieve their goals?

2 Explain the role the individual plays at an individual and community level. Give examples.

3 Explain the role the individual plays at a regional level. Give examples.

4 How important is the role of the individual to help deepen regional integration?

Case study

The Caribbean Festival of Arts, commonly known as CARIFESTA, is an international multicultural event organised by the countries of the Caribbean. The main purpose is to gather artists, musicians, authors, and to share the folklore and artistic talents of the Caribbean and Latin American region.

The festival was introduced by the heads of government of the Caribbean Community (CARICOM) in 1972. At each festival, CARICOM Member States must bid to host in their country, similar to a bid to host the Olympics or World Cup. Originally, the festival was to be held every four years; but is now held every two years. The festival usually involves a grand market, music, dance, theatre, film, visual arts, literary arts fashion and food showcases, community festivals and tours, a youth village and many more events and activities are scheduled over the course of the festival.

The opening ceremony of CARIFESTA X111 at the Kensington Oval in Barbados, 20th August 2017.

Research

Carry out research into the last CARIFESTA, find out where it was and what events were held. Write a paragraph explaining how it encouraged regional integration.

Exercise

5 Name three ways an individual can help with regional integration at an individual level and a regional level.

6 Give examples of things that citizens should stay informed about.

Key vocabulary

goal

Questions

See how well you have understood the topics in this unit.

1. Match the key vocabulary word (**i–vii**) with its definition (**a–g**).

   i) regional integration

   ii) integrate

   iii) social integration

   iv) racial integration

   v) economic integration

   vi) interdependence

   vii) region

   a) when people of all cultural groups, sexes and ages live and work together in an area

   b) an area of the world – for example, the Caribbean

   c) the joining or working together of countries that are near to each other, in order to make them economically and politically more powerful

   d) when two or more things or people rely on each other or help each other

   e) bring together ideas and people so that they work together or become part of the same group

   f) when people from different cultural groups live and work together on an equal basis

   g) cooperation in business, such as trading and finance.

2. Which organisation was the first attempt at integration by Caribbean states?

3. Match the dates (i–v) to the events (a–e):

   i) 1958

   ii) 1962

   iii) 1965

   iv) 1973

   v) 1989

   a) CARIFTA formed

   b) CSME formed

   c) West Indian Federation formed

   d) West Indian Federation disbanded

   e) CARICOM formed.

4. Explain what is meant by:

   a) social integration

   b) racial integration

   c) economic integration.

5. When did Caribbean countries try to lessen their dependence on former colonial powers?

    a) 1940s

    b) 1950s

    c) 1980s

6. True or false: Bilateral agreements are arrangements of economic support between three countries.

7. CARIFTA stands for _____.

    a) Caribbean Fair Trade Association

    b) Caribbean and Recent Trade Association

    c) Caribbean Free Trade Association

8. Whose flag is this?

    a) Jamaica

    b) The West Indies

    c) The Caribbean

    d) Trinidad and Tobago

9. What does this flag represent?

    a) CSME

    b) CARICOM

    c) CSME

    d) CARIFTA

10. Explain two of the aims of CARIFTA.

11. True or false? The CSME helps allow free movement of trade and money.

12. Correct this statement: From the 1950s, Caribbean states tried to increase their dependence on former colonial rulers in order to strengthen their economies.

13. Explain, in 100 words, the other benefits of greater interdependence, apart from economic, giving examples.

14. What is the 'Windies'?

15. Explain what is meant by UWI?

16. What is CARIFESTA, and how does it strengthen cultural bonds between people?

17. Make a list of ways that disaster management is better organised by CDEMA.

18. Explain how free trade leads to better quality of life.

Grade 7 Unit 9 Summary

Communities and the relationships between them

In this chapter, you have learned about:

- What it means to participate in regional integration
- How to differentiate between social, racial and economic integration
- The purpose of cooperation
- How Caribbean countries established bilateral agreements and lessened their dependence on European colonists.

Community cooperation

In this chapter, you have learned about:

- The interdependence of the Caribbean as a means of strengthening the region
- Organisations in Jamaica that promote community development
- West Indian Federation as the first attempt at regional integration in 1958
- The objectives for the countries that participated in the West Indian Federation
- The reasons for the dissolution of the West Indian Federation in 1962
- The Caribbean Free Trade Association (CARIFTA)
- The Caribbean countries that participated in CARIFTA and their main objective.
- The factors that encouraged the evolution of CARICOM and CSME from CARIFTA
- How the number of Caribbean countries with full membership status has increased
- CARICOM's creation of CSME in response to the effects of globalisation on the region.

Cooperation through sport, education and medicine

In this chapter, you have learned about:

- The main purpose of the CARIFTA Games and the countries that have hosted them
- Internationally successful athletes who began their careers in the CARIFTA Games
- The West Indies cricket team as an example of regional cooperation through sport
- The University of the West Indies which shows the region's cooperation in education
- How CARICOM promotes health as an area of regional cooperation
- How CARIFESTA demonstrates regional cooperation in culture
- The establishment of CDEMA to respond to disasters that affect the member and associate member states of CARICOM.

Benefits of integration and the role of the individual

In this chapter, you have learned about:

- The benefits and achievements of regional integration and participation
- The role of each Caribbean citizen in enhancing regional integration.

Checking your progress

To make good progress in understanding different aspects of Caribbean integration and global links, check to make sure you understand these ideas.

Understand the term *regional integration* and the history of the integration process in the Caribbean.

Understand objectives and membership of institutions/bodies which form part of the integration.

Explain the benefits of regional integration.

Identify areas of cooperation within the Caribbean region.

Analyse ways in which the individual, businesses and countries benefit from regional integration.

Discuss the ways young people and adults can help promote Caribbean integration and the development of a Caribbean identity.

Discuss ways the individual, businesses and countries can deepen regional integration.

Explain the role of businesses in regional integration.

Explain how cooperation is benefical.

Discuss the role of the individual in regional integration.

Explain ways that interdependance is strengthened through sports and cultural events.

Research how integration affects your education and job opportunities.

Unit 10: Sustainable Use of Resources: Protecting Our Environment

The importance of sustainable use of resources

- examine the features of Jamaica's physical/natural heritage: sustainability and ecotourism
- demonstrate ways of caring for the environment: recycling
- explain how the '3 Rs' help to look after our environment.

Responsibility for our environment

- demonstrate ways of caring for the environment
- gather information from multiple sources and use it to explain the need for sustainable use of resources and protection of the environment.

How do production and consumption patterns contribute to sustainability or sustainable development?

- discuss the ways in which production and consumption patterns of individuals, communities and countries can contribute to sustainable development practices.

Protected areas and endangered habitats and species

- use geographical skills and tools to present and interpret information related to protected areas in Jamaica and the rest of the Caribbean
- understand what we mean by endangered habitats and species.

Conserving our resources

- implement and improve conservation practices within the school and community environment
- compare and critique the work and activities carried out by the different environmental groups, organisations and watchdogs in Jamaica.

The importance of sustainable use of resources

We are learning to:

- examine the features of Jamaica's physical/natural heritage: sustainability and ecotourism.

Sustainability

Sustainable activities do not damage the resources that make them possible. For example, if tourists visited a river and polluted or littered the environment, or removed fish, then the natural environment could be destroyed for future generations. This type of tourism is unsustainable.

Ecotourism is a type of tourism that focuses on protecting the environment and local culture. Ecotourism means:

- travelling to undisturbed or unspoilt natural areas
- enjoying, studying or experiencing the natural environment without damaging it
- treating the environment responsibly and carefully
- benefiting local communities
- supporting conservation projects
- providing education to travellers and local communities.

In Jamaica, there are specialist tourist operators that run holidays and tours for visitors who wish to see the natural heritage without damaging it. **Eco-friendly** accommodation tends to be smaller than big hotels and resorts. They are often lodges that can accommodate small groups, and usually have activities organised that help to support local sustainable initiatives. For example, Hotel Mockingbird Hill.

Unspoilt beach, Jamaica.

Project

Design an eco-friendly hotel. Suggest ways to make your hotel eco-friendly in terms of its size, materials, style of design, and the activities that it may offer.

Discussion

What do you know about the Rocklands Bird Sanctuary, in Wiltshire, Jamaica? Discuss in groups and then with the whole class.

Exercise

1. In your own words, define sustainability and ecotourism.
2. Do you think ecotourism is good for Jamaica? Explain why/why not.

Research

Copy or trace a map of Jamaica. Find out the locations of at least three different ecotourism projects. Insert these on your map.

- Hotel Mockingbird Hill in Port Antonio has received 21 international awards for environmentally friendly tourism. Their facilities include solar energy, no plastic bottles, recycled stationery, and environmentally toiletries, and locally produced food is used.
- Blue Mountain and Wilderness retreat and camp in the Blue and John Crow mountain range. This is supervised by the Jamaican forestry department. Rainwater is recycled and used and solar powered energy is used.
- Zion Country eco beach cabins are located in Long Road in Portland, where rainwater is used and bottles, paper and plastics are recycled.

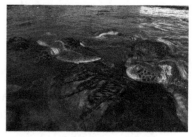

Green sea turtles in a turtle farm, Caribbean Sea.

Case study

Ambassabeth Cabins

Situated deep in the Blue and John Crow Mountains National Park, this unique tourist facility uses only solar powered energy and uses water sourced from a local spring. The food served is locally produced, and activities include trail hiking, visits to observe traditional farming techniques and field trips to learn about the natural flora and fauna.

Questions

1. Suggest three geographical features that make Jamaica an ideal island for ecotourism.

2. Why is sustainable tourism important for the economy of Jamaica?

3. Explain why each activity on this page could be described as an ecotourism project.

4. Name two geographic features and three animals that have provided opportunities for ecotourism.

Activity

Choose an ecotourism project in Jamaica and do a case study on it. Find out where it is, the history of the project, the kinds of activities it offers, and which aspects of the environment it focuses on. Write up your case study in a booklet, providing pictures and information.

Did you know...?

Manatees are endangered worldwide and there are less than 100 along the south coast of Jamaica.

Key vocabulary

ecotourism

eco-friendly

Sustainability and sustainable practices

We are learning to:

- demonstrate ways of caring for the environment: recycling
- explain how the '3 Rs' help to look after our environment.

No single person can stop the damage that humans do to the environment. However, there are ways we can become more responsible in the way we use resources.

Sustainability

Sustainability refers to making sure that an activity can occur over a long period of time without causing any resources to run out. Sustainable practices are where people have adapted their activities to ensure that the environment is protected. For example, ecotourism, where people can visit a place without damging it or causing any resource to become damaged.

The 3 Rs

Consumer culture encourages people to want new things, from technology to clothing. However, the more new things people buy and consume, the more rubbish goes into the Earth's landfills.

Many households still throw all their rubbish into bins, and it ends up in dumps or landfills. The contents of a normal household bin (see opposite) include a large proportion of materials that can be reused or recycled. There are many materials that can be recycled:

- paper
- plastics
- glass
- aluminium cans
- used automobile oil
- tyres
- iron and steel from old cars and appliances.

There are three principles that can help us make a smaller impact on our environment – the '3 Rs': reduce, reuse and recycle.

- Reducing starts with buying fewer products and having less 'stuff'. Next, reduce the amount of disposable materials that you use. Many foods are already in packets, so they do not need to be put in bags.
- Reuse products, especially packaging, wherever possible. For example, instead of using disposable cups, food containers and plastic bags, use items that can be reused.
- It is possible to recycle materials such as glass, aluminium, paper and plastic. Find out about recycling programmes in your area, and separate your rubbish into materials for recycling. Fruit and vegetable cuttings can go onto a compost heap.

Activity

Brainstorm ways of how you could reuse or recycle any of these materials: paper, plastics, glass and cans.

Case study

The National Solid Waste Management Authority (NSWMA) serves whole of Jamaica. It is a non-profit making organisation whose mission is 'to provide solid waste management services to safeguard public health, while helping to create an environment that is healthy and visually pleasing for both residents and visitors to enjoy.'

Non-biodegradable materials are items that cannot decay or be broken down through natural decay. Examples include plastic products (a water bottle, for example), metal products (a food tin can), rubber (car tyres) and electronics (a computer). NSWMA provides:

- the collection of non-biodegradable materials
- the initial processing and exportation of non-biodegradable materials
- education to the public about recycling
- tours and demonstrations at the recycling faculty
- the distribution of recycling bins
- the loan of recycling bins for special events.

Source: adapted from National Solid Waste Management Authority website.

Glass, aluminium, plastic and paper are all recyclable materials.

Research

Do a research project on how materials Jamaica are recyled. Show your findings on an illustrated poster.

The benefits of the '3 Rs' ⟫⟫

Reducing, reusing and recycling has many benefits both for consumers and the environment:

- The consumer saves money by spending less on new goods, especially bags, jars and bottles.
- Less land gets used up for landfills.
- There is less need for waste disposal services, saving money from the national budget.
- Fewer toxic chemicals pollute the water, land and air.
- There is less disease and illness from pollution.
- Natural resources become more sustainable.

Discussion

In groups, discuss the importance of the '3 Rs'.

Exercise

1 What is the mission statement of NSWMA? What services does NSWMA provide?

2 Give some examples of non-biodegradable materials.

3 Describe the recycling symbol and suggest how the symbol shows its meaning.

Key vocabulary

sustainability

consumer culture

reduce

reuse

recycle

Responsibility for our environment

We are learning to:

- demonstrate ways of caring for the environment.

Keeping our environment free of litter

The food you eat, the way you use energy at home, the amount you travel and the types of products you own and use all make a difference to the environment.

Litter is waste material that gets dropped or left in the environment instead of being disposed of properly.

- Do not drop litter.
- Always find a bin for your waste.
- If you cannot find a bin, collect your litter in a bag and dispose of it properly at home.
- Reuse items such as bottles, jars and tins. Many glass and plastic items can be used for other purposes rather than thrown away.
- Recycle items made from glass, plastic and aluminium.
- Kitchen waste, such as vegetable and fruit peelings, cores and eggshells, can go onto a compost heap to make compost for a garden.
- Items that contain chemicals, such as printer cartridges, batteries and paint, need to be taken to collection points so that they can be disposed of properly.

Did you know...?

Did you know that energy-saver light bulbs use between 25% and 80% less energy than traditional bulbs? They can also last up to 25 times longer than the traditional bulbs.

Research

Research how to create a compost heap. In groups, create a short video on how to make a compost heap easily and cheaply at home or at school.

Use our resources sensibly!

Use water wisely:

- Take a shower instead of a bath.
- Use a water-saving shower head to use less water during a shower.
- Turn off the water when you brush your teeth.
- Choose **water-wise** plants in your garden – these do not need a lot of water.
- Fix leaky pipes and taps.

Use electricity wisely:

- Turn off appliances and lights when you are not using them.
- Use energy-efficient light bulbs.

Exercise

1 What is litter?

2 Why should each of the following NOT go in a normal bin? Explain what you should do with them instead:

    a) printer cartridge   **b)** glass bottles.

10.3

Conserve fossil fuels and reduce the amount of air pollution by following these guidelines:

- Do not make unnecessary trips by car or plane.
- Use shared rides and public transport when you can. When possible, ride a bike or walk rather than driving.
- Modern cars need catalytic converters on their exhaust systems to cut down their carbon emissions. Make sure your car's exhaust system is always well maintained.

Food

- Use fruits and vegetables that are in season. This helps to make sure that your produce comes from local producers, without wasting resources.
- Choose meat, fish and vegetables that use sustainable farming methods.
- Do not hunt or eat endangered species, such as shark.
- Try eating less meat. The production of meat causes around 20% of the world's greenhouse gases.

Ethical consumerism

People are becoming increasingly aware that all the products they buy and use have an impact on the local and global environment. An **ethical consumer** is someone whose shopping reflects their values and beliefs.

Have you seen any labels on products saying 'free range', 'fairtrade' or 'organic'? Each of these labels tells us that the company making the product wants the public to know that they are taking care of their impact on the environment.

Buy local, think global

Another principle for ethical consumers is to buy local rather than imported products. By supporting local producers, you can reduce negative consequences for the environment and help to support your country's economy.

Activity

In groups, brainstorm an idea to look after the environment in your school or community. It could be a plan to clean up litter or to give advice on the '3 Rs'. Carry out your plan and produce a report, with pictures, of how you carried it out.

Fairtrade sticker on a banana.

Exercise

3 Explain how each of the following can reduce your negative impact on the environment:

    a) sharing transport **b)** eating locally produced fruit
    c) eating less meat.

4 List two ways that you can save water and electricity.

5 What do you understand by 'ethical consumerism'?

Key vocabulary

litter

water-wise

ethical consumer

How do production and consumption patterns contribute to sustainability or sustainable development?

We are learning to:

- discuss the ways in which production and consumption patterns of individuals, communities and countries can contribute to sustainable development practices.

The way that goods are produced, or **production** is important in achieving sustainability. This is because the process of producing the majority of the goods we use requires a lot of energy. When we use energy, it is important to try to be as energy efficient as possible because:

- it saves energy, known as **energy conservation**
- it reduces energy costs
- by using less energy, or conserving energy, we ensure sustainability. In other words, we can carry on using energy for longer
- if we use less energy, there is less impact on the environment. For example, avoiding printing means less paper is needed and fewer trees are felled.

A wind farm.

Case study

National Energy Policy 2009–2030

Jamaica's National Energy Policy was set up to find affordable, environmentally sustainable energy solutions. This was to make sure that Jamaica's economy develops and at the same time, to ensure that the environment is protected. The plan involves using more renewable forms of energy, such as wind farms and relying less on fossil fuels such as petrol, which are non-renewable.

Solar panels.

Activity

Do some research on the following types of renewable energy sources:

- solar
- wind
- hydro
- biomass.

Identify a strength and weakness of each.

Jamaica: how renewables are changing island energy sources

Jamaica is a leader in the transition to sustainable energy systems in the Caribbean. The country's National Energy Policy (2009) is seen as a model for law makers region-wide.

The policy lays out targets for a 30% renewable energy share and a 50% reduction in energy intensity by 2030. New research suggests that, by further developing its renewable resources of solar, wind, hydro and biomass, the country can comfortably meet 40% of its total anticipated electricity demand by 2027.

The country currently sources 95% of its electricity use from petroleum-based power plants. Because Jamaica lacks domestic petroleum resources, it depends entirely on imports, resulting in significant economic and environmental costs for the country.

Achieving sustainability by being energy efficient also applies to our **consumption patterns**, or the way that we buy and use goods and services:

- Where we have a choice, we should choose to buy environmentally friendly goods and services.
- People should try to use public transport, or walk, rather than drive.
- People should buy goods that are energy efficient.
- People should try to work for companies that have good energy efficient, environmentally friendly practices.

> **Did you know...?**
>
> By 2030, Jamaica can save up to $12.5 billion in energy system expenditures by transitioning to renewables.

Case study

Eco Tings

One business that is now considering the need for eco-friendly items is 'Eco Tings', an online business that sells reusable drinking straws, metal coconut openers, tea infusers, wooden forks, ceramic knives, nutmeg bags, vegetable peelers, storage bags, loafer pods, reusable storage bags, soap bags and other items made of bamboo, metal, wood, glass and non-toxic silicone. The business owner explained that he did not want to use plastic cutlery and utensils, so that perhaps was the inspiration for the business.

> **Did you know...?**
>
> In January 2019 the Jamaican Government banned the use of plastic bags, plastic straws and Styrofoam packaging to prevent waste and save energy.

What is sustainable development? »

Sustainable development is economic and social growth or improvement without damaging the environment. The main aim of sustainable development is to ensure both

Key vocabulary

production

energy conservation

consumption patterns

present and future generations can enjoy the resources of the Earth and benefit from them. It requires careful planning and sometimes additional costs to establish more environmentally friendly practices and systems.

Case study

Sustainable Development Goals

The United Nations Sustainable Development Goals are a global call to action to end poverty, protect the Earth's environment and climate, and ensure that people everywhere can enjoy peace and prosperity. Some of the goals include:

- By 2030, achieve the sustainable management and efficient use of natural resources
- By 2030, halve global food waste at the retail and consumer levels
- By 2020, achieve the environmentally sound management of chemicals and all wastes, and significantly reduce their release to air, water and soil in order to minimise their adverse impacts on human health and the environment
- By 2030, substantially reduce waste generation through prevention, reduction, recycling and reuse
- By 2030, ensure that people everywhere have the relevant information and awareness for sustainable development and lifestyles in harmony with nature.

Discussion

Imagine you are building a new school. How could you build it in a way to make it more sustainable? Write up your suggestions using a drawing of your new school.

SUSTAINABLE DEVELOPMENT GOALS

Exercise

1 Explain what is meant by
   a) energy consumption
   b) renewable energy
   c) sustainable development.

2 Identify three forms of renewable energy.

3 Identify an advantage and a disadvantage of a renewable energy form.

4 What is the National Energy Policy?

5 What has recently been banned to prevent waste in Jamaica?

6 For the UN SDGGs, what are some factors that may prevent us from reaching these goals? How can we overcome these obstacles?

Jamaica Plans for new sustainable tourism

Airline passenger numbers to Jamaica have grown significantly in recent years and the island is seeking to further increase its global share of international tourists by tapping into new and existing markets. The Jamaica Tourist Board has set a target of securing 5 million visitors by 2021 (up from 3.84 million in 2016) and the indicators for 2017 already show the country is on course for record-breaking growth. If the visitor targets for 2021 are achieved, the nation will generate $5bn in tourism earnings, increasing the total direct jobs to 125 000.

However, it's important that these new opportunities are sustainable and benefit every Jamaican. The Travel Foundation is working in Jamaica with the aim of increasing the scale and spread of tourism revenue to local businesses and communities.

The Ministry for tourism proposes 'Five Pillars of Tourism Growth', designed to tap into new markets; develop new products; promote investment; build new partnerships, and develop human capital. These are centred on five networks designed to attract tourists and spread the benefits as widely as possible among Jamaicans, namely: good food; sports and entertainment; health and wellness; shopping; and knowledge.

Activity

1. What are the potential damages to the environment with an increase of tourism in Jamaica?

2. List 3 benefits of increasing development

3. How can tourism be made more sustainable?

Did you know...?

2017 was the 'International Year of Sustainable Tourism for Development'.

Discussion

How sustainable is your school? Think about ways that your school could reduce waste and increase efficiency in using energy.

Log rafting is a sustainable tourist activity.

Hiking in the Blue Mountains is a sustainable tourist activity.

Why we need to protect the environment

We are learning to:

- gather information from multiple sources and use it to explain the need for sustainable use of resources and protection of the environment.

There are many **protected areas** of Jamaica. A protected area refers to a defined geographical space that is managed through legal or other official ways to make sure that there is long-term conservation of nature. That includes making sure that **biodiversity** (the variety of animals and plants) and other resources are protected, as well as Jamaican cultural heritage.

In Jamaica, protected areas and national parks are taken care of by the National Environment and Planning Agency (NEPA). The role of this agency is to protect the country's environmental resources such as land, wood, and water. As well as this, the Jamaica Protected Areas Trust, Ltd. (JPAT) is an organisation, set up in 2004, which works with the government and businesses that seek to protect the natural resources and biodiversity of Jamaica.

In the last 50 years, Ocho Rios has grown from a fishing village to a major resort city and cruise port. It benefits from its attractive coastal setting and the nearby Dunns River Falls, Jamaica's most visited tourist site.

Roles played by conservation agencies in Jamaica

The Jamaican government, together with JPAT, has played an important role in taking care of the nation's protected areas and national parks. This is through their activities, which include:

- bringing together different groups in both the private and public sectors. Making sure these groups work together to enhance their cooperation and efforts of conservation
- overseeing proper use of conservation funds by monitoring the ways that these are organised and shared
- playing an important role in ensuring that policies such as Jamaica's National Biodiversity Strategy and Action Plan are carried out properly
- offering support in various forms such as technical support, resource management and support to manage these protected areas
- creating awareness on protected areas through the news, education, and other ways of spreading information.

In Jamaica, protected areas include forest reserves, national parks, fish sanctuaries, and forestry management areas. The main protected areas include:

- Bogue
- Cedar Valley
- Bull Head
- Cockpit Country
- Dover
- Portland Bight Protected Area
- Mason River Protected Area
- Blue and John Crow Mountains National Park (UNESCO World Heritage Site).

Cockpit Country is one of the most important economic protected areas of Jamaica. It is located in the west of the central island and is made up of 22 327 hectares of forest reserves. It contains important cultural and natural heritage of Jamaica. Cockpit Country is home to various flora and fauna including 27 of the 28 endemic birds of Jamaica and over 1 500 species of plants. **Endemic species** are those which belong to a particular geographical area. Due to its rich biological and cultural resources, it is really important that Jamaica's wildlife is preserved and protected.

Did you know...?

There are 28 endemic species of birds in Jamaica, including five different types of flycatcher.

Rufous-tailed Flycatcher in Cockpit Country.

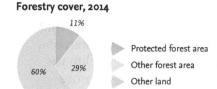

Forestry cover, 2014

11%
60%
29%

- ▶ Protected forest area
- ▶ Other forest area
- ▶ Other land

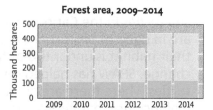

Forest area, 2009–2014

Thousand hectares

500
400
300
200
100
0

2009 2010 2011 2012 2013 2014

Exercise

1 Name three protected areas found in Jamaica.

2 What percentage of land in Jamaica is protected forest area?

3 Why do you think it is important that forest land is protected?

4 What has happened to the amount of forest area on Jamaica over time according to the graph above?

Key vocabulary

protected area

biodiversity

endemic species

Protected areas of the Caribbean

We are learning to:

- use geographical skills and tools to present and interpret information related to protected areas in Jamaica and the rest of the Caribbean.

Jamaica is not the only Caribbean country to have rich biodiversity and protected areas. This has led to countries working together in order to protect wildlife.

Specially Protected Areas and Wildlife (SPAW) ⟫

In 1990 the United Nations set up '**The SPAW Protocol**' which seeks to take the necessary steps to protect, preserve and manage in a sustainable way:

1. areas that require protection to safeguard their special value, and

2. threatened or endangered species of flora and fauna (plants and animals).

Case study

Sea turtles

Sea turtles in the Caribbean are one of many species that are in need of protection. Their eggs are often taken and their habitat is under threat from pollution and climate change. SPAW has helped set up action plans to protect turtles where there are no plans in place. This involves making sure that people are educated in the need to protect this species The police, vets and other stakeholders are also involved in the protection of wildlife. SPAW plans also make sure that the number of turtles are managed carefully.

Activity

Make a list of the top ten animals and plants that are in need of protection in the Caribbean. Explain why each of these is in need of protection, suggest ways to protect these species.

Did you know...?

Globally, the number of hawksbill sea turtles may have declined by as much as 80% over the last century due to sale of their shells, poaching, habitat loss, being accidentally caught in nets and pollution in the sea.

Hawksbill sea turtle.

- Sharks and other large predatory fishes are constantly and gradually falling in number.
- Sharks are very important since they keep marine **ecosystems** healthy and productive, by balancing many fish populations and cleaning the ocean of carcasses of dead animals.
- SPAW makes it a legally binding agreement to protect and manage sea life.

Sharks fins for sale.

> **Did you know...?**
>
> Worldwide 100 million sharks are killed every year because of fishing and shark finning.

Exercise

1. What do UN and SPAW stand for?

2. The text says that Jamaica has a 'rich biodiversity' What does this mean?

3. Why might countries need to work together to protect wildlife more effectively?

4. Explain why sea turtles are in danger.

5. Carry out research into why shark numbers are falling in the Caribbean.

6. Write a paragraph explaining why regional integration is important for protecting wildlife.

Key vocabulary

The SPAW Protocol

ecosystem

Endangered habitats and species

We are learning to:

* understand what we mean by endangered habitats and species.

Threats to our heritage ⟫

When we say that something is **endangered**, we mean that it is under threat and in danger of becoming **extinct** or totally destroyed. Human activities such as growing cities **threaten** the habitats or existence of our **flora** (plants) and **fauna** (animals).

Case study

The Jamaican iguana

The Jamaican iguana is endemic to Jamaica and Jamaica's largest native land animal. In 1948, the Jamaican iguana was considered extinct. However, in 1990, the species was rediscovered by Mr. Edwin Duffus who was hunting pigs in Hellshire Hills, St Catherine. Extensive surveys found a small number of adult individuals and virtually no young ones. Out of that, an emergency conservation strategy was initiated . Even with active conservation programs, the Jamaican iguana remains on the list of endangered species.

The Jamaican iguana.

Endangered habitats ⟫⟫

Many animals become endangered because their habitat, or where they live, changes or disappears. The Jamaican iguana population was drastically reduced by a mixture of habitat loss and hunting by alien species. Agricultural and urban development, together with timber extraction for charcoal production, has degraded and broken up the Jamaican iguana's tropical dry forest habitat. Where habitat is still in good condition, dogs, feral cats, and wild pigs prevent the iguana's existence, impacting the whole forest ecosystem. The iguana's tropical dry forest home of the Hellshire Hills is one of the most endangered ecosystems in the world. Forest health depends on the iguana; it feeds on fruits and flowers and helps the germination of seeds and their dispersal, thereby benefiting many other species in the forest.

Source: adapted from IUCN website

Exercise

1   Explain how habitat loss led to iguanas in Jamaica becoming endangered.

2   Why does the health of the forest also depend on iguanas?

3   What does this example tell us about the importance of protecting both flora and fauna?

Discussion

In groups discuss what you think is the greatest threat to our natural heritage today and why it needs to be preserved.

Illegal poaching

Poaching is the illegal hunting or capture of wild animals. In Jamaica, sea turtles are vulnerable to poaching since they nest on sandy beaches. Hawksbill and green turtles are still illegally hunted for their meat and eggs as they can sell for a high price. Both species are endangered.

Economic development

Physical resources are valuable and essential to the economic development of a country. In Jamaica, our natural resources, such as oceans, lakes, waterfalls, flora and fauna have helped to attract tourists and develop the tourism industry.

However, this increased use of our natural heritage is having a damaging effect on the environment. Today, the threats to our natural habitats mainly result from human activities. For example:

- squatting, poaching or illegal hunting
- land clearing (fires) cattle grazing, logging, slash and burn agriculture, overfishing
- invasive alien species
- drilling for oil or gas, quarrying or pollution (such as oil spills and chemical leaks)
- global warming or climate change.

The cane toad is a native of South America, but was introduced into the Eastern Caribbean as long ago as the 19th century. It is an omnivore and will eat small animals, as well as being poisonous (including its tadpoles). By 2013 it had 'invaded' The Bahamas.

The casuarina (commonly called the Australian pine) is widespread in the Caribbean, where it suppresses the native vegetation and can cause beach erosion. This stand on Paradise Island in The Bahamas has since been removed.

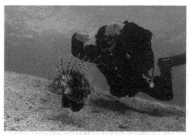

The lionfish is an Indo-Pacific species that is a voracious carnivore with poisonous spines. It has invaded the entire Caribbean, probably starting from the US coast, where some are believed to have escaped from an aquarium, then spreading south through The Bahamas. It can be eaten and this is one way of reducing its numbers.

Key vocabulary

endangered

extinct

threaten

flora

fauna

poaching

Exercise

4 Why do you think that illegal poaching takes place in Jamaica?

5 What is meant by 'invasive alien species?'

6 In about 100 words, outline which human activities put our natural habitats at risk.

Conserving our resources

We are learning to:

• implement and improve conservation practices within the school and community environment.

Why should we conserve our resources?

• **Moral** reasons – as human beings we have a moral duty not to destroy other species or our environment

• **Ecological** reasons – plants provide food and shelter for animals as well as resources for humans such as wood. Animals provide foods and other products that come directly from nature. If we destroy the environment, we reduce the chances of helping ourselves.

In most parts of the world, the environment is harmed by air, land and sea pollution. Pollution can destroy habitats as well as fauna and flora. This is why Jamaica has set aside areas of land that are given special protection in order to allow the flora and fauna to survive. They have also brought in laws to protect forests and other environments.

Discussion

Discuss the reasons why we should conserve our resources, placing them in order of importance. What should be the consequences of not conserving the environment.

Laws to protect the environment in Jamaica (home, school, community)

To make sure that everyone protects the environment in Jamaica, there are a number of laws and policies in place. These laws relate to homes, schools and the community, which also includes businesses. The National Environment and Planning Agency (NEPA) is the agency which ensures that laws and policies are respected and enforced.

Their aims include:

• **Conservation and protection**
  Management of species, habitats, and ecosystems; protected, watershed, coastal and marine areas management; wild fauna and flora protection, rescue and relocation.

• **Environmental management**
  Pollution prevention and control; pollution monitoring and assessment; pollution incident investigation and reporting.

• **Planning**
  Building and developing areas in a way which ensures that the environment is protected.

• **Education and outreach**
  Teaching school children and the wider community about the importance of protecting our environment.

The National Environment and Planning Agency (NEPA) is the agency which oversees the following Acts and Regulations:

- The Beach Control Act (1956, 1957, 1978)
- The Clean Air Act (1964)
- The Endangered Species (Protection, Conservation and Regulation of Trade) Act
- The Land Development and Utilisation Act (1966)
- The Natural Resources Conservation Authority Act (1991)
- The Wildlife Protection Act (1973)
- The National Solid Waste Management Act (2001).

In addition to NEPA personnel, other roles involved are: forest officer, fishing inspector, game warden, inspector, marine officer, marine park ranger, national park ranger, member of the Jamaica Constabulary Force, member of the Jamaica Defence Force, and traffic wardens.

Activity

Pick two of the laws above and carry out research into what they aim to do. Write a summary and produce a PowerPoint to present it back to the rest of your class. Visit the NEPA website to help you.

Case study

Mangroves

In 2017 NEPA began a new project to protect the mangroves in Jamaica. Some places in Jamaica, like other Caribbean islands are at a high risk of flooding and other hazards. Mangroves and coral reefs offer important flood protection benefits. However, mangroves and coral reefs are increasingly threatened by human development and climate change. This project seeks to consider ways to restore and protect mangroves to reduce the risk to people and property in Jamaica.

Mangroves.

Did you know...?

Mangroves currently cover approximately 9 800 hectares across Jamaica. More than 700 hectares of mangroves have been lost in recent decades.

Exercise

1 What does NEPA stand for?

2 Why are mangroves important?

3 What does it mean that 'human development' threatens mangroves and coral reefs?

4 Carry out some research about the animals that live in mangroves. Design a wall display in your classroom explaining the importance of mangroves in Jamaica.

Key vocabulary

moral

ecological

Environmental groups in Jamaica

We are learning to:

- compare and critique the work and activities carried out by the different environmental groups, organisations and watchdogs in Jamaica.

As well as government organisations, there are several voluntary organisations that seek to protect the environment in Jamaica. These sometimes work with the government, schools and the community. They act as **'watchdogs'** to make sure that individuals, companies and communities all act in ways that are responsible and avoid harm to the environment where possible. Here are some examples of these organisations and the work they do:

The Jamaica Environment Trust (JET)

JET carries out projects under three main focus areas: environmental education, law and conservation. Their projects include Jamaica's longest running environmental education programme for students and teachers, the Schools' Environment Programme, which began in 1997. They organise environmental events in Jamaica, including the annual International Coastal Cleanup Day. Other conservation work has included monitoring of sea turtle nesting and the patrol and management of the Pedro Bank fish sanctuary.

The Jamaican Environmental Trust.

National Environmental Societies Trust (NEST)

The mission of NEST is to help design and implement solutions to environmental problems.

Formed in 1989, NEST is dedicated to restoring Jamaica's natural resources, which are being eroded at an alarming pace. For example, in the early 1990s, the island had the highest rate of deforestation in the world at 4.5% per annum, according to one report. NEST believes that the key to ending the destruction lies in the hands of the people who are directly affected. Their objectives are to:

- provide a framework for encouraging citizens' participation in environmental conservation
- secure the necessary resources to support the conservation efforts of environmental organisations throughout Jamaica

- help environmental groups to maximise their positive impact on environmental problems at the community level
- work with environmental groups in planning, implementing and evaluating community-based conservation projects.

Activity

Carry out research into Birds Caribbean, an organisation which protects birds in Jamaica and the Caribbean. Find out how they do this by visiting their website.

Produce a PowerPoint presentation, with images and information on the aims and projects of Birds Caribbean and present it to the rest of your class.

Discussion

What can you do in your school to encourage individuals and the school staff to use sustainable practices? Develop a programme of activities and a slogan to use in the school. Present these in an environment awareness day.

Exercise

1 What is meant by a 'watchdog'?

2 Explain the role of the JET and NEST, using your own words.

3 Write a paragraph explaining why voluntary organisations are important in protecting the environment.

4 Find out about a voluntary organisation that works in your area to protect the environment. Write a leaflet explaining the work it does.

Key vocabulary
....

watchdogs

Questions

See how well you have understood the topics in this unit.

1. A/An _____ is a type of animal or plant that is threatened.

   a) extinct

   b) protected

   c) endangered species

   d) endemic species

2. A creature or plant that belongs to a specific place is known as a/an _____ species.

   a) endemic

   b) rare

   c) endangered

   d) protected

3. A/An _____ is an area where there are laws and policies about preventing building and changing the environment in specific ways.

   a) urban area

   b) protected area

   c) tourist resort

   d) forestry land

4. The three R's stand for:

   a) reduce, reuse recycle

   b) replace, reduce, reuse

   c) redo, reduce, replace

5. True or false? Mangroves in Jamaica are an important part of flood defence systems.

6. Correct this statement: The government of Jamaica do not get involved with conserving the environment, they leave it to other organisations.

7. Explain what is meant by 'biodiversity'.

8. Write a short definition of the following terms:

   Environmental watchdog

   Poaching

   Sustainable development

9. Make a list of species that are in need of protection in Jamaica.

10. Which two of these are environmentally friendly practices?

   a) Recycling
   b) Cycling instead of driving a car
   c) Using air conditioning

11. Explain how consumption patterns can contribute to sustainable development practices.

12. Explain what is meant by energy efficient.

13. Name two laws which have been created to protect the environment in Jamaica.

14. Explain the effects of 'invasive alien species' on Jamaican flora and fauna.

15. What can you do as an individual to protect the environment, at home, at school and in your community? Write 100 words.

Grade 7 Unit 10 Summary

Sustainable resources and the environment

In this chapter, you have learned about:

- What is meant by sustainability
- Ecotourism projects
- How the sustainable use of natural resources protects them for future generations
- Ecotourism and ecotourism projects in Jamaica
- Reduce, reuse and recycle as the 3 Rs of sustainable practices.

Taking responsibility for the environment

In this chapter, you have learned about:

- The importance of keeping our environment free of litter
- How individuals can participate in sustainable practices through responsible travel
- The significance of responsible agriculture
- Why ethical consumerism and supporting local producers matters.

Production and consumption

In this chapter, you have learned about:

- What is meant by sustainable development
- The link between production and sustainability
- The importance of using less energy
- The meaning and the goals of sustainable development.

Conservation

In this chapter, you have learned about:

- The roles that conservation agencies play in protecting Jamaica's environment
- The protected areas in Jamaica
- The protected areas of the Caribbean
- The habitats and species that are endangered by unsustainable practices
- Conservation practices that can be implemented in our school and community
- The effectiveness of the work of Jamaica Environmental Trust and National Environmental Societies Trust.

Checking your progress

To make good progress in understanding sustainable use of resources and how we can protect our environment, check that you understand these ideas.

- Explain and use correctly the term *sustainable practices*.

- Describe the difference between reusing and recycling.

- Explain the impact of recycling on the environment.

- Explain and use correctly the term *preservation*.

- Name the ways that Jamaica preserves its natural habitat.

- Explain the role of laws in protecting Jamaican wildlife.

- Explain and use correctly the term *biodiversity*.

- Name the governmental agencies involved with protecting the environment.

- Explain the role of conservation groups in Jamaica.

- Explain and use correctly the term *endemic species*.

- Describe the ways that sustainable practice is carried out in the community, home and school.

- Explain the role of projects to ensure energy conservation in Jamaica.

End-of-term questions

Questions 1–8 〉〉〉

See how well you have understood ideas in Unit 8.

1. Explain the reason why there are seasons.

2. How often does the Earth orbit the Sun?

3. Match these definitions to the correct terms:

   a) gravity

   b) orbit

   c) axis

   i) An imaginary line around which the Earth turns
   ii) A force that draws objects in a particular direction, towards the centre of a planet
   iii) To take a curved path around an object.

4. Briefly describe how life on Earth is supported through the movement of the Earth.

5. What is a solar system?

6. How does the Earth's rotation enable life to form and thrive?

7. Explain what is meant by a summer solstice and a winter solstice.

8. What is the role of the Moon in relation to the Earth?

Questions 9–17 〉〉〉

See how well you have understood ideas in Unit 9.

9. What are the three types of integration?

10. What are the benefits of interdependence in the Caribbean?

11. Why was the West Indian Federation set up?

12. What is meant by 'free trade?' Give examples.

13. What is globalisation and why does it mean regional integration is even more important?

14. Apart from economic integration, what other types of integration are important in the Caribbean?

15. How can the individual support regional integration?

16. Match these events to when they happened.

    a) 1958

    b) 1962

    c) 1965

    d) 1973

    i) West Indian Federation disbanded

    ii) Caribbean Community or CARICOM formed

    iii) West Indian Federation formed

    iv) Caribbean Free Trade Association (CARIFTA) formed.

17. Explain how citizens can help at local, national and regional level.

Questions 18–30 »»

See how well you have understood ideas in Unit 10.

18. Explain the term ecotourism.

19. Give three examples of ecotourism.

20. Explain how the 3 Rs can contribute to helping the environment.

21. How might consumer culture be bad for the environment?

22. Explain why saving water is important for the environment.

23. Give an example of how a person can become an ethical consumer.

24. Describe three protected areas in Jamaica and give examples of the biodiversity found in each.

25. Why is regional cooperation necessary to protect sea life?

26. Describe three endangered species of Jamaica, explaining why each has become at risk.

27. Describe the role of environmental watchdogs in Jamaica.

28. Explain how production and consumption patterns contribute to sustainability or sustainable development.

29. Outline the roles played by conservation agencies in Jamaica.

30. Explain what these acronyms stand for, and what the agencies do to help conservation in Jamaica.

    NSWMA

    NEPA

    JPAT

    SPAW

Glossary

abolition the act of abolishing.

active citizenship a citizen who is active in their community.

alien someone who is not a legal citizen of the country in which they live.

ancestor the people from whom you are descended.

ancestry the family you come from, especially their ethnicity or cultural origins.

animal hide animal skin.

appoint to assign officially, as for a position, responsibility, etc.

associate professional someone who works supporting a professional worker

authority the power or right to give orders and directions to others, to make decisions and to enforce those decisions

autonomous independent of others.

axis an imaginary line through the middle of something.

belonging to feel accepted or part of a group

bilateral agreement agreements between two countries.

biodiversity the great variety of life forms on Earth.

biological function having children.

blood ties a connection based on common ancestry, such as having one or more shared parents.

brain drain the problem of highly skilled people leaving a country to find opportunities elsewhere

breadwinner the person who earns the main income for a family or household.

capital money; anything that an economy needs in order to produce goods and services.

carbon dioxide a gas produced by breathing out, and by chemical reactions.

career a job or profession that someone works in.

CARICOM The Caribbean Community.

CARIFESTA Caribbean Festival of Arts.

CARIFTA Caribbean Free Trade Association.

CDEMA Caribbean Disaster Emergency Management Agency.

characteristics the characteristics of a person or thing are the qualities or features that belong to them and make them recognisable.

charismatic authority power that comes from one's exceptional personality or character, or powers of persuasion

Charter of Fundamental Rights and Freedoms a charter of fundamental rights of everyone living in the European Union, covering civil, political, economic and social rights.

citizen someone who is a member of a country and who has certain rights in that country, but also has duties towards that country.

civic activities activities related to society, for example voting.

civic responsibility your duties to your country.

classification a division or category in a system which divides things into groups or types.

clerical support worker workers who carry out tasks related to the recording, organising and storing of information.

climate zones any of the eight principal zones, roughly demarcated by lines of latitude, into which the Earth can be divided on the basis of climate.

coat of arms a special design in the form of a shield that they use as a symbol of their identity.

colonist a person who settles or colonizes an area.

common-law union a couple who live together as husband and wife without getting married.

community organisation an organisation which aims to make improves in the community.

competition when two or more people try to achieve the same thing.

compromise an agreement in which both parties make concessions (allowances).

conservation protecting, restoring and preserving something.

constitution the principles and laws by which a country is governed.

consumer culture a culture which encourages people to want new things.

consumption patterns the process by which people purchase and consume products and services to satisfy their needs.

contract a legal agreement, usually between two companies or between an employer and employee, which involves doing work for a stated sum of money.

controlling when someone tries to get people to behave in a particular way, for example their behaviour.

cooperation working together.

courtship the art of seeking the love of someone with intent to marry.

Crown colony a country ruled by the monarch of another country.

CSME the Caribbean Single Market and Economy.

cultural relating to a particular society and its ideas, customs, and art.

cultural background the beliefs and traditions that a group of people share.

cultural bonds cultural ties that bring people together.

cultural festival a festival featuring arts and events specific to a particular culture.

cultural/educational function skills, acquired within a family that contribute to a child's education.

cultural heritage the cultural traditions that we have inherited from past generations.

culture the customs, arts, shared language, history and ideas of a group.

custom a way of behaviour that has been established for a long time.

deforestation the removal of trees and vegetation to create open spaces for human activities.

democracy a system of government in which a country's citizens choose their rulers by voting for them in elections.

dependence relying on someone or something.

deportation the act of expelling an alien from a country; expulsion.

descent a movement from a higher to a lower level or position.

development the gradual growth or formation of something.

digital citizen a person who is using technology to be a good citizen.

disability a permanent injury, illness, or physical or mental condition that tends to restrict the way that someone can live their life.

disband to cease to function or cause to stop functioning, as a unit, group, etc.

dispute resolution methodologies a wide range of dispute resolution processes and techniques that act as a means for disagreeing parties to come to an agreement.

dyad group of two.

dynamic relating to or tending toward change or productive activity.

eco-friendly not damaging to the environment; sustainable.

ecological tending to benefit or cause minimal damage to the environment.

economic citizen someone who becomes a citizen of a country because they have invested money into that country in some way.

economic development improving a country's standard of living.

economic function bringing in income to fulfil basic needs for food, shelter, security and clothing.

economic integration when two or more states in a geographic area set common economic goals and reduce the barriers to trade between them.

economic policy a set of aims or goals or laws set out by the government to grow the country's economy by creating jobs and earning revenue.

economy the system of how industry, trade and finance is organised in a country, region or worldwide to manage wealth.

ecosystem a system formed by an environment and the living and non-living things within it.

ecotourism tourism that does not damage or destroy the natural environment or local culture.

education the act or process of acquiring knowledge, esp systematically during childhood and adolescence.

elected voted to a role in an election.

elementary occupations low-skilled work made up of simple tasks.

emissions gases that are given off during a chemical process.

employee someone who is paid to work for someone else or company.

employer a person or organisation that employs people.

employment the fact of having a paid job.

Encomienda (in colonial Latin America) a large estate under the control of a Spaniard.

endangered in danger of extinction.

endemic species those which belong to a particular geographic area.

energy conservation the prevention of the wasteful use of energy, esp to ensure its continuing availability.

enslavement the system by which people are owned by other people as enslaved people.

equality the right of different groups of people to have a similar social position and receive the same treatment.

ethical conduct a set of moral principles people live by.

ethical consumer someone who makes careful choices of what they buy in order to show their values.

ethnic group a group of people who have common cultural backgrounds. They belong to an ethnic group because of their ancestors, their language or religion, or because of where they live.

exploitation the overuse of something.

extended family a larger family, with additional family members besides the nuclear family.

extinct the process where an animal or plant species disappears forever.

extracted taken out.

family group of people who may live together and are related by blood, marriage or another union.

family tree a tree-like diagram that shows the structure of a family.

fauna animals and wildlife that are found in a country or region.

flag a piece of cloth which can be attached to a pole and which is used as a sign, signal, or symbol of something, especially of a particular country.

flora plants that grow in a particular region.

focus the point, underground, at which an earthquake happens.

folklore unwritten literature of a people as expressed in folk tales, proverbs, riddles, songs, etc.

folkway any way of thinking, feeling, behaving, etc. common to members of the same social group.

forest an area thickly covered with trees and shrubs.

formal group a group that has written rules, a clear division of work and power, and procedures for replacing members.

free trade trade which allows people to buy and sell goods freely, without restrictions.

freedom the power to act and speak as you choose.

frostbite when skin is exposed to very cold temperatures and freezes.

function the purpose of a particular thing or person.

genealogical related to the history of the past and present members of a family or families.

global citizen a member of the world community.

Global Positioning System (GPS) a navigation system that provides data about time and location.

global warming an increase in global temperatures.

goal the aim or object towards which an endeavour is directed.

goods material objects that people can see or touch, and which they can buy.

grandparents the parents of your parents.

gravity the force of attraction that moves or tends to move bodies towards the centre of a celestial body, such as the Earth or moon.

group a group is made up of two or more people who do things together to achieve their common goals.

group cohesion a group's ability to stick or stay together and last.

hemisphere one half of a sphere or globe.

heritage features that belong to the culture of a society that were created in the past and have an historical importance to that society.

Heritage Week National Heritage Week is observed annually the week leading up to the third Monday in October, National Heroes Day. The week-long observation includes a national religious service organized by the CPNRS and replicated in each parish. The week closes with the National Honours and Awards Ceremony.

hero a person distinguished by exceptional courage, nobility, fortitude, etc.

Heroes Day a holiday commemorating the seven national heroes from Jamaican history.

heroine a woman possessing heroic qualities.

heroism the qualities and actions of a hero or heroine; bravery, nobility, valour, etc.

hierarchy a system in which people are ranked according to their status or power.

honest someone who tells the truth or deceives anyone.

honesty sincerity or fairness.

Honours system the system by which people are honoured in Jamaica.

human resource development educating and training the workforce.

human resources people and their knowledge, abilities, experience and talents.

human rights the basic rights which all people should have, for example the right to liberty, equality, respect, freedom of expression.

humid moist; damp.

identity the way you think about yourself, the way the world sees you and the characteristics that define you.

impressionable easily influenced; easily learning from what happens around them.

indentured labour system when one person works for another for a specific period of time in exchange for a reward.

independence being able to do things without assistance or direction.

indigenous native to, or originate in, a particular region or country.

informal group an informal group does not have written rules or objectives or a strict hierarchical structure.

innovation something newly introduced, such as a new method or device.

intangible imprecise or unclear to the mind.

integrate involving people from all groups and cultures.

integrity someone who is honest in their principles.

interact people spending time together or working together.

interdependent/interdependence relating to two or more people or things dependent on each other.

island landform surrounded on all sides by water.

Jamaica Day a national holiday celebrating Jamaica.

Jamaica National Heritage Trust Act an act which speaks to how historical sites can be used and should be treated.

kinship the relationship between members of the same family.

knowledge the understanding someone has about a particular subject.

labour the work that people do to provide goods and services.

labour force the part of the population that is able and available to work.

land an area of ground, especially one that is used for a particular purpose such as farming or building.

latitudes horizontal lines circling the Earth showing distance from the Equator. The Equator is the most well-known line of latitude, circling the Earth at 0°, followed by the tropics found at 23.5° north and south of the Equator.

law abiding adhering more or less strictly to the laws.

leader an individual who influences the behaviour or actions of another person or who directs and guides a group towards decisions

leadership when a leader (or leaders) influences a group to achieve a common objective.

learned having great knowledge or erudition.

legacy something handed down or received from an ancestor or predecessor.

line of latitude an imaginary line on a globe, map, etc, indicating latitude.

line of longitude an imaginary line on a globe, map, etc, indicating longitude.

litter to make (a place) untidy by strewing (refuse).

lobby group a group of people who seek to influence the government make changes to or act on a particular issue.

manager someone who is responsible for running part of, or all of a company or business.

Maroons freed enslaved Africans and their descendants, who escaped British rule when the British defeated the Spanish in 1655.

marriage the state or relationship of living together in a legal partnership.

material culture culture that can be touched, it is tangible and includes symbols, cultural buildings, heritage sites and objects used in traditions.

mediate to intervene (between parties or in a dispute) in order to bring about agreement.

moral concerned with or relating to human behaviour, esp the distinction between good and bad or right and wrong behaviour.

more the traditional behaviour or way of life of a particular community or group of people.

multicultural consisting of many cultures.

multilateral agreement an agreement between more than one country or international organisation.

multinational corporation organisation that has business interests in more than one country.

national hero are individuals (or groups and community activists) who are recognised for their significant contributions to their national heritage or the development of their country.

national identity a sense of who you are and that you are part of a country.

natural disaster a natural event which causes a lot of damage and kills a lot of people.

natural resource/physical resource something that forms naturally or on the Earth and that we use for other purposes.

naturalise to give citizenship to (a person of foreign birth).

non-material culture culture that is not physical, it is intangible. It must be learnt and practiced and has to do with how people in a culture think about the world around them, others and themselves.

non-renewable resources resources that cannot be replaced.

norm a way of behaving that are considered normal in a particular society.

nuclear family a family unit that consists of father, mother, and children.

oath ceremony a special event for 'new Jamaicans' as they are formally welcomed.

orbit the curved path in space that is followed by an object going round and round a planet, moon, or star.

Orders of awards types of awards.

origin the beginning, cause, or source of something.

oxygen a colourless gas that exists in large quantities in the air.

patriotic showing a deep love for, and devotion to, your country.

pendulum something that changes its position, attitude, etc fairly regularly.

people trafficking the practice of bringing immigrants into a country illegally.

permanent worker full-time employment OR to be in full-time employment.

poaching catching (game, fish, etc) illegally by trespassing on private property.

political system the process for making official government decisions.

population the total number of people living in a specific geographic area at a particular point in time.

poverty being very poor, not having enough money or food.

power control and authority over people and their activities.

practice a usual or customary action or proceeding.

preservation maintaining an original state.

primary groups a small group in which people frequently interact (often daily), know each other very well, and can depend on each other, for example a family.

primary industry an industry that harvests raw materials OR involved in the extracting and developing of raw materials.

primary socialisation socialisation carried out by family members, friends, religious ideas and practices and possibly also by the media, such as the television programmes a child watches.

prime meridian the line of longitude, corresponding to zero degrees and passing through Greenwich, England, from which all the other lines of longitude are calculated.

production the process of manufacturing or growing something in large quantities.

professional relating to a person's work, especially work that requires special training.

protected area a defined geographical space that is managed through legal or other official ways to make sure that there is long-term conservation of nature.

quality of life measure of happiness that a person has in their life.

quaternary industry an industry which provides knowledge and skills, such as information technology, research and development, innovation industries and the media.

racial integration when people from different cultural groups live and work together on an equal basis.

Rastafarian/Rastafarianism a religion based in Jamaica.

rational-legal authority a form of leadership in which people come to positions of power through a fair system of rules and laws.

raw material when natural resources can be used to make something.

reconstituted family a family where one or more parents have children from previous relationships.

recycle to process a material into a new material; e.g., we can recycle old broken glass to make fresh glass.

reduce to make or use less of something.

referendum when all the citizens of a country can vote on a specific issue.

Reggae a type of West Indian popular music having four beats to the bar, the upbeat being strongly accented.

region a large area of land that is different from other areas of land, for example because it is one of the different parts of a country with its own customs and characteristics, or because it has a particular geographical feature.

regional integration the joining together or working together of countries that are close together, in order to make them economically and politically more powerful.

relationship the quality or state of being related; connection.

reliable someone or something that can be trusted.

religion belief in a god or gods and the activities that are connected with this belief, such as praying or worshipping in a building such as a church or temple.

renewable resources natural resources that can be replaced.

resource a source of economic wealth, esp of a country (mineral, land, labour, etc) or business enterprise (capital, equipment, personnel, etc).

respect due regard for someone or something.

responsibility job or task we are expected to complete OR the things we are expected to do as part of our role.

responsible If someone or something is responsible for a particular event or situation, they are the cause of it or they can be blamed for it.

restoration something restored, replaced, or reconstructed.

reuse to use something again.

revolve to move or cause to move around a centre or axis; rotate.

rights moral principles or norms that describe certain standards of human behaviour.

role a part we play in relation to others OR a pattern of behaviour that comes from your position in the family.

rotate to turn or cause to turn around an axis, line, or point; revolve or spin.

salary a payment made to a worker by an employer at regular intervals for work done.

sales workers a person whose job is to sell things, especially directly to shops or other businesses on behalf of a company.

sanctions a form of punishment, used to make sure that group members follow the group rules.

sanitation having a clean supply of water and good sewage system.

season a period of the year characterized by particular conditions or activities.

secondary groups large groups which are not as close or intimate as primary groups, for example a sports club.

secondary industry an industry mostly involved in processing and manufacturing OR manufacturing industries which make products from raw materials.

secondary socialisation refers to the internalisation of norms and values that takes place from the age a person begins school throughout their entire life.

self-employment providing one's own work or income, without an employer.

services public utilities and facilities that are provided for settlements where people live.

services workers workers working in industries such as travel, housekeeping, catering, personal care, working and selling in shops or retail and public services.

shared divided or apportioned, esp equally.

sibling brothers and sisters.

sibling household a household in which the parents are absent, so the older brothers and sisters take care of younger siblings.

single parent family a family that consists of one parent and his or her children living together.

social of, relating to, or characteristic of the experience, behaviour, and interaction of persons forming groups.

social group two or more people who work together to achieve a common purpose or goal.

social integration when people of all cultural groups, sexes and ages live and work together in an area.

social skills the skills that are necessary in order to communicate and interact with others.

socialisation function how we interact and communicate with others and how we form relationships.

socialised When people, especially children, are socialised, they are made to behave in a way which is acceptable in their culture or society.

solar system the Sun and all the planets that go round it.

standard of living the level of comfort and wealth that a person or family may have.

structure the way something is made, built or organised.

sustainable/sustainability something that can be continued without destroying the resources that make it possible OR able to continue at the same level without destroying the resources it relies on.

symbol a sign or image that is used to represent something.

taboo If there is a taboo on a subject or activity, it is a social custom to avoid doing that activity or talking about that subject, because people find them embarrassing or offensive.

technician someone whose job involves skilled practical work with scientific equipment, for example in a laboratory.

temporary work/worker short-term employment OR to be engaged in short-term employment.

tertiary industry an industry that provides services OR service industries which sell manufactured goods OR involves providing services and making goods available to customers, like banking for example.

The Jamaica National Heritage Trust an organisation responsible for making sure that Jamaica's cultural heritage continues and is developed.

The SPAW Protocol a regional agreement for the protection and sustainable use of coastal and marine biodiversity in the Wider Caribbean Region.

threaten to make threats against; express one's intention of hurting, punishing, etc.

time zone one of the areas into which the world is divided where the time is calculated as being a particular number of hours behind or ahead of GMT.

trade agreement an agreement between two or more countries in relation to providing goods and services.

tradition a custom or belief that has existed for a long time.

traditional authority a form of leadership in which people come to a position of power through traditions or customs, because it has always been that way.

triad group of three.

underemployment the state of having work that does not fully use one's skills or abilities.

unemployment the state of not having work.

UNICEF an organisation which provides funding to many charities and organisations which protect children.

union an association, alliance, or confederation of individuals or groups for a common purpose, esp political.

United Nations an organisation whose role is to encourage international peace, co-operation, and friendship.

unity being joined together or in agreement.

universal suffrage the right of all adults to vote.

unskilled worker workers who have no formal training, education or skill.

unsung hero one who does great deeds but receives little or no recognition for them.

urbanisation increasing numbers of people living in the cities is referred to as urbanisation.

value what we believe is important in life.

visiting relationship a long-term partnership where the partners do not live together, but one visits the other from time to time; they may have children.

voting the person with the most votes gets the position of authority.

wage a payment to a worker for work done in a particular time period.

watchdog a person or committee whose job is to make sure that companies do not act illegally or irresponsibly.

water-wise refers to plants that evolved in regions with lower precipitation, thus requiring less water throughout the growing season than most residential landscape plants.

wealth all goods and services with monetary, exchangeable, or productive value.

West Indian Federation a group of ten Caribbean states that formed a federation from 1958 to 1962.

work ethics the rules and standards of conduct that are acceptable in the workplace.

Index

Acknowledgements

The publishers wish to thank the following for permission to reproduce photographs. Every effort has been made to trace copyright holders and to obtain their permission for the use of copyright materials. The publishers will gladly receive any information enabling them to rectify any error or omission at the first opportunity.

p6: Drotyk Roman/SS; p6: Liderina/SS; p7: Niyazz/SS; p7: Perfect Angle Images/SS; p7: Danita Delimont/SS; p8: alenagungor/SS; p10: Creative Family/SS; p11: Cavan Images/Alamy; p12: White Space Illustration/SS; p14: agefotostock/Alamy; p17: Yuriy Boyko/SS; p18: Hafiz Johari/SS; p19: Djohan Shahrin/SS; p20: Child Protection and Family Services Agency; p21: logoboom/SS; p22: AFP/Stringer/Getty; p23: Garey Lennox/Alamy; p23: wavebreakmedia/SS; p24: Respect Jamaica; p25: Extinction Rebellion Jamaica; p25: JSPCA; p30: Karol Kozlowski Premium RM Collection/Alamy; p30: Karol Kozlowski Premium RM Collection/Alamy; p31: PHLD Luca/SS; p31: Aflo Co. Ltd/Alamy; p31: Filipe B. Varela/SS; p35: vkilikov/SS; p35: Prachaya Roekdeethaweesab/SS; p35: Benjamin John/Alamy; p36: Prachaya Roekdeethaweesab/SS; p36: Prachaya Roekdeethaweesab/SS; p37: Georgios Kollidas/SS; p37: Janusz Pienkowski/SS; p38: Ron Case/Stringer/Getty; p38: Everett Collection Inc/SS; p39: Hulton Deutsch/Getty; p40: Everett Collection Historical/Alamy; p41: Xinhua/Alamy; p41: 360b/SS; p41: WENN Rights Ltd/Alamy; p41: Shahjehan/SS; p42: David Corio/Contributor/Getty ; p42: Filipe B. Varela/SS; p44: Kwanza Henderson/SS; p45: agefotostock/Alamy; p46: Aflo Co. Ltd./Alamy; p46: Allstar Picture Library Ltd/Alamy; p47: Jan Kruger/Stringer/Getty; p47: Jeff Morgan 15/Alamy; p49: Debbie Ann Powell/SS; p54: Debbie Ann Powell/SS; p54: Tim Graham / Alamy; p55: Ossie Gee/SS; p55: Debbie Ann Powell/SS; p55: Eric Laudonien/SS; p57: Kkulikov/SS; p57: Robert Landau/Alamy; p57: AFP/Stringer/ Getty; p57: Paul_Brighton/SS; p58: Ozphotoguy/SS; p58: Mira/Alamy; p58: Debbie Ann Powell/SS; p58: Alla Danilchenko/Alamy; p59: agefotostock/Alamy; p60: railway fx/SS; p60: Photo 12/Contributor/Getty; p61: Danita Delmont/SS; p61: JIANG TIANMU/SS; p61: twiggyjamaica/SS; p61: YuRi Photolife/SS; p62: twiggyjamaica/SS; p62: MediaWorldImages/Alamy; p70: Debbie Ann Powell/SS; p70: Album/Alamy; p71: AS Food studio/SS; p72: Arvind Balaraman/SS; p72: JeniFoto/SS; p73: akepong srichaichana/SS; p74: donatas1205/SS; p74: CamBuff/SS; p75: Lewis Tse Pui Lung/SS; p75: Brent Hofacker/SS; p76: Denise Andersen/SS; p78: David Levenson/Alamy; p80: Yardie Inc/SS; p81: Grey Villet/Getty; p82: norikko/SS; p82: Cosmic_Design/SS; p82: Bash Mutumba/SS; p84: Ozphotoguy/SS; p85: Yakov Oskanov/SS; p94: Wirestock Creators/SS; p94: Marc Stephan/SS; p95: Kostenyukova Nataliya/SS; p95: Giovanni Bailey/SS; p95: LBSimms Photography/SS; p97: Ed Connor/SS; p97: OurDesigns/SS; p98: Joseph Thomas Photography/SS; p102: Jaemin Sohn/Alamy; p102: Steven Frame/SS; p103: Goncharovaia/SS; p103: CampSmoke/SS; p103: damann/SS; p103: Tarzhanova/SS; p104: Greg_Cohen/SS; p105: Pat Canova/Alamy; p105: Leonardo da/SS; p105: G-Zstudio/SS; p105: superoke/SS; p105: Wojciech Woszczyk/SS; p105: Ilya Images/SS; p105: Andre Place/SS; p105: Debbie Ann Powell/SS; p107: Patty Orly/SS; p107: Steven May/Alamy; p107: Oleksandr Malysh/SS; p107: mike_green/SS; p111: Royal Geographical Society/Getty; p111: Gino Santa Maria/SS; p112: Robert Fried/Alamy; p112: Penny Tweedie/Alamy; p120: SeventyFour/SS; p120: Craig F Scott/SS; p120: Buena Vista Images/Getty; p121: Photo Spirit/SS; p121: Juliet Highet / Art Directors/Alamy; p122: Wavebreakmedia Ltd UC77/Alamy; p122: Monkey Business Images/SS; p124: Jason Winter/SS; p126: dani3315/SS; p127: Everett Collection/SS; p128: Vision 2030; p129: michaeljung/SS; p130: Danil Evskyi/SS; p132: Gelpi/SS; p136: Daniel M Ernst/SS; p137: StockLite/SS; p138: Mike Goldwater/Alamy; p138: Christian Lagerek/SS; p139: michaeljung/SS; p140: Ozphotoguy/SS; p141: ANGELA WEISS/Getty; p142: Bloomberg/Getty; p143: wavebreakmedia/SS; p144: Hongqi Zhang/Alamy; p144: Debbie Ann Powell/SS; p145: Debbie Ann Powell/SS; p146: Iakov Filimonov/Alamy; p147: XM Collection/Alamy; p154: Lisa Strachan/SS; p154: Billion Photos/SS; p155: Krakenimages.com/SS; p155: Karol Kozlowski Premium RM Collection/Alamy; p155: Andrey_Popov/SS; p156: Tim Graham/Getty; p156: Salim October/SS; p161: Helene Rogers/ArkReligion.com/Alamy; p163: Art Directors & TRIP/Alamy; p163: Rosemarie Mosteller/SS; p164: SS; p164: Danita Delimont/SS; p165: SS; p166: SS; p167: Bloomberg/Getty; p168: dbimages/Alamy; p172: wavebreakmedia/SS; p173: Art Directors & TRIP/Alamy; p174: michaeljung/SS; p175: zimmytws/SS; p177: Georges De Keerle/Getty; p179: stuar/SS; p184: Rawpixel.com/SS; p184: Ron Giling/Alamy; p185: fizkes/SS; p185: Neil Cooper/Alamy; p185: LightField Studios/SS; p187: SS; p189: Stefano Manocchio/Alamy; p192: galastudio/SS; p194: pixelheadphoto digitalskillet/SS; p195: wavebreakmedia/SS; p198: MANDEL NGAN/Getty; p201: ricochet64/SS; p202: CPFSA; p202: Ozphotoguy/SS; p203: pixelheadphoto digitalskillet/SS; p210: GizemG/SS; p210: JoaoCachapa/SS; p210: Vinnikava Viktoryia/SS; p211: TomVolkov/SS; p211: Peyker/SS; p212: mapichai/SS; p212: ONYXprj/SS; p215: Inna Bigun/SS; p218: Universal Images Group Limited/Alamy; p219: Portrait Essentials/Alamy; p223: Lukasz Pajor/SS; p224: bogadeva1983/SS; p226: Brian A Jackson/SS; p227: biletskiy/SS; p232: David Levenson/Alamy; p232: Brian A Jackson/SS; p233: arindambanerjee/SS; p233: Yaw Niel/SS; p233: Pressmaster/SS; p234: Rodney Legall/Alamy; p235: MANDEL NGAN/AFP/Getty; p236: Horst Könemund/Alamy; p238: yui/SS; p240: Dana.S/SS; p241: Philip Wolmuth / Alamy; p242: 506 collection/Alamy; p243: Niyazz/SS; p244: Anfisa focusova/SS; p245: Gareth Copley/Getty; p246: Robert Fried/Alamy; p247: PJF Military Collection/Alamy; p250: mavo/SS; p252: mangostock/SS; p253: Rodney Legall/Alamy; p258: akinotombo/SS; p258: Lucky-photographer/SS; p259: Kononov Oleh/SS; p259: Kris-Tee/SS; p260: shipcfactory/SS; p261: Wolfi Poelzer/Alamy; p262: Preres/SS; p263: EdBockStock/Alamy; p265: cm studio/Alamy; p266: Doug Miles/SS; p266: lalanta71/SS; p268: Deni Nandar Sukanwar/SS; p269: Giovanni Bailey/SS; p269: ajlatan/SS; p270: Susan Santa Maria/SS; p271: Agami Photo Agency/SS; p272: blue-sea.cz/SS; p273: CatwalkPhotos/SS; p274: National Geographic Image Collection/ Alamy; p275: Gillian Holiday/SS; p275: Pierre-Yves Babelon/SS; p275: Frolova_Elena/SS; p277: JackViaggiante/SS; p278: Jamaica Environment Trust.